free to
be single

"I have learned to be content, whatever the circumstances may be."

(Philippians 4:11 Phillips)

free to be single

ELVA McALLASTER

CHRISTIAN HERALD BOOKS
Chappaqua, New York

Unless otherwise noted, Scripture citations are from the *New English Bible*, copyright 1961 and 1970 by Oxford University Press and Cambridge University Press, and are used by permission.

Library of Congress Cataloging in Publication Data

McAllaster, Elva Arline, 1922-
    Free to be single.

    Includes bibliographical references.
    1. Single people—Religious life.   2. McAllaster,
Elva Arline, 1922-   I. Title.
BV4596.S5M32   248'.4   78-64838
ISBN 0-915684-45-4

We acknowledge with appreciation permission to quote from:

Gerard Manley Hopkins, "As Kingfishers Catch Fire" (Poem 57), and "God's Grandeur" (Poem 31), *Poems of Gerard Manley Hopkins,* 3rd ed. (New York and London: Oxford University Press, 1948), pp. 95, 70.
Edna St. Vincent Millay, "Renascence," *Collected Poems*, ed. Norma Millay (New York: Harper and Row, 1956), p. 13.
C.S. Lewis, *A Grief Observed* (New York: The Seabury Press, 1961)

First Edition
CHRISTIAN HERALD BOOKS, 40 Overlook Drive, Chappaqua, New York 10514
Printed in the United States of America

DEDICATION
TO EVERYONE
WHO HELPED ME
(KNOWINGLY
OR UNAWARE)
TO WRITE
THESE PAGES:
WITH
GRATITUDE

Contents

An Invitation
to Dialogue

It is the morning of Epiphany as I start to write these paragraphs; it is January 6, the day that Christians have observed for centuries as a revealing: the revealing of Christ to the Gentiles, in the persons of the Wise Men. Ever since I spent a sabbatical year in England, Epiphany has been very special to me because of the way the Christmas season is observed there. And today is more than usually special, because now I am starting to dialogue with you.

I half-wakened (or one-twelfth wakened) very early this morning, thinking about you, and this invitation, and a lot of other things, while I was in my blanketed cocoon. At 6:30, still too foggy-minded and sleep-numbed to start talking with you, I got up to welcome in Epiphany. I lighted four candles and went back to bed, musing and glowing inwardly while I watched their glowings, and asking God again to make me a wick for the Light to shine from.

An hour later, after prayer and breakfast with Bach's Christmas Oratorio, I began to think about my writing. For some time now, as I have thought about this book, I have jotted down rather randomly the names of some persons I know, to whom I would like to be speaking in such a book as this. Or with whom. Persons who might care to read a book on "Christian and Single." Care to; need to; want to.

Christian persons, and some who aren't Christian but may be curious about my ideas anyway.

Single persons. Persons who aren't single themselves will be heartily welcome to read; after all, each of them was single once, and many will be single again sometime. But on the clipboard at this Epiphany breakfast, only the names of persons who are now single. As I sipped peppermint coffee, I added twenty names, and more. It's with you I want to dialogue. And with many others like you.

9

Jerry. Age 22 or 23. Bearded. Splintered by emotions since his newest girl friend ceased being his girl friend.

But his name really isn't Jerry. Let me make that a part of the contract, right at the outset. I'll be alluding to a good many people whom I actually know, all through this book, but I shall try very scrupulously to protect all identities that should be protected. If I refer to someone by a given name only, be assured that it's a fictitious given name — and please don't ever, ever ask me to reveal all I know! In the home of my childhood, a very firm parental maxim was, "I don't tell names and stories both." That will be my usual principle. If the surname appears, the whole name will be authentic and the reason for a salute of recognition will probably be quite obvious.

Jerry.

June. Age, similar. Employed in a big, big city, half a continent away from any relative.

Marian. Past eighty, widowed, living in a retirement center.

Betty. Mother of three small children. On her own, now, ever since an auto crash left her an instant widow.

Marge. Vivacious. Fiftyish. Executive with fifteen people or so under her brisk direction.

Bill. University professor. Slim-handsome, energetic, gray-sprinkled.

Olive. About to have her first child, an illegtimate. On welfare. High intellectual capacity.

Sue. Lives in a world without sounds. Reads lips well. Trained for a good job in a laboratory science.

Cathy. Completing a master's degree. Almost ready for employment as a librarian, with a good many special skills.

Ruth. Working at Kroger's, trying to get funds together for grad school, living with her parents and arguing with them daily, questioning her own identity, questioning everything she has ever read.

Darrell. Preaching, thinking, praying. Begging God earnestly to help him locate Mrs. Darrell, and soon. Or sooner.

Alvin. Nearly forty. Yesterday's mail mentioned that this Christmas was different and difficult. Yes, it was. His wife divorced him since last Christmas, and his psyche is still oozing blood.

Teresa. On her own now, after intolerably heavy family responsibilities. Mid-twenties, but with more experience in nursing homes, funerals, and disposal of real estate than many people who are mid-fifties.

Willa. Tied, she thinks, to a job she isn't fond of. Out of college for ten years. Tired of her city, tired of the boring people around her. Disillusioned. Hoping many hopes, though.

John. In the army. Learning a lot, he says. "Learning too much, John, of the things nobody really needs to know?" wonder his friends.

Vincent. Fifteen years a widower, but still married in memory, still utterly devoted to the Ann of his twenties.

Thelma. A missionary for several terms. Public speaker. Organizer. Thinker. Still in culture shock after return to the USA. Health problems.

Ralph. Teaching in public schools. Talks a lot about his enjoyment of music and drama. Talks a little, a very little, about his roommate — but talks with an inflection that makes us know what we haven't wanted to know. And lives in an area that's becoming notorious for its approval of homosexuality.

Dorothy. Twenty-eight or thirty-two or somewhere between. Blonde innocence of appearance, as though she were seventeen. Left her husband in order to do more with her art. Probably "genius" is not an inaccurate word to use about Dorothy.

Alyce. Tolerates her job, tolerates some of her relatives; college drop-out; likes marijuana, sometimes; likes philosophy books, sometimes; likes some of the recollections she has of Sunday School and church, sometimes.

Hazel, Kathryn, Laura, Lisa, Ethel, Sherri. Each is approaching thirty-nine, or laughs about being thirty-nine again, and again. Each is an educator, and very good indeed at her work. Each is a longtime Christian. Each is active in her own church. Each knows more of anger and frustration and bitterness than she often tells anyone, anyone at all.

Sandra. Pretty. Vivacious. Doing very well in medical school. Thinking hard about the chapters ahead: professional chapters, personal chapters.

Sally. An executive secretary. Dynamic and capable. A very loving person. Divorced half a dozen years ago when her preacher husband put aside his fidelities to each vow he had made at each successive altar.

Anne. Great skills in homemaking: in cooking, interior decorating, gardening. Loves children. Is now a college administrator, but looks very thoughtfully at descriptions of other jobs.

Lori. Among the many biographical facts, the one she would mention first to some friends and last to others is that she is currently dating a charming divorced man. Very charming. But divorced.

Beth. Has a good job; good, but very limiting. Lives in a community which bores her almost intolerably. Has several married siblings. Feels she has to plan all of her weekends and holidays around the needs of her ailing father.

Ellen. Unemployed. Lives with a relative. Gets by on foodstamps. Discouraged about job-hunting. No known social life.

Mel. Yes, he's a Christian, he would say. Well, that would depend on who asks. He really does care (sometimes) about his church. He really does (sometimes) acknowledge God. But some of his friends do not know that Sometime-Mel at all; they know about the kind of beer he drank at their last party, and about his ribald humor.

*   *   *   *

But Mel came to breakfast at my table this morning. And a lot of others came too, along with Jerry and Marge and Ruth and Willa and Hazel and Lori, and all the rest of you.

With you this Epiphany morning I want to share my thoughts about being single.

Rather than working on some new poems (which, in a way, I'd prefer to be doing) or on new fiction or literary studies, I'm opening a series of discussions with you. Rather than protecting some areas of my private experience and private thinking (which, in a way, I'd prefer to be doing), I'm sharing. If I can help anyone, anyone, here I am.

That, essentially, is the agreement between us.

As I said a while ago, I'll be drawing thoughts and illustrations from other people whom I know or have known, during all of the fascinating people-watching days of my years.

I shall endeavor to speak Truth, and to speak truths. I shall not promise to speak "the whole truth." That honored courtroom vow is really nonsense, if one thinks hard enough about it; who in human existence could tell "the whole truth" without exhausting whole forests for newsprint? It took James Joyce a very big book to report "the truth" from one day of one supposed life in *Ulysses,* didn't it? But the phrase "so help me, God" protects the integrity of the one who testifies in court, of course; as God shall help me to select quickly and accurately and rightly, I shall speak the truth.

And a similar phrase is the next aspect of my agreement with you. I shall endeavor to speak, here, as God himself will help me to do. I have asked him earnestly to guide my thoughts. What is it that should be said about being Christian, and being single? What have other books neglected to say, or blurred in the saying? What has been said before, but needs reiteration? What thoughts of mine will stir new thoughts for you? (You, Lori and Beth and Ellen and Mel? You, and you, and you, and you.)

I shall be saying "it seems to me." That's all I can say. I pray that the Holy Spirit will quicken my recollections and nudge me about the way I pull experience and assertion and hypothesis together. But

I'm not a prophet. I'm not even a sociologist. I haven't been instructed to hurtle declarations. I shall be saying "it seems to me." And I'll be saying, "Let's talk it over."

All of my students could tell you — the thousands of them, by now, from several campuses — that I very seldom lecture for many consecutive minutes. For good or for ill, my classrooms are cooperative enterprises; I toss out the questions and coordinate the responses. I've often said that in the literature classroom I'm more like the conductor of a symphony than like a solo pianist. Here, too, as one can through the printed page, I'd like to be the facilitator of a discussion, with you, and with you, and with you, in what I am saying.

In the saying, of course I'll be trying to draw upon what life has been teaching me ever since I first started to sort things out in ways that made sense to me, ever since I first started asserting my own lifestyle — long before I ever heard anyone say "lifestyle." I was fascinated by words, early on, and I knew "antidisestablishmentarianistically" before I was out of pigtails, but I didn't know "lifestyle." Well, I didn't know it as a word, but I knew it as an experience. (Sometime I may yet write a short story about the moment in a Sunday school program when I, at about eight or nine or ten, suddenly started to be an adult; I knew that the right way for my "piece" to be done was not, not, not the way They had told me to do it.)

During recent days, thinkings toward these pages have led me to dredge up episodes, occasions, and friendships that I hadn't thought about for a long time. Discussions in dorm rooms. "Relationships," to use a very weary word. Men I smiled at, but not much. Men who smiled at me, but not much. Or not marriage-much, in either case. Men whose names I don't even remember now, though certain etchings of emotion are far from effaced.

From what I have learned, decided, believed, considered, unlearned, reconsidered: these pages. I've been hiking off in my woods, and now bring these baskets of wild flowers. If any of them will be useful in your bouquets, here they are.

Or maybe, if you'd prefer to put it that way on Epiphany, these canisters. I'm not all that wise and I don't come in a camel caravan, but I bring to you, because of God who is within you, what I have of "gold, and frankincense, and myrrh." He will know what to do with it, if it is really intended for you. Ask him.

That's your part of the contract: ask him.

part one

FIRST THINGS FIRST: ON SELF-IDENTITY AND THE SINGLE

First Things First 1

I am a believer.

That is the one most significant fact about me. Not that I'm poet, teacher, counselor, woman. Not that I love outdoor nature, love to hike, enjoy travel. Not that I know certain wonderful human beings. Not anything else. The rest is peripheral, subsidiary, radiating out from the hub like spokes from a wheel.

"I believe in God the Father Almighty, Maker of heaven and earth, and in Jesus Christ his only Son our Lord —"

And I believe (utterly, urgently) that when one is a believer in Jesus Christ, first things must come first in one's life. We may stumble, we may blunder, we may grope to understand what would be clearer to us if we were purer of heart, but if we are believers we, like St. Paul before Agrippa, are not disobedient unto the heavenly vision.

Everything else I have to say on any topic has to acknowledge this primacy. Certainly any thought at all that I have to say about being Christian and single has to presuppose and recognize this primacy. First things must come first. The life of serenity and joy and security in Christ, now and in the everlasting corridors of forever, is contingent upon placing first things first.

The sicknesses and the sores in our family relationships come about when first things are not first. Dire sicknesses and ugly sores in our individual lives come when first things are not first.

This is not to say that pagan persons and semi-Christians may not be persons of much charm and much strength. The goodness of God permeates his created world ("like shining from shook foil," as Gerard Manley Hopkins exclaimed), and all our disobediences have not dispelled his light that glows in human minds, human personalities.

But first things need to come first.

Our Lord himself said it in strong words, in the Sermon on the Mount: "But seek ye first the kingdom of God, and his righteousness; and all these things shall be added unto you."

Last evening, thinking on these topics of priority and primacy, I reached for my copy of the New English Bible. It is a copy with additional emotional overtones to me, because it was my last Christmas gift, in 1970, from my mentor and friend, Dr. Mary A. Tenney. But the words would burn like dry ice against the skin, whoever the donor or purchaser, in verses I have underlined from time to time.

First things first.

Verses (to change the metaphor) for the Christian single to stand upon or to quarry within, as he thinks about being Christian and single. As he thinks about being Christian, in any circumstance life may hurl at him.

Matthew 14:24-27. "Jesus then said to his disciples, 'If anyone wishes to be a follower of mine, he must leave self behind; he must take up his cross and come with me. Whoever cares for his own safety is lost; but if a man will let himself be lost for my sake, he will find his true self. What will a man gain by winning the whole world, at the cost of his true self? Or what can he give that will buy that self back?' "

Mark 8:35-37. "Whoever cares for his own safety is lost; but if a man will let himself be lost for my sake and for the Gospel, that man is safe. What does a man gain by winning the whole world at the cost of his true self? What can he give to buy that self back?"

Luke 7: 30b. ". . . but the Pharisees and lawyers, who refused his baptism, had rejected God's purpose for themselves."

(How many, I ask myself quietly, how many of the 45 million singles in America have thus far "rejected God's purpose for themselves"? How many of the Americans who have stepped into matrimony during this year have, in doing so, "rejected God's purpose for themselves"?)

Luke 17:32-33. "Remember Lot's wife. Whoever seeks to save his life will lose it; and whoever loses it will save it, and live."

Galatians 5:22-25. "But the harvest of the Spirit is love, joy, peace, patience, kindness, goodness, fidelity, gentleness, and self-control. There is no law dealing with such things as these. And those who belong to Jesus Christ have crucified the lower nature with its passions and desires. If the Spirit is the source of our life, let the Spirit also direct our course."

(Joy. That's what humanity craves: joy. But how topsy-turvy we human beings are in our questings after joy. We look for it in good and evil things, wholesome things and nefarious things; we look for

it in jobs and sports and shopping and travel; we look for it in desperate marriages and — heaven help us! — in group sex. We look for
it in secondary places, in gleanings that may eventually lead to it, as
C. S. Lewis recorded so splendidly in his autobiography, *Surprised
by Joy.* We look for it in the thorn fields where it has not even been
planted. We gather substitute fruitage, the wild grapes and the wood-
bine berries. But all the time, the harvest of the Spirit is joy.)

Ephesians 2:7, 10. ". . . so that he might display in the ages to
come how immense are the resources of his grace, and how great his
kindness to us in Christ Jesus. . . . For we are God's handiwork,
created in Christ Jesus to devote ourselves to the good deeds for
which God has designed us."

(Does it sound like the distant sound of a trumpet? A resonant,
scalp-tingling summons to all you ever faintly wished for and knew
that somehow you might be, if only things were different in your
circumstances? It shivers in the marrow, and reminds us of our un-
tried destinies: "for which God has designed us.")

Colossians 3:12, 17. "Then put on the garments that suit God's
chosen people, his own, his beloved: compassion, kindness, humility, gentleness, patience. . . . Whatever you are doing, whether you
speak or act, do everything in the name of the Lord Jesus, giving
thanks to God the Father through him."

Colossians 4:17. "This special word to Archippus: 'Attend to the
duty entrusted to you in the Lord's service, and discharge it to the
full.' "

(I wonder about him, about Archippus. He was mentioned to
Philemon, too, as a comrade-in-arms. The word to him is valid for
any now-Christian, for any Christian single: discharge the duty:
discharge it to the full.)

2 Thessalonians 1:11. "With this in mind we pray for you always,
that our God may count you worthy of his calling, and mightily bring
to fulfillment every good purpose and every act inspired by faith, so
that the name of our Lord Jesus may be glorified in you, and you in
him, according to the grace of our God and the Lord Jesus Christ."

First things first.

After leafing around in the New Testament last night, I reached
for some scribble paper and started thinking very hard about what
the priorities really are; for the time, I wasn't working on translating
principles into what we slangily call "the nitty-gritty." That transla-
tion is a lifetime process, believe me. (After a while I did notice,
with some wry amusement, that the scribble paper I was using was
the back of a 1974-75 budget report from God's local enterprise
called Greenville College, and that there was an electricity bill of
$47,927.17. That's fairly nitty, and gritty!)

What is of ultimate, absolutely ultimate importance to me? Would you try these with me? How near to the ultimate are they?

— *To be a friend of Almighty God, and a co-worker with him.* I pick up my falling-apart old King James Bible and turn again to a page that is now mottled beige-yellow from many thumbings; I read 1 Corinthians 3:9 again: "For we are labourers together with God." The awe of it astounds. To be a wick, lighted by God's own flame! I think of Annie Dillard's burning moth, in her book, *Holy the Firm.* We, with God.

— *To follow the admonitions to me of the Holy Spirit.* The huge ones, the tiny ones. Two days ago, a letter mailed away to a bitter lass whose alienation from her mother almost drips pus. Yesterday, a prayer that God would forgive me for a conversation I had bungled through pride. This morning, the dialing of a telephone number two states away. Once, my first signature on a contract for Christian college teaching. Once, a quiet "No, I cannot" when a handsome graduate student wanted me to apply with him where he was applying, so that in teaching together we could get to know each other better and think further about marriage.

— *To grow in Christian character; to let sin be cleansed away and virtues purified.*

— *To be a strength to other persons.* Again I echo St. Paul; Galatians 4:19 (NEB): "For my children you are, and I am in travail with you over again until you take the shape of Christ." And 2 Corinthians 12:15: "As for me, I will gladly spend what I have for you — yes, and spend myself to the limit."

From St. Paul's words, I turn to George Eliot's iambic pentameters, in "The Choir Invisible," to lines I have read many times with yearning that echoed hers:

> O may I join the choir invisible
> Of those immortal dead who live again
> In minds made better by their presence: live
> In pulses stirred to generosity.
> In deeds of daring rectitude, in scorn
> For miserable aims that end with self,
> In thoughts sublime that pierce the night like stars,
> And with their mild persistence urge man's search
> To vaster issues. . . .
>   May I reach
> That purest heaven, be to other souls
> The cup of strength in some great agony,
> Enkindle generous ardor, feed pure love,
> Beget the smiles that have no cruelty —
> Be the sweet presence of a good diffused,

> And in diffusion ever more intense.
> So shall I join the choir invisible
> Whose music is the gladness of the world.

And, turning to Eliot, I pray it again; grant it, O God. "The cup of strength in some great agony." That's near, surely, to the ultimates of what I really would want.

— *To serve the present age.* It was our senior class motto, when I was a senior at Greenville College. We sat in Room 17 of Hogue Hall, which is now a part of the business offices. Then it was a classroom, where we studied philosophy and ethics, where we held senior class meetings. Marv Galbreath presiding, we thought hard, and decided crisply. Our class would echo Charles Wesley's hymn, "A charge to keep":

> To serve the present age,
> My calling to fulfill;
> O may it all my pow'rs engage
> To do my Master's will!

I should sing it again and again, I tell myself wryly this morning, whenever my eyes (as soggy as stewed onions) go to sleep, willy-nilly, over the papers I'm grading; often when I shape a new poem; often when I'm summoned to a committee that threatens numbing sludges of tedium. For this now, as I can: To serve.

Miss Ruby Dare urged us to that in a chapel talk she gave when we were juniors — juniors, I think; maybe seniors. She took her text from a filling station ad, and told us it was the way of life for a Christian: "Service is our business." And she lived by that motto. Typically, Miss Dare's very last deed, after a strenuous day of work in the library that now bears her name on our campus, was to bake a pan of brownies for her library staff. Then a massive stroke, and whatever "service" immortality is providing to her. (I wonder if immortal Dare thoughts will sometimes be in Greek and in Latin; maybe in something even better!)

— *"That I may know Him."* Paul summed it up. Philippians 3:10 this time. "That I may know him, and the power of his resurrection, and the fellowship of his sufferings, being made conformable unto his death." (KJV)

Like a South African diamond mine, that verse? You could dig there for several lifetimes, and not exhaust it, surely.

"The fellowship of his sufferings." Even the merest, feeblest Christian learns a little about that fellowship as life moves from one decade to another. The hurtings are here: the pinpricks, the dreadful amputations. I think of the sickly purple bruises on my spirit recently when an insolent acquaintance was deliberately rude, and I wonder why I didn't use Philippians 3:10 for witchhazel against the bruises. I think of long distance telephone calls to our community that have jolted lives like earthquakes. (Accident. Murder. Agony.) Suddenly we were cockle-shell ships on hurricane seas.

I think of a Dietrich Bonhoeffer. He knew the fellowship of the sufferings. I think of Corrie ten Boom. I think of St. Shephen.

And then I think of the other sorts of martyrdoms: Christian businessmen ridiculed for their scruples. Jimmy, limited in every moment of his life by cerebral palsy; Tom, in the diurnal and desperate agonies of rheumatoid arthritis.

They have all known, in some measure already, the fellowship — and the power: Dietrich, and Corrie, and Stephen; Jimmie, and Tom.

And Peter too. Calloused old fisherman Peter, the first of the Peters that Christian history knows about. In 2 Peter 1:4, he stated his ultimate of ultimates: "that by these ye might be partakers of the divine nature." Or, as the New English Bible puts it, "and come to share in the very being of God."

The mind staggers. It's like having a huge spotlight flung into one's eyes, like hearing a Niagara after deafness. Man, mere and mortal man, is to share the very being of God!

One more topic I jotted down last night, and in cool morning daylight my heart cries "Amen" and "Amen":

— *To obey, in little things and large things, God's will for my life as I comprehend it.* A sense of my own temerity shakes me. I, to venture that kind of declaration? I, blundering and fallible and —

But he says to hush, and to get on with it. (If I'm hearing rightly, that's what he says.) It's like being on a mountain ledge, and no step to take except forward and upward, none at all. I may be mouse-high beside Brother Martin, but my arm swings with the same curving of his as I nail my theses to my Wittenberg door; here I stand, and God helping me, I can do no other.

It is a today-new nailing of the theses, and yet it is not a new thing.

At other times I have built my altars, like the patriarchs on the hills where Israeli tourist buses chug today. (Hebron, Bethlehem, the Golan Heights.) And now and again the fire has touched my altars.

One such time that I actually do not even recall was brought to my awareness in a way that moved me to the very depths. During our college Homecoming in November of 1977, a girls' service club, the Ladies of Elpinice presented a "This Is Your Life" program. It's a tradition around here; they've been doing such a program annually for some twenty years. Well, that year the spotlight fell upon my unexpectant face in the audience, and I was led to the platform for roses and visitors and various kindly reminiscent words.

My surgeon brother, Wendale, could not be present, but he sent several pages of rememberings and greetings, from which the girls selected some fun and chuckles for their script. Later when I saw his whole letter I smiled to read about pony-saddling and about my juvenile lectures on "the exquisite beauty of various parts of a squash blossom." Then another paragraph. I read it, and read it again — and knew an overwhelming awe.

"Really the most outstanding memory," wrote Wendale, "is a Sunday evening when Elva was about 14 years old. At a neighboring Free Methodist church (Stone Church) she sought the Lord in complete consecration. As she raised her head in acceptance there was an iridescent illumination of her face which I have never seen before nor since. I had no idea what Elva's Christian work would be but I was acutely aware that it would be many things that only she could and would do. No prophecy was spoken but the feeling was universal among the handful present. That is a cherished memory that is too sacred to be expressed well in mere words."

I truly do not remember that evening prayer time, but I am very grateful to Wendale for remembering, and for recording. And I thank God that his flame touched the altar of the teenager I then was.

Another moment, a different hue of the flame, when my age had doubled. Yes, I must have been about twenty-eight. I was teaching at Seattle Pacific College, having joined the staff there right after the winding up of the Ph.D., after a very strong sense of "Macedonian call" for that era of my life. I was working very hard, loving my work, learning immense amounts, and feeling the deep inner stability of God's place, at God's time, for this life which had been committed to him.

It came to me then, almost like biting upon a pebble in an elegant crab louis, to have an older woman take me aside one day for some firm advice. She was — oh, who knows about ages? Maybe 42. Maybe 46. Spinsterly, certainly, in the more pejorative shadings of "spinsterly," and tending toward the harsh, the sour, the bitter. "You shouldn't be teaching at Seattle Pacific, you know," she told me firmly. "There isn't really much chance to meet new men around here. You're still young, you know. You ought to be working somewhere else, where you would be meeting men. . . ."

I wonder what I said. I do not recall. I do remember my incredulity. I remember the glow, inside me, of a renewed altar flame. To move from what I counted his appointment in order to search for a husband seemed to me to be a singularly ridiculous possibility for a Christian. No. First things must come first.

One Splendid Elm, and Other Landscapes 2

On Sunday before last, I took myself out to dinner at the Holiday Inn in Vandalia. One of the boons of singleness: at a moment's impulse, I can take myself out to dinner without tangling up anyone else's schedules. On such occasions, I often have really good times in discussing ideas and events and circumstances with myself. Maybe I'm a little like John Henry Newman, the great 19th century writer, of whom it was once remarked, "Never less alone than when alone."

Well, on Sunday before last, one topic of our discussion was a magnificent American elm which stands near Highway I-70 between Greenville and Vandalia. It stands alone in a field, with the soybeans or the corn stalks around its toes, like minions doing homage to some Oriental potentate. If they were nearer, other elms or oaks or maples of impressive size could be doing obeisance too, for that one elm is of truly superb height and circumference. And it is proportioned beautifully. If I were a craftsman in oils and acrylics, I think I would want to set up a canvas near it and try for a painting of its great symmetrical boughs. Looking at it, one feels a *frisson* of emotion up the spine, like the ripples of joy when a great cathedral organ sends out fortissimo chords.

It ought to have a name. Maybe, for my conversations with me, I should give it one. All right. The Tenney Tree. That's the way I have been thinking about it for these two weeks.

It isn't the only tree that stands alone among the fields of this rolling farm country in southern Illinois, The Tenney Tree, although it's certainly one of the finest of them all. Frequently, as one drives around the country roads of Bond County — as I like to do, especially when goldenrod and black-eyed susans and ironweed are filling roadsides with yellows and purples — as one drives toward Hillsboro or Centralia or Carlyle or Carbondale or St. Louis, alert eyes see them often: the solitary trees, on hill crests or in field edges. An elm, an oak, a maple. Not crowded by adjacent trees. Sturdy. Gracious. Emanating a sense of self-respect, ease, power, poise, grace. Gloriously proportioned symmetry.

They have grown alone, and they have grown splendidly. If the elm seed that has grown, in the course of fifteen decades or so, into The Tenney Tree had fallen along a nearby creek or in a thicket two fields away, it would now be blurred into the landscape. It would be spindly-slim and badly proportioned – but no one would notice the proportions, because it would be just a part of the woods.

Ever since I moved to southern Illinois, the splendid solitary trees have seemed to me to present an interesting analogy with what can happen to a personality: alone, and with room to grow.

Such a person, who touched my life in indelible ways when I was an undergraduate, was Dr. Mary Alice Tenney, for whom I now name this great elm. In graduate school I used to say jokingly that she was my patron saint and guardian angel, but there was always earnestness under the jesting. She was my revered and inspiring friend until she died in 1971, and a photo of her continues to admonish me from my bookshelves. She was tough-minded but gentle; quick to challenge shoddy thought in a classroom or in a conversation; quick to notice the needs and moods of other human beings. She was a disciplined scholar, a historian of early Methodism whose research was even translated into Japanese for use in seminary study in the Orient. She was a wise counselor, solicitous about everyone but domineering over no one. She was also merry in spirit, full of infectious good humor. She touched thousands of lives, and touched them all for good. At her funeral her neighbor and colleague. Dr. Ralph Miller, a professor of physics at Greenville College, said thoughtfully, "She was everyone's best friend."

And Miss Tenney's solitudes had enabled her to grow to that kind of splendid spiritual height, to that kind of symmetry of soul. Had her Lord directed her into matrimony, she would have been a really wonderful wife; we all thought that. In fact, our undergraduate dorm-room discussions did not spare the conjectures about a man whom we thought she ought to have married, and we had our times of wrath with him for marrying another instead of our beloved Miss Tenney. But God had led her into the solitudes, and led her in them, and her soul grew and grew and grew.

Whom else shall we name?

Doesn't everyone know the solitary trees – the souls that have grown very deep roots and very wide branches by standing alone, the trees that stand out against a skyline?

Yesterday's mail brought a note from a mutual friend quoting a few lines from another of them — Bertha Munro, dean emerita of Eastern Nazarene College. I wish I knew Miss Munro better; I have seen her only a few times, but her whole life is a very tonic. I turn to my bookshelves for her autobiography, *The Years Teach,* and note again what Samuel Young wrote in the foreword: "Dean Munro writes from the epic of her maturity with clarity and strength that build confidence and faith. Her gentle humor and humility afford a fragrance that is unmistakable. She makes it easier for all who read her writings to believe in God. . . ."[1]

As I think now about Miss Tenney and Miss Munro and others of their soul-strength, I think other thoughts — about the whole landscape of contemporary America. About what people have been telling me concerning the singles in America. The landscape, I'm told, needs some scrutiny, and I have come to believe that it does.

There are more than 45 million of them, I'm told — the singles in America. Sociologist Peter Stein checked the 1975 census records and found 47,104,000 of us at age 18 or older.[2] Nicholas Christoff reports the 1976 census up to 48,926,000.[3] How many of those millions, I wonder, face their present singlehood with the soul-deep and eternal aloneness of not knowing Christ? How many are Christians, but keep their Christianity in one box and their lifestyle in another box?

I'm told further that "one in three of marriageable-age adults" is now single "at any point in time."[4] One in three. We hear a great deal, see a great deal in print, for the two-thirds; books and articles on the good marriage abound. And new ones keep rolling from the presses. Marriage counselors are familiar personages, to help the married to be well married. But how many publications are talking about preparation for good singlehood? Who is counseling with the singles? I stopped in one church library and looked with interest; I found quite a shelf full of books on marriage and the home, but only one slim volume about the singles — and it with a title that made me want to push it away, or maybe to put it in a plain brown wrapper if I would check it out. I stopped in at a college library. (And let me note that it is counted a very good college library, where faculty members have repeatedly found materials that they did not find in their universities, for graduate courses they were taking.) Well, I thumbed the card catalog, and between *The Singing Wilderness* and *A Single Six-Year Term for President,* I found exactly four cards — and two of them were for one book, since *Single* was both subject and title.

Singles need, nevertheless, to talk things over sometimes. They're facing the stereotypes of society: that singleness is merely a preface to matrimony, and not a very significant state to the one who is within it. That singleness is the circumstance of those who have somehow failed. Or, another stereotype, that singleness is for "swinging singles," who want to live an irresponsible life of casual sex and other self-indulgence. Some singles, comments sociologist Stein, "are discovering that their preferred life styles do not have to comply with the scripts written for them; and they are choosing to write scripts of their own — a difficult task."[5] What churches, what discussion leaders, are helping them with the script-writing task?

Too little, thinks Mark W. Lee, is known about happy singles. "We do know," he says, "that many married people are deeply unhappy, and that many singles are happy."[6] Well, let's think. Let's ask. Let's know.

Many younger singles, the teens and twenties and some of the thirties, are living a vaguely expectant kind of life which we might call "the hope chest syndrome," deferring decisions and opportunities by their "if-I-get-married-I-will" substratum of thought. Certainly many singles of all sorts and conditions are drifting along in an unexamined kind of life. They haven't really let themselves, nor any counselor, nor God himself, put certain disconcerting questions to them, yet a painful crisis of self-examination might lead to valuable and creative changes and growings. What about the unexamined single life in twentieth-century America?

And the unexamined stereotypes and attitudes of society, in twentieth-century America? Stereotypes! Let me illustrate. I came across an allusion recently to a "classic discussion of early adulthood," and I was informed that the "classic discussion" listed eight tasks which young adults "must learn" on their way to adulthood. Um-hum, eight. And the first four, in order, were: mate-finding; learning how to be a spouse; beginning a family; rearing the kiddies. I do not use the sociological words of the "classic discussion." As I read, I blinked and smiled, and felt like drawing some cartoons for the *New Yorker*. (If I were a cartoonist.) "Must learn," forsooth. Some young adults indeed "must" learn those tasks, but millions and millions must not. Need not. Will not. The stereotypes need examining!

If people find themselves in a faulty marriage, what do they do about it? Suffer. Endure. Go to a counselor. Get help. In our culture, more and more frequently, they get a divorce.

If a person finds himself in a faulty singleness, what does he do about it? He suffers. He endures. Will he go to a counselor? Who is counseling the singles? He can't get a divorce from himself — unless it's the ultimate and dreadful separation of self-slaughter. There is a possible route of "divorce" from his singleness, through a marriage. And from his faulty singleness he may hurry into that kind of "divorce" so unthinkingly that he will only prepare the way for yet another divorce a few years later.

Singleness needs to be thought about.

Among sociologists, there seem to be some beginnings. Among all the university and college courses on marriage and the family, the University of Southern California has been offering a course, I'm told, on "The Challenge of Being Single," and Marie Edwards has gained quite a reputation as its instructor during weekend workshops on the various campuses of U.S.C.

The real implications of Christianity need to be thought about. For twenty centuries, the real implications of Christianity have needed to be thought about.

And now, in our present now, the thinkings need to be brought together: to be Christian, and single. What does it mean, what can it mean, and what might it mean, to be Christian and single?

Let's talk about it. I'm no voice of utter wisdom on these topics, but I like to look at landscapes. And out there is the landscape of America — on which there are some splendid solitary trees.

Notes to Chapter 2

1. Bertha Munro, *The Years Teach: Remembrances to Bless* (Kansas City: Beacon Hill Press, 1970).
2. Peter Stein, *Single* (Englewood Cliffs, New Jersey: Prentice-Hall, 1976), p. 1n. This figure includes the widowed and the divorced.
3. Nicholas B. Christoff, *Saturday Night, Sunday Morning: Singles and the Church* (New York: Harper and Row, 1978), p. 132, in Appendix B, "Recent Census Reports on Singles," pp. 132-141.
4. Mark W. Lee, "The Church and the Unmarried," in *It's Okay to be Single,* edited by Gary R. Collins (Waco, Texas: Word Books, 1976), p. 43.
5. Stein, *Single* p. 62.
6. Lee, pp. 54-55.

Why Do the Others Marry? **3**

Good Morning.

Welcome to the seminar of the morning. Of this wintry morning. It is not the day of the Epiphany now, but it is still that season. A professional voice has just been saying on the radio, "Temperatures right around the zero mark in metropolitan St. Louis . . . three degrees right now . . . winds will remain strong." You should have seen me (or, no, you should not have seen me!) some minutes ago when I put on fuzzy-lined boots and oddly assorted other protectors, including my oldest coat, while I carried the garbage can out to the curb. I used oldest gloves, too — a now-threadbare pair which I pull on with a new glee each time that I reach for them, because I first reached for them in Edinburgh. Today, as the season turns, I left on top of the garbage can a wreath of pine twigs and cones which has announced Advent and Christmas and Epiphany from my front door.

Now, on from there.

That's a basic principle of human experience, isn't it? — on from there, whatever the "there" of one's life has been, up to now. It's a principle I want to explore in all of our thinkings together.

Now, for the seminar of this morning. Probably the teens and the twenties are largely the ones in attendance today. Right? Maybe a sprinkling of thirties, though anyone is welcome. Anyone at all.

I glance out the window at a woodpecker drilling his way up a maple trunk, and I clear my throat to propound the query. Why do the others marry? Why have the others married? You are single, at seventeen or nineteen or twenty-four or twenty-seven. The others are married. Since we were mid-teens, the others have been marrying around us. (I smile, and remember how I celebrated my own sixteenth birthday by giving a small shower for a neighborhood bride. My birthday gave a convenient excuse for a surprise to her.) Why did they marry?

No big mystery, you mutter. Look out the window again: the woodpecker pecks wood; that's his nature. Birds mate with other birds. That's their nature. We are biological mammals, and the mating instinct has been within us as long as *Homo sapiens* has walked upon this planet.

Well, you're partly right, but only partly. Man is a mammal, but he is more than a mammal. Much more, to his glory or to his shame. ("What is man, that thou art mindful of him?" cried the Psalmist to Jehovah. "For thou hast made him a little lower than the angels, and hast crowned him with glory and honour. Thou madest him to have dominion over the works of thy hands —")

I repeat: Why do they — Some of you grin a little, and titter a little, and shake your heads. How naïve can one be? you wonder. Anybody knows that they get married because they Fell in Love.

An interesting idiom, that, I murmur. Mischief-smiles are twitching at my lips. They Fell in Love.

Why do the songs never say, or the movies never declare that one might Ascend into Love, or Climb into Love, or Grow into Love, or Rise to Love? Why are people always Falling in Love? Is there some linguistic link with the primal fall? Laughter ripples through the room. When it subsides, I ask more seriously: Do we wish, semantically and subconsciously, to declare an experience which actually is beyond all rational control?

Without a doubt, our culture constantly proclaims and implies that people are expected to fall in love, and many would say they marry as a consequence of that fall. Love — which popular culture blurs pretty much with the sex drive — is constantly extolled as the acme of experience, the total need of the human being, the solid and adequate foundation for any marriage. "She's in love" is thought to explain everything; it's all she can possibly desire. "He's in love," and all the problems of mundane existence are expected to disappear like Houdini's kerchiefs.

Indubitably, to be in love is a very powerful force among mortals. But there is quite a little more to think about.

Why do they marry?

Gail Sheehy, the brilliant and cynical author of *Passages,* reports firmly that among 115 depth interviews which she carried through in preparation for her book (of which the full title is *Passages: Predictable Crises of Adult Life*), no man who was past thirty when he was interviewed even mentioned that he was "in love" when he married a wife. Nor, she adds, did any of them suggest "that sex had been an inducement." (I'm looking at page 152 of the Bantam paper-back, if you want to check it out.)

With all due allowance for what she calls "the amnesia factor," and for the possibility that a researcher may find what the researcher wants to find, her comment can stimulate some useful ponderings. Why have the others married? Why have you not married? If you do marry, what will the reasons be? The ostensible reasons, the real reasons?

Some of us marry because our society expects us to. That's at least one strand in the corded "why," and sometimes a pretty thick strand. Little girls hardly past kindergarten receive bride dolls to play with. In and out of the classroom, junior high and high school students get the message. College campuses vary, but the indoctrination, both subtle and unsubtle, may be unrelenting: you are expected to marry. It may give rise to a phenomenon which is laughed about with humor-less laughter in dormitory rooms: Senior Panic, the desperate last efforts to find her, or him, before "Pomp and Circumstance" and the diplomas. Meanwhile, magazine advertising and TV advertising and department stores, serving their own commercial interest, din the message: "You are expected to marry. You are expected to marry. You are expected to marry." Later on, alumni magazines, appropri-ately enough, give major column space to Weddings and to Births. But from them, too, the message is reiterated: "You are expected to marry."

Not more than hours ago, I heard a resonant ministerial voice (I'll carefully not mention the kind of microphone through which his voice was being transmitted to me) in an eloquent plea: ". . . and you young people, you will marry and have children of your own, and you should be thinking now about. . . ." I felt a little like tweaking his coatsleeve, if it had been in reaching distance, and protesting, "Sir, sir, you're building pressure that these kids don't need. *Some* of them will marry. *Some* of them will not marry. Don't add your fine voice to the pressure from society which will push some of them into a choice that's wrong for them."

Society has expected it, and they themselves have come to expect it. Maybe they are in love with love, actually; maybe they haven't tripped nor stumbled nor otherwise fallen into love.

Within society, parents particularly have expected marriage to happen. Happily married parents want their children to have equally great happiness in life. Unhappily married parents want their chil-dren to find a security they have not found. Any parent may look forward to the vicarious excitement of a romance, an engagement, a marriage. Any parent may know, and express without hesitation, his desire to be a grandparent.

Society expects the task of parenting to continue in a primary way until the young person is "on his own, and married, and settled down." The parents want their task to be completed in a way that brings honor to themselves, and the message lingers: "You are expected to marry."

Parents push toward marriage in another way, too. I'm thinking now of a young woman to whom I wrote just this morning; Olivia is involved in a common-law marriage which seems to have just about everything wrong with it, and it seems to be clearly an example of what Gail Sheehy has called "jail-break" marriages. (The book *Passages* again.) Young people, especially the teen-age brides and grooms, especially the runaway brides and grooms, may feel such a compulsion to be adult persons, rather than ordered-around children, that they "break jail" and marry.

Maybe they call it love. Maybe it is a kind of love. Maybe it is primarily desperation and a need to escape, to break free. After the jailbreak, a wonderfully good marriage may yet grow into being, but it isn't likely. (I pause to think again about Olivia, and about the stark tragedy of her last letter to me, and I wonder again whether I should telephone a minister I know who lives near her. Who can help you, dear Olivia? Your brilliant mind, your winsome spirit; the misery you have stepped into; the deeper and deeper steps. And I turn from our seminar to breathe a prayer: Touch her today, O God. In the midst of the wretchedness, touch Olivia. Show her the best courses for rebuilding her life.)

Along with the jailbreakers are the other naïve ones who have a problem, a yearning, a need, and think that marriage is the full solution to it all. In a way, we're all of us always like the squalling infants we were when life began; we want to be taken care of, to be warmed and fed and rocked and soothed and cuddled. We want — late teens and twenties especially want — to be protected, assured, calmed. It's a stressful world, but marriage, we feel sure, will ease the stress, ban the worries, calm the tensions. And marriage may solve some things — or it may not solve anything at all. For many young people, an old set of problems is simply replaced with a new set, a bigger and fiercer set. And the divorce statistics curve upward.

Lynn. Now I'm thinking about Lynn. When she was in college, she was essentially friendless, except for the fellow whom she was dating. Other students would have called her thoughtless, over-impulsive, opinionated, insecure, selfish, jealous. She was a problem to the head resident in her dormitory; nobody wanted to room with her. *Nobody.* And nothing was solved when Lynn got married before finishing college. She still has all the problems she brought along in her college-youth luggage, plus other ugly baggage now, labelled "divorce." I wonder how Lynn earned her groceries last month. I wonder.

Some of them marry for a certain sort of prestige, wouldn't you think? Partly for that; another strand in the rope. Suppose George is tired of going alone to the social events in his university department, or of finding a date when the local expectation is "couples only" for departmental dinners. Suppose George feels he will be more totally a person in the community if he becomes part of a "we" rather than a solitary "I." George marries.

Loneliness has harried him. And loneliness can be a gnawing, beastly associate.

Or practicality. If Joyce's father is a senior partner in Richard's law firm, and it would be such an advantage to everyone for Richard and Joyce to be married. If Richard needs a hostess for his receptions when he goes on in politics. If Richard needs a coordinator for his social life, his laundry lists, his shopping and his shirts. Joyce is available. Joyce is pleasant. And, now, at least for the present, Joyce is married.

Suppose that Sara has a deep, deep hunger for approval. When she was three, she clung to her father's knees and longed for his pats on her curls. When she was a schoolgirl, she lived for her teacher's approbation. Her mother has always been able to send her mood up or down like mercury in a March thermometer by praise given or praise withheld. Suppose Sara meets Tony, who approves of her so much that he asks her out, and then so incredibly much that he proposes. She will be dizzy with happiness. But if the marriage didn't have much else to build upon, what odds would you give it?

Not much better, probably, than Ellie's marriage had. Actually, we all thought Ellie had a pretty good thing going. Gil was handsome, considerate, poised, with good job experience behind him and better prospects ahead. He was a campus leader, a brisk and efficient executive in student organizations. Ellie and her family gave a big party to announce the engagement, and everyone's gladness seemed solid and durable. But in quiet fact Ellie's marriage was an illustration of what you talked a little about at the very beginning of this morning's seminar; it was a mating of mammals, and (I reiterate) man is more than a mammal. If I had said to anyone at Ellie's wedding reception, "This is one of the ones that will splinter into divorce," I would have been thought quite mad. I didn't even think it. But I remembered afterward, when Ellie's mother was going about with shadowed eyes and tight-closed lip muscles, how Ellie had once startled a listener with a self-assured quip about how Gil was marrying her, she guessed, because she had a few pounds of avoirdupois in just the right places. She was buxom, but she and Gil needed more than a good pair of mammary glands to meet all the years and fears and heartaches that were yet to come into their two lives.

Last night, thinking toward this seminar, thinking about the Ellie's and the others, I had already turned off my bedside lamp when a verity struggled its way into my brain. It had such muscle that I turned on the lamp again and reached for a pen to jot down an aphorism: People — some people — get married because they are unsuccessful at being single.

Think so?

If a marriage seems not to be working, people may try for an out by the painful, scarring process of divorce. If singleness seems not to be working, some people try for an out by hurrying into a marriage. Any marriage. A wrong-for-them marriage. An illusion-of-happiness marriage.

Sometimes I look at their wedding photos in the newspaper — all those seventeens and eighteens and nineteens, and all those twenties, too — and feel like asking them: Why, you innocent? Why, you, and why you, and why you? Why, really? Do you marry for good reasons? Are you indeed entering what Peter Marshall called "the highest halls of human happiness," or are you entering new prisons of the spirit? "Well, why do you *think*?" they'd probably answer. "We fell in love!"

Someone stirs in this seminar group. Look, someone protests. Don't be so doleful and derogatory. People do fall in love and stay loving. Don't you know any happy stories?

Yes, friends, I do. Heaps of them. And I thank the Lord for them, each and all! The contacts I have had with many, many happy marriages have been a brightness through my whole life, believe me. This story, for example, doesn't require any supposes; it is utterly and totally for real:

When I was a junior in college, my Sunday School teacher, who was also my esteemed professor of Greek, brought in a guest lecturer to speak to us one day; the lesson was to be on the Christian home, and Miss Dare wanted us to hear the viewpoint of a faculty wife. In particular, she wanted us to hear from Mrs. Wilson C. LaDue, whose husband taught modern languages.

Anyone who has had any contact with Greenville College during the past fifty years — nearly anyone — will know about Mary LaDue. She came to the campus as a very young instructor in music, married, and stayed on, after Dr. LaDue's death in 1969, until her own retirement. Everyone knows that they were sweethearts until the moment of his death, that he wrote poetry for her and cherished her with flowers, that high earnestness and bubbling humor and utter fidelity bound them together. Everyone knows (she is still glad to talk about him with her many visitors) how they loved to travel together, to enjoy music together, to delight together in the careers of the children they adopted.

Well, I knew something of all that already when I was a student, and Miss Dare asked Mrs. LaDue to speak to us. The LaDues were our junior class sponsors, and I had been in their home repeatedly. They were aunt and uncle, fondly, to all of us. The thing she really wanted to share with us, Mrs. LaDue told us that day, was a finding; after her father-in-law died, she and Uncle Wilson had acquired the diaries kept by that saintly man. He had been a popular Bible teacher, respected and revered, with the campus nickname of "The Rabbi." Their first eagerness, lovers that they were, was to turn together to see what The Rabbi might have written on the date of their marriage. "My son Wilson was married today," they read, "to Mary Helen Watson. I am very sure God wills it."

I have never forgotten — obviously I have not — the awe and joy and triumph in Mrs. LaDue's voice as she told us about it. That was the deep foundation of their home, she assured us: to be very sure that God willed it. Uncle Wilson had been sure before he proposed it to her, and she had been sure before she accepted his proposing. And it delighted them to have the written record of The Rabbi's affirmation; he too had prayed earnestly about the decision, and had become calmly sure in his conviction: "I am very sure God wills it."

When such a marriage happens, surely the joy bells ring, on this earth and beyond it. It is not just a trite phrase, to speak of marriages that are "made in heaven." That is where true marriages are to be made.

With which, let's close this seminar.

Oh. The temperature is up to six degrees Fahrenheit now, outside, and the woodpecker has gone, and a tree has been felled in the little woods beyond my studio window. For this day: Adios.

Are You, or Aren't You? And If Not, Why? 4

Recently when I picked up a book about singles — I'm trying carefully not to remember which book it was — I smiled in lively amusement over one assertion, which struck me as really comic in its superficiality and inaccuracy. The majority of those who are single, said the author calmly, are so because they have never given or received a proposal of marriage. Well. That's a neatly tied package, now, isn't it?

In reality, if you are single, why *are* you single?

If it chances that you have never spoken nor listened to a "Marry me!" plea, why (really and truly, in the broader implications) have you not?

One can spend far too much mental energy on such queries, but now and again a retrospective and evaluative probing of one's own biography can have its uses, can be a readying of the house of life for new constructive projects, or new interior decoration, or a new kind of joy to be lived out inside the house. The unexamined life, thought Socrates, is not worth living. Have you examined yours lately?

Once when I was in the vicinity of 33 or 34, an article of mine in a national magazine brought a commendatory letter from a professional journalist. His note beckoned toward a response; eventually I heard from him quite a few times, and gained good learnings from him. Early on in the correspondence, he appended a terse postscript: "Are you, or aren't you? And if not, why?" Rightly guessing that he meant marital status, I thought very carefully about the sentences that I finally wrote — though I wrote them lightly and briskly enough when they moved through the typewriter. (I could wish that I might put my hands now on what I said then; it would be interesting to review.) That journalist did me a good turn — greater than he could then have guessed; it was valuable for me to do some self-interviewing, some considering of considerings. A special sort of New Year's Day scrutiny, out of season.

To a similar sort of New Year's Day scrutiny, whatever the calendar says while you read, I now invite you.

First off, is marriage an open option in your life? Would you consider marriage this month, this year, if a winsome candidate appeared on your horizons? If you say "No, no!" or a milder "No," or "Probably not," or "I doubt it," your responses to the rest of this interrogation will have a difference of texture. But thinking through the rest of the interrogation may still be valuable in clarifying to you, and increasing for you, the serenities of your life. Is marriage, then, an open option? Yes? No? Maybe? If you'd say "Maybe," what are the qualifiers?

Take some scribble paper, if you like, and jot down the qualifiers. Or postpone that part of the self-scrutiny until later.

Let's turn, then, to my journalist correspondent's blunt question: "And if not, why?"

Here's a check list. Think your way through it. Add to it. You may want to put an X beside each item that describes you partially, and double or triple X-marks for emphasis beside more important items. Your self-evaluation and self-esteem will become clearer through the process, I think, as my own self-evaluation and self-esteem were certainly (and usefully) clarified when I was writing back to my inquisitive acquaintance, the journalist. You may begin a collection of ideas that you will want to talk through with a friend, with a counselor, with a discussion group. If so, blessings to you!

WHY, REALLY, AM I SINGLE?

_____ 1. For me, it's a good life. I like the degree of independence I have for travel and hobbies.

_____ 2. I like my own ways of doing things around the house.

_____ 3. I was married before, and emotionally I am still married.

_____ 4. Well, I have always been shy.

_____ 5. I like being able to spend my income entirely as I choose.

_____ 6. I wouldn't care to give up the home that I have chosen (inherited, designed).

_____ 7. I'm too fully responsible for my parents' (mother's, father's) welfare to consider marriage now.

_____ 8. I'm past the marrying age; that's all there is to it.

_____ 9. I like being able to go out with a lot of different people rather than being tied down to one.

_____ 10. My career is my total priority, and marriage would interfere with it too much.

_____ 11. I'm too fully committed to my present housemate (housemates); she (he, they) would be desolate if I were to marry and leave her (him, them).

_____ 12. I like not having to adapt constantly to another person.

_____ 13. During high school and college, I was too involved with my studies (or work, or family, or sports) to date much, and now I don't know how to bridge the gap.

_____ 14. My emotions are still too deeply committed to a person who was formerly the center of my life.

_____ 15. Guys seem to be frightened off because I'm superior to them in job skills.

_____ 16. My work does not put me in touch with any persons whom I'd care to marry.

_____ 17. Singleness is the way of life that contributes most to my personal growth and well-being.

_____ 18. I'm just not that affirmative about the idea of marriage, and never have been.

_____ 19. My community, my church, my whole social life do not put me in touch with persons whom I'd care to marry.

_____ 20. I have always disliked housework and resisted the housewife's roles.

_____ 21. As a single, I am more free and flexible for some kinds of Christian service.

_____ 22. I'm not all that good-looking, and men (women) don't give me much attention.

_____ 23. I'm affirmative about the idea of marriage, but, up to now, God has led me away from the friendships that moved toward an engagement.

_____ 24. Men (women) bore me.

_____ 25. The divorce hurt too much; I haven't recuperated enough to consider another marriage.

_____ 26. I like my present freedom to make my own choices.

_____ 27. The responsibility of having a mate does not appeal to me.

_____ 28. The responsibility of having children to rear does not appeal to me.

_____ 29. The marriages I see among my closest associates make me think how fortunate I am not to be in their shoes.

_____ 30. I have physical handicaps (illnesses) which would make marriage very improbable.

_____ 31. The men (women) I have dated were too inferior to me intellectually to interest me very much.

_____ 32. I really don't know how to socialize in pre-dating and dating situations.

_____ 33. I find that I usually withdraw from strong emotion, and especially from the emotions of a courtship.

_____ 34. There are more women than men in our society, and I guess I have been less aggressive than other women are.

_____ 35. I have not yet had the financial security that would permit me to marry.

_____ 36. I don't especially need or crave the sexual part of marriage.

_____ 37. I simply have not encountered a man (woman) whom I like that much.

_____ 38. The one person I would have wished to marry is married to someone else.

_____ 39. The one person I would have wished to marry is no longer living.

_____ 40. I'm basically very selfish, and my singleness enables me to look after my own happiness.

_____ 41. I'm basically very unselfish, and my singleness enables me to help a lot of other people.

_____ 42. My childhood gave me deep prejudices against marriage; my parents were not happy together.

_____ 43. When I was younger, I wasn't free to marry; now, there's no one in sight that interests me.

_____ 44. I don't need to get married to escape from anything.

_____ 45. I'm timid and hesitant, usually, about any big decisions or involvements.

_____ 46. I'm comfortable in living with my parents; why change?

_____ 47. I take seriously St. Paul's counsel to the Corinthians, that singleness is a preferred choice for disciples of Jesus Christ.

_____ 48. Being single is a good choice for meeting my personal goals.

_____ 49. No one has yet offered me a better life than the singleness I have.

_____ 50. I believe deeply that a loving God is guiding my life, and that for now he has guided me to my present single role.

*   *   *   *

So, what is the picture that emerges from the darkroom of the ego, from the developing fluid of such an interrogation?

Revise these queries, or add fifty more, or leave them as they are. What do they show you about yourself? What do they show you about singles in general?

Would these be some of the conclusions?

First, the "why" of anyone's being single is exceedingly complex. A network of a thousand decisions, ten thousand decisions — one's own decidings, other persons' decidings — have fitted together to make now into now.

Second: some of the factors are beyond the single's own deciding. Those the Christian can entrust (after strong cryings and tears, perhaps; after his own personal Gethsemane experiences, it may be) to his sovereign Lord. Those he imprints daily, daily with reiterated Scriptural affirmations, backward and forward from Romans 8:28. Maybe he lingers, deeply and often, inside the tenting of Psalm 84:11-12.

Third: The past is not always the measure of the future. Perhaps your thus-far years have been basically full of selfish reasons for being single; maybe the years ahead will have more creative and altruistic "whys." Maybe your past self had limitings, self-imposed or otherwise, which your future self will not have. Maybe there are some good growings and changings ahead for you, as you now see your single self more clearly and truly.

Fourth: More than many singles have even said aloud to themselves, and more than society in general would know how to admit, singleness may be right and good and chosen — for those individuals to whom it is indeed right and good and chosen.

I would realize, of course, that for some of us — and maybe sometimes for all of us — the inclination is not to take a cool and rational look at any "whys" that can be identified on any check list. We are more inclined to yell "why" toward the heavens, or to whisper it into pillows. We pray it, aloud or silently, consciously and subconsciously: *"Why, God, why?* You gave me this body. You gave me these emotional capacities. You put the longings inside me. *Why, God, why?* Other people find mates. Why can't I? Why haven't I? *Why? Why? Why?"*

When that is the scream, when that is the mood, it is time to reach again for the Psalms, for Isaiah, for St. Paul's letters. God may not send any tall glowing angels to explain just "why," and he may not change one smidgen of your immediate circumstances, but he will let you know that he is present with you, in each nook and pressure of the circumstance.

While I have been thinking about this complicated query, "And if not, why?," two mental mental pictures have kept appearing and reappearing on the projector screens of my mind. Maybe they are worth flashing across other screens for a moment. Two very dissimilar photographs.

The first is of a spry, energetic, vigorous man whom I last saw when he was past eighty and moving from his then-locality to marry a woman whom he had come to know through a computer dating service. A widower for several years, Mr. X had apparently decided that another marriage was what he wanted, and he had wanted it enough to pursue it with resourcefulness and *élan*. Many of you have not made it that fully the business of your lives, to find a marriage; you would give Mr. X your happy blessings, but you would not ask him for the mailing address of his computer service.

My second photo comes from a criminal courtroom and its environment. I was required, one autumn, to be a prosecution witness in a murder case, after the detectives had come to me for handwriting samples from a murdered young man whom I had taught. While I sat in a hard straight chair in a courtroom corridor, awaiting the summons of the baliff, I had to notice a woman near me who also awaited the instructions of the courtroom. She was grimy, dingy, bleak, bedraggled. Under her sandals, a visible crust of dirt beneath the bare toenails. Later I had occasion to learn a little about that dismal woman, and then a little more. Married, yes. Probably her fourth marriage now, actually. Or fifth? No, fourth, they thought. Inside the courtroom, after my words had been spoken to the lawyers and to the judge, I saw her with her current husband, and I had to think immediately of how his profile would look in "Most Wanted" posters for post office walls. The ache of her whole situation still writhes inside me. (Such a husband! Such a harshness, such a hardness in a human face!)

Apparently that woman had wanted to be married. She had needed to be married. She had made it the business of her life to be married. And she was. After a fashion. In spite of her obvious limits in appearance and in graces, she had found marriage after marriage. Obviously, for a good many millions of single Americans, both Christians and pagans, marriage is not so necessary a goal as it had been both for that sad woman and for the successive men who had married her. She exemplified pretty pathetically what I have heard said — what you have probably heard said: that anyone can get married, anyone at all, who is willing enough to lower his standards, and to lower them far enough.

For many Christian singles who have tended to blush or stammer, to evade or laugh away the "If not, why?" query, perhaps there is a new level of affirmation awaiting: "Why not? Because, for now, I'm free to be single. Because God's leadings thus far have led me to singleness. Because he is giving me a role as a single to fill for him."

I reach again for a devotional book I used within minutes after my eyes came open this morning. From an ancient Methodist covenant service, the words resonate strongly for the single Christian in his now:

> "I am no longer my own, but Thine. Put me to what Thou wilt, rank me with whom Thou wilt; put me to doing, put me to suffering; let me be employed for Thee or laid aside for Thee, exalted for Thee or brought low for Thee; let me be full, let me be empty; let me have all things, let me have nothing; I freely and heartily yield all things to Thy pleasure and disposal.
>
> "And now, O glorious and blessed God. Father, Son and Holy Spirit, Thou are mine, and I am Thine. So be it. And the Covenant which I have made on earth, let it be ratified in heaven."

For many single Christians, that is why; for now, their now, that is precisely *why*.[1]

Note to Chapter 4

1. From *A Diary of Private Prayer,* ed. Elizabeth Goudge (New York: Coward-McCann, 1966), p. 15. Copyright 1966 by Elizabeth Goudge, who gave acknowledgment to The Epworth Press "for the prayer from *The Methodist Book of Shorter Offices.*"

The Courage to Stay Single 5

The morning mail is always a suspense until it arrives. Sometimes, after I flip the dial on my box in the college mailroom panel, the rest of the day carries its coruscations, and I go around with extra measures of sunshine tumbling from class lists or text books, from file drawers and snack bar counters. Sometimes, the bleak emptiness of a junk-mail-only day. Sometimes, turbulent and shaking pain scuttles from the mailbox and lands somewhere around my diaphragm.

And sometimes the odd mixtures.

Today was a mixture day. Today, a lovely fold of pastel cardboard telling me that Bettina and Matt have been "united as one in Christ." The folder carries a printed Scripture passage which talks about God's plans for his people, and I know that Bettina and Matt chose that Scripture with deep thought about their part together as his people. They were married, I learn, at a chapel which has been steeped in decades of earnest prayer; obviously they are aligning, in the sacredness of their marriage, with all the sacred traditions of that chapel. How good, how good!

I look again at the folder, and think about the things Bettina has done. She has had the courage to stay single longer than many of her friends have chosen to do. During these several years, her wit and charm — real charm, very genuine — her vivacious beauty and her entertaining skills have made their contributions to several different Christian enterprises, and she has been one to "adorn the doctrine of God our Savior."

And now it's Matt. If he is as fine a person as his photo suggests, I think Bettina will be glad she had the courage to stay single until God's plan was clear.

But in the same mail, a word about Ocie, and if it would do any good I could wail like a banshee.

Ocie is clever, sensitive, gifted. Musical skill thrums inside her. In writing classes, she could bend words to her will in unusual ways. But Ocie wanted so desperately to be part of a twosome a year or so ago that she started going around with a man whom the people who loved Ocie thought to be — well, deplorable. His personal life was tangled, and she didn't want to stay single until he could or would go through a legal ceremony with her, so she moved in anyway. Or maybe he moved in.

Now, in a centuries-old story of the deserted girl, she is just that: a deserted girl. She called a cab at 1:30 one morning, checked herself in at a hospital, and gave birth alone to his child.

Ocie has spunk and grit, and she will need all she has of those qualities. But if she had had mustered more courage to repel the attention of Mr. Deplorable from the outset. . . . If she had possessed more courage of the kind that can keep one serenely single. . . .

How many of her friends, I wonder, could wail like banshees for Ocie now, if it would do any good? But it will not help.

While I wonder what will come in tomorrow's mail besides grocery coupons and ads for unwanted appliances, I think about the courage to stay single. It is a topic, I'd surmise, that is thought about far too little by teenagers and college kids and grad students, by the twenties crowd and the thirties crowd.

A certain sort of courage is needed, anyone would say, to enter intelligently into a marriage. Anyone who says "I do" without a quota of trepidation first must surely be trivial, or thoughtless, or stupid, or incredibly arrogant, or all of those things. One learns from time to time of engagements broken and then restored, of wedding dates postponed while a timorous groom or a timorous bride re-thought and re-thought. In the moderately recent past, I was chatting with a colleague — call him Jerry — and one of us had occasion to mention the deeply loyal marriage of Bill and Trudie, and how Bill and Trudie both smile now about their on-again-off-again courtship. Jerry suddenly became very, very thoughful and his voice trembled a little deeper into gruffness than it usually sounds, as he reminisced about his own utter terror on the day before his wedding. Not because of anything about his Renée; he adored her, and has continued to adore her through several decades. But the fear was there. The sense of finality, of immense change, of a change that would affect all of life until its very end. If there had been a way to run away and a place to run to, he said candidly, he would have skedaddled.

Okay. It takes courage to get married. And it certainly takes courage to stay married. People do not arrive at the silver anniversary and the golden wedding day without having endured, and worked through, and transformed much that was neither silver nor golden while it happened.

Yet, in proportion, probably far too little has been said, ever, about the kind of courage it takes to stay single. It takes courage to stay single for a while, as our winsome Bettina has done. It may take another measure of courage to stay single at other eras and epochs of one's life.

Anyone may not judge another life accurately; we may evaluate with folly or with ineptness. Yet anyone, working around a college campus, sometimes almost feels like shouting out, "Courage, my dear! Summon your courage! Have the courage to stay single for this now! Don't you *see* what you are getting into?"

Faces whirl before me.

Pretty Mara had the courage. She was already wearing a diamond when she began to realize that Larry's moods were so unpredictable that, in spite of all the qualities for which she adored him, he was not good husband material. Nor was he ready to be a father. She thought of his moods — those black moods, and she shuddered, and stood by her courage.

Deena failed the courage test. When I first saw her in the college corridors, she was one of the most promising students on the entire campus. Only a freshman, she organized programs and directed projects in amazing ways. Her good humor and brilliant mind made her a sparkler in any course, any club. She was so genuinely warm and winsome that other students, less gifted, did not resent her abilities. She had great zeal for Christian witnessing, and we thought she would make some rich and good contribution to the Kingdom. If a poll had been taken, probably she would have been high on any list of "greatest promise" or "contributing most to the campus" or "a really fine person." But the freshman year ended without a lasting romance, and the sophomore year, and the junior year, and Deena had deep cravings for a husband and a home.

When pleasant Sam started escorting her here and there, she quickly started assuming little wifely airs. ("Oh, I thought they were a married couple," a new faculty member said to me in surprise when he heard someone exclaiming about the dating interest that Deena had just found.) Deena was proprietary — and the rest of us were heartsick. Sam was not reliable. Sam was not a person of fidelity. Sam was not one whom any of us could really imagine as a teammate for Deena in her Christian service dreams.

She dated. She clung. She didn't confide much in the rest of us, nor ask counsel much. She knew what her friends would have said, and she didn't have the courage to hear it, nor to keep on alone.

And the glow on Deena's face (so radiant a glow when she was a freshman) became dimmer and dimmer and dimmer. When she married Sam, people phrased their greetings very carefully, very carefully indeed, at her wedding reception.

Such a waste, of such a life. If she could have had more courage! If only she could!

I think about gentle Toni. Toni wanted a house with oak wood-work, and an antique rocker in it, she wrote in a theme after she had visited my home for the first time. Maybe she thought Perry would like oak woodwork and antique rockers. She liked the kind of music that Perry liked — or persuaded herself that she did. She liked Perry's kind of humor — or persuaded herself that she did. She did errands for him. She obeyed the flick of his eyebrow. She didn't notice other men much, though other men really had much better eyebrows, and better personalities, and better kindnesses, and better dependabilities.

She dropped out of college to marry him. And, hardly into her twenties, gentle Toni was a divorcée.

If only Toni could have had more courage!

College boy Woody did have courage. Lana thought he was great, and was edging him toward the altar day by day. Woody had real misgivings. One day I was working on a project in one of the big offices at Woody's college (my college, too), when he came whooping into the room — he, who was usually a person of mild chuckles and quiet conversations. "I'm a misogynist!" he told us. "I'm a misogynist!" Someone calmed him down enough to find out that he had summoned the needed mettle, and had told Lana their romance was through. Broken up. Kaput. Quit. Ended.

And then Woody, having explained, rushed off to the snack bar, to bring an ice cream cone back for everyone in the office at that moment, so that we could all celebrate his liberation with him.

Actually his vocabulary wasn't very accurate. A year or so later he started dating Martha, and everyone saw that he most certainly was not a hater of womankind. Their Christmas cards bring affirmings back to the campus of their continuing deep affection, and news about the smaller women, his daughters, whom he certainly does not hate.

If he ever, ever thinks of Lana now, I'm sure that Woody thanks God very fervently that he had the courage to stay single for a while longer than Lana wanted him to, until what everyone would believe to be God's better plan for him became clear.

Mervyn had courage, too. He was already engaged, as a matter of fact, when he began to feel ominous intensities of penned-in and nailed-down limitation. He knew it would make him feel like sixteen varieties of a heel to break the engagement, but he knew increasingly that Erma was wrong for him. Wrong, wrong, wrong. When Erma nervously wanted the wedding to be sooner than they had first planned, her insecurity liberated Mervyn's emotions, and his emotions liberated his whole future — as he would now describe it.

For Mervyn, as it happened, bachelordom didn't last long. Someone quite unlike his clutching Erma came across his path, and there was a very rapid courtship (he would say, a heaven-guided courtship), and a splendidly good marriage. Mervyn is very glad (when, once in a blue moon, he pauses to remember) that he had some courage toward the end of the Erma episode.

Now, Lee. All his friends thought for a while that Lee might stay single for all his days after he broke an engagement. It had not been an engagement lightly or casually made, but it had a wrongness about it. I remember vividly the day that Lee's mother called me and asked urgently that I please, please pray about Lee. She didn't explain much about the nature of her concern, but later on Lee told me soberly what he had finally realized; June just wasn't the kind of Christian that he could team up with for a truly Christian home.

It took him a long while to recuperate. He held good jobs, helped other human beings in some special ways during the freedom of his single years, matured in emotion. And after a time the courage of the decision to stay single was, for Lee, changed over into the other courage, to take on matrimony.

Belle. Her narrative has to be another "if only." Belle was already married when I first knew her; I don't know about the courage she had lacked when she was eighteen and nineteen. At twenty, she was much admired for her poise, her speaking ability, her unusual intellectual powers. If I remember rightly, students talked about her as a candidate for student body president. But they certainly didn't talk about her Lance for student body president. His potential seemed passably good; Belle's potential was superb. "It's a shame," said the college dean one day when someone spoke about Lance. "He will always be just 'Belle's husband.' "

But he wasn't just her husband for very long at all. And her intensity was fierce and agonized when she wrote me about the divorce.

I wonder what our handsome, brilliant Belle is doing now. Once I wrote a graduate school recommendation for her. Once? Or more than once? When she was only a junior, she wrote a term paper that I urged her to polish and try for publication. I wonder. . . .

I wonder why Belle did not have the courage to stay single a little longer. With the courage, I wonder what her life might have been. I wonder. . . .

In *Passages,* author Gail Sheehy reported that one study (among the many from which she gathered her source material) revealed that the mental health profile of wives showed up "unfavorably," compared with that of single women; "phobic reactions, depression, passivity, and mental health impairment" were more frequent among them.[1] One could conclude that the lot of married women is not, in truth, as satisfying as all of the popular literature of bride's magazines and love lyrics would say; one might conclude, also, that it does, indeed, take courage to remain single, and that the courage is useful in meeting the continuing stresses of life.

One of my friends in graduate school told me that she had thought up a short story with what she considered a splendid final line; I wonder if she ever wrote the story. (Would you let me know if you have seen it in print?) A woman of intellect and good taste was to be the main character. She was to become infatuated with a day-laborer who had received little training for his inferior mind, a person rather like T. S. Eliot's "Apeneck Sweeney." She would marry him, after due plot complications had been snarled and unsnarled. At the end, the bride would say to herself, as she took Apeneck's arm and strode down the aisle from the altar, "Oh well, it don't make no difference now."

But in the narrative we are all writing day by day, it does make a difference. Everything makes a difference. And the courage to stay single may be a very joyful part of a joyful difference.

Once when I was a senior in college, and dorm-room chatterings had turned to often-talked topics, I commented laughingly that I would rather be single than always wishing I were. Still with my gleams of laughter, I'd affirm it again. And in the meantime, I have come away from various weddings and other events thanking the Lord that I wasn't tied to *that* one for the rest of my life. I'm not sure that "courage" is a right label for all of those happenings, but I'm quite sure that courage is often needed by all of the singles. Will society be stronger as more people have more courage to walk alone?

Wilma would say a resounding "yes" to that inquiry. Wilma is a brilliant young professional woman, some ten years out of college. "I am so *glad*," she told me recently, "that I knew Miss X and Miss Y when I was a senior," (she was naming two of her professors) "and I learned from them that one could have a really good life without being married. Of the marriages I know well," she went on thoughtfully, "I would say that three-fourths are bad marriages, in varying degrees of badness."

Yet there are the *good* marriages! Let us not forget about them! Connubial joy does exist. A few days ago I helped friends celebrate their silver wedding anniversary, and the sheer joy which permeated the occasion was awesome and shining and splendid. In the mail recently came a really delightful little book from other friends; it's a collection of nuptial poetry written by a middle-aged lover, Virgil, to celebrate twenty-five years with his Pauline. Virgil is very sure, say his poems, that God himself gave Pauline to him.

Sometimes the courage to stay single turns out to be a very temporary need. Have you noticed that? God doesn't treat us all alike, as if we were auto parts on a conveyor belt. It is our individual assignment to find his will, whatever it is, and, finding, to follow.

I'm thinking now about Harold, who was married before he was twenty and has adored Marie for more than forty years. His reminiscences would convince you that Harold in his teens had faith like an old Testament prophet's, that he had a great hunger to do the will of the Eternal. His friends now are not about to question whether he obeyed, back then.

The courage of obedience. That, in brief, is what we need, all of us. And for many of us, for now, that is another wording for the courage to be single.

Note to Chapter 5

1. Gail Sheehy, *Passages: Predictable Crises of Adult Life* (New York: Bantam Books, 1977), pp. 286-87.

What Next, God? 6

"But you don't — uh — um — you aren't *opposed* to marriage?" Mark and Margie wanted to know. They sat in my living room, talking some things over. Margie was an English major; Mark was a member of the campus writing club who had been in my home a good many times. Both of them liked to talk things over, and just now they were into some prickly thinking because of the chapel talk I had given a few days before: "God doesn't Promise Matrimony — He Promises Himself."

Oh, no, I assured them. Oh, no! I didn't mean that at all!

Not for you, Mark. Not for you, Margie. Not for hundreds of other people.

When Delafern Durr and I were both summer employees of Mrs. Alice Hoiles, during our college-girl era, and Fred Baumberger proposed to Delafern, Mrs. Hoiles was away, and wrote us a chuckle-some letter: knowing "how Elva loves a romance," she wrote, she knew there was a lot of excitement around her house.

I've enjoyed bridesmaiding, and doing other assistings for Cupid. After our senior year, I went off to Iowa by bus to read a new sonnet in the wedding that made Alice Fickess into Alice Rice. I went gladly. Much more recently, I went off to Kansas to share another poem in the wedding of Faye and Alden Nay. I went gladly. When I was fourteen, I was the bridesmaid for the wedding of my brother Allan and his bride Evelyn — I in lavender voile (probably from Sears Roebuck), and carrying garden flowers. When I was past forty, I was bridesmaid for a departmental colleague — I in blue and silver brocade. I've had a gleeful part in initiating various romances. And I couldn't begin to count how many weddings I have given my blessings to, with smiles and words written or spoken, and china or linens or crockery bestowed. I'm glad in all their gladness.

Once, even, I essentially managed a wedding. Mel Harrison tele-phoned to his Florence during a summer school, that he was being "shipped out" by the army, and he wanted to be married first. They talked long and persuasively to their parents, and decided: yes, to be married that weekend. All the other girls in the dorm that summer were in tight class schedules, but I was doing independent study in German. Naturally, I dropped the lists of German verbs to help Florence. When Mel arrived, expecting to go over to the parsonage for quiet vows, he was surprised and deeply gladdened to find that he was to have a wedding: flowers in Burritt Hall parlors, someone to play, someone to sing, a ceremony with dignity and grace. (And the next day I was still so wedding-minded, and so exhausted, that I totally forgot a valued invitation to a meal at a faculty home!)

No, I'm not opposed to marriage *per se*.

Not for other people, and not for myself. I have never felt a voca-tion to celibacy.

In principle, however, I should note that I am not opposed to celibacy either. It is hard for most Protestants to keep perspective on that topic. Certainly there were many flagrant abuses of celibate vows during medieval times and leading up to the Reformation. Anyone who has read Chaucer's poetry and/or a few history books would know that the power lodged in the hands of men pledged not to marry led to grievous sins in the ecclesiastical palaces, in monas-teries, in bedrooms of all social levels. Nevertheless, countless numbers of holy persons knew the call of God, and fulfilled it, and served the Kingdom of our Lord Christ with a wholeness of self and of purpose which they could not have done if they had been living usual family lives.

In today's world men and women who have taken vows of celi-bacy are devoting their lives to teaching, to prayer, to nursing, to social work, to serving all the needs of other mortals. And many of them are heroic. How much sadder our world would be without a Mother Teresa of Calcutta, and her ministry to the dying outcastes, the poorest of the poor! Only God himself knows the pure worship he receives daily from the Jesuits, the Franciscans, the Dominicans and the others of his celibate children.

The Anglican Revival of the 19th century saw a renewal in the Church of England of set-apart lives, of the monastic. If our present Protestantism were following Christ more closely, maybe we would hear a great deal more about set-apart lives, about the monastic. And St. Paul himself would be right there in the cheering section, (or seated up in the Amen Corner, to use the vocabulary of our frontier evangelists); I'm looking at 1 Corinthians 7:32-33, of course.

Francis Schaeffer, the world-renowned Protestant Bible teacher, has reportedly affirmed that, granted our present conditions of over-population and world hunger, the truly Christian model for the future might be celibacy and childlessness.

But for myself — no, there has never been a definite "call" to celibacy. In fact, I remember telling my typewriter a few years ago (in a self-identity piece which, as it turned out, didn't move on to publication) that if I liked a man enough, if the inner green light of Guidance were present, I would cheerfully leave everything in my present life, everything, except some jeans to wear while I walked across from my life into his. (Actually, though, I would probably have asked to take along my brain children, especially my new poems in their various notebooks!)

I'm rather glad I haven't known outcomes in advance, while I have been living through the various episodes. "What next, God?" is a comfortable question to be asking, as a principle of one's life. To keep saying, "What next, God?" is to live with an attitude of expectancy, of flexibility, of curiosity, along with the basic stance of obedience to the will of God as one knows it.

Sometimes, of course, it is an agonized question as well as a comfortable one, while one questions and wonders and searches for intimations of the guidings. That's the paradox of being human, and Christian. God does not make us into his puppets when we accept him, and he does not give us full game plans before any game begins. He leaves us free to choose — free to blunder, yet free to obey. We are always Adam, all of us, with ever-new pieces of Eden to retain or to forfeit. (And it's the further paradox that "Eden" is also spelled "Gethsemane," within obediences. St. Stephen. Dietrich Bonhoeffer. Missionary martyrs.)

What next, God? What next?

If I liked a man enough. . . . If I loved a man. . . .

What next?

So far as I can comprehend, "what next?" is the attitude God would want us to live with, from the time we first begin to make decisions on our own. "This is what I have determined to have, and I'll get it no matter what" is not the posture of the Christian. Nor is it the posture of the happy person. Relaxation and serenity do not go along with the desperate quest for a mate. If one goes into "Senior Panic" or "Grad School Grabs," the steering mechanism of his life may be so locked that the right guidings simply cannot happen.

I think of Lil, whom I knew in graduate school. I think she was one of the most utterly unhappy persons I have ever known. As I recall, she called herself a Christian and was active in Inter-Varsity Christian Fellowship. I remember her name (which wasn't Lil), and the throbbing intensity with which she said one day, during the kind of dorm-room chatter that goes on between research papers and exams, "I would marry *any man* who was not a drunkard or a dope fiend." Any man. Any man. Her voice shook with the intensity of the saying. I wonder what, or whom, she settled for. Maybe our Lord rescued her, in spite of herself. His ways and his guidings are beyond mortal knowing.

In contrast, I think of Tessie, whose story Catherine Marshall told in *Beyond Ourselves*. Page 173 to 180. Check it out. After a series of determined efforts, Tessie finally came to the point of saying, "Well — I think God is trying to tell me to relax and let him take over now. If he wants me to remarry, somehow I think he's capable of arranging it." And he did arrange it, in a way that left Tessie dazzled and breathless, and left Catherine Marshall jubilant at seeing a miracle happen.

What next, God? It will be interesting to discover. Will You help us to keep asking? Will You help us to keep listening?

What next, God?

In the little country church we attended when I was a child, we often sang a gospel song with a strong personal affirmation:

> "Where he leads me, I will follow;
> Where he leads me, I will follow;
> I'll go with him, with him all the way."

Surely that affirmation is the center of life for the Christian. If "where he leads" is into lifelong celibacy, the Christian thanks him for the guiding and says "Yes" to him. If "where he leads" is into matrimony, the Christian thanks him for the guiding and says "Yes" to him. If "where he leads" is into present singleness, the Christian thanks him and says "Yes" to him.

Another gospel song from our little frame church on a Kansas hill reverberates deeply in my memory today. "This bondage to love sets me perfectly free," it said.

Perfectly free.

Free to be married, if the person and the time accord with his guidings, and "married" is right for me.

Free to be single, if the big decisions and the little decisions are in accord with his guidings, and "single" is right for me.

What next, God?

Singles, Yes; Spinsters, No! 7

Dictionaries have their fascination. I've been looking in the desk dictionaries here in my study, and they give some interesting gleams of light. Single, an adjective coming down to us from Middle English and Old French, has a variety of specific straightforward meanings: *one only*; *one and no more*; *individual*; *unmarried*, along with a dozen more other phrases. Try "spinster": one who spins, and besides that, an old maid. Try "old maid." Old maid: *A fussy, nervous, timid person,* says Webster's Collegiate. *A prim, prudish, fussy person,* says Webster's New World.

Observe, please.

According to the lexicographers, "old maid" is, then, not a women-only term. It's a "person." Prim, prudish, fussy men are old maids. Have you known quite a few of them? I talked to one just a day or two ago: jittery and skittery, with no more quietude of spirit than a basketful of beetles. Married women may be old maids. My friend Mae told me once how hard it was for her to establish rapport with Alleen, who had lived through some thirty years of matrimony and twenty-five years of parenting, but was definitely an old maid; "she is such an *uptight* person," Mae said carefully.

Now obviously such words as we're looking up have moved into the dictionaries because of the traits of certain unmarried women, hordes of 'em, who had old maidish traits as well as singleness. But to be single is not necessarily to be an old maid nor a spinster. Hooray, and hallelujah! I thank God for the people I have known who didn't happen to wear wedding bands on the left hand, yet were serene, fulfilled, free-in-spirit, joyous human beings. I'd like to be like them, not like Mae's friend Alleen, not like that skittery, jittery, old maid of a man whom I just mentioned to you.

I've been pondering lately on some of the specific differences which might be isolated between the "old maid" species and the "wholesome single" species. The distinctions aren't quite like those in an ornithology fieldbook, or in a manual of botany that might give sketches and diagrams for identifying the flowering shrubs of the Appalachian region. Still, some characteristics can be sorted out. Let's try some; thinking about the differences ought to give some useful guidelines on decisions and lifestyles and attitudes. As we probe, we may see things to talk with God about. Some of the traits of old maidishness move over beyond amusing or dismaying personality traits and into the category of sins of the spirit, it would seem.

How do these sound? Would you agree with the distinctions?

The Old Maidish Singles	The Wholesome Singles
1. Prim, prudish, fussy	1. Tolerant, gracious, accepting
2. Nervous, timid	2. Venturesome, zestfull

Let's pause. Let's pause often, as we work through the list. Okay? To note now: there would obviously be a wide continum of individual differences, not just an "either/or" grouping. And many qualifiers, many "yes, but —" notations, many exceptions coud be specified anywhere along the way. But the basic differences are there — and people do keep moving from one column to the other as they harden into old maidishness, or grow into more grace. From time to time ancedotes may be useful. As I look at "venturesome, zestful," I think of the real glee I felt inside myself when a faculty wife said to me in a gently puzzled voice, "Elva, you shock me sometimes." At a time when jeans weren't yet in vogue on our campus, I had put on an old shirt and a very battered pair of pedal pushers and had gone down to the corner of Scott Field to trim a hedge; I wasn't on the custodial staff, but I thought the untrimmed hedge looked too sloppy to be a pleasant greeting to the new students who were about to arrive, and I thought I could do something about it. It was a small venturesomeness, a small zest, but I'm glad I perpetrated it.

3. Unduly preoccupied with their singleness.	3. Primarily a person, a follower of a vocation, a Christian.
4. Humorless. Sometimes matter-of-fact, sometimes cantankerous.	4. Mirthful; prone to smiles, chuckles, hearty laughters.
5. Driven by duty.	5. Exuberant about tasks.

"Ought" is a good word, and we need more use of it in our society in general, but it can become a little dictator inside us. I used to know a really wonderful woman whose good works in her community were innumerable, but she always made me uncomfortable by her bustling and her attitude of "I should, I must, I will." Through gritted teeth, she envisioned what a Christian would do in her town, and through gritted teeth she did, and did, and did. Alas! And we shrank back a little as she caused us to know where she had last been bustling, as Tom Sawyer's Aunt Polly caused Tom and his comrade Huck to shrink and wince.

6. Rigidly righteous: repelling others.	6. Aspiring and inspiring; pulling others heavenward.

Have you looked lately at Matthew Arnold's great poem, "Rugby Chapel"? It deserves being read at least once a year by every human being! Arnold pays tribute to his educator father, Dr. Thomas Arnold, as one who, "zealous, beneficient, firm," led others with him through the wastes of life and over its steep high mountain trails. So ought we to be!

7. Gauche, awkward, tactless.	7. Gracious.

We're all learning, always. We hope we are. How does one move from here to there? Basically, by thinking about other people and their needs, by thinking with one's heart. John Henry Newman suggested that in his "Definition of a Gentleman." Newman's sentences would be another good reason to pull a Victorian literature book off the shelves at least one a year. Newman's "gentleman," whether in a masculine or a feminine version, would be the exact opposite of an old maid, ditto. The gentleman "can recollect to whom he is speaking," he "makes light of favors while he does them, and seems to be receiving while he does them." And he has other similar traits. I know one old maid (tall, broad of sholders, masculine in gender, rather handsome) who really ought to read Newman's essay and work on living up to it; Jake can manage to make more people more uncomfortable by his inattentiveness to what they are saying and thinking than you would imagine. In any company, however genial, he seems to be an intruder. He is so concerned with himself that himself becomes a social excrescence.

8. Provincial. Limited in interests, limited in outlook.	8. In the best sense, a citizen of the world.

It isn't just a matter of where one lives. It isn't just a matter of having traveled or not traveled, though for the open-hearted person travel can be windows on anywhere and vistas to everywhere. One of the more provincially old-maidish persons I've ever met, I suppose, was a girl of about 22 who was on the ship with me when I returned from a summer at the University of London. Apparently she had gone away thinking that New York was the only spot on the globe worth her concern, and she was returning to her niche with an even more narrow mind. What one might and might not wear to work in New York City interested her; not much else seemed to. As we neared the end of the voyage, I remarked at the dinner table that it seemed a little sad not to have further opportunities to get to know all the people who had been our shipmates for those few days. With a quiet sneer, she asked whether I thought there was anybody really worth getting to know "on this ship." Poor girl.

Maybe even more of the spinster, now that I think of it, were some American college students I got to know during European tours: blasé about everything, interested in almost nothing except the availability of Cokes or iced tea. Provincial, really provincial. They stayed in their home towns, no matter where the tour guides took us. One even sat on the bus, too bored and weary and full of ennui to enter the building, while the rest of us toured a royal palace.

In contrast, consider the eager-eyed villager who asks "Is it —" and "Will they —" and "Do you think —" on every conceivable topic, who gains ideas from every associate by intellectual osmosis, whose letters go out to India and Hong Kong.

9. Out of touch with children and teen-agers.

9. Has good contacts across all generations.

This one is really important, it seems to me. Really important. Singles can easily withdraw into themselves and become dessicated, or they can keep reaching out and reaching out, can keep caring.

When my friend Rosella Wilson and I visited the Knorrs at their Colorado ranch, she could easily have lingered in the house in pleasant conversation with hostess Gail, or she could have found a book. The Knorrs were not even relatives; Gail is my cousin, not hers. But she was alertly questioning when Kerry and Holly talked about their prize sheep, and she was delighted to go out to the corral to see them grooming and training their sheep, in preparation for the state fair. And as we drove on toward Colorado Springs, she was that much more remote from the spinsterly!

10. Deeply discontented, and lets it be known.

10. Uncontented —*i.e.*, reaching and growing, not stagnant — yet deeply contented, restful, serene.

Is this the basic dividing point between two types? The discontented one fusses, "I wish, I wish, I wish . . . ," and pities himself. The contented one has come to a point of creative acceptance, a deep inner consenting to what is, a life of creative acceptance, a mood of gladness, an expectant hope for the future and joy in now. *Acceptance* is different from *resignation*. I think. Resignation seems to shrug shoulders, fold hands, dump possibilities into the waste basket; acceptance nods and looks for new bulbs to plant. The discontented one says, "They ought, they ought, they ought. . . ." The accepting one says, "Let's try it *this* way! Come on, give me a hand," and exclaims, "It's great that. . . ."

There's Derrick. I like getting mail from him, and yet I don't. He's always viewing with alarm. His bosses have always just made wrong decisions. He always has some anger, always some throaty grumble.

There's Ellen. Just now she is shrill about the unfair treatment of women in her offices, but if she weren't twitter-shrieking about that she would have some other vexation to report. She doesn't know how to be deeply happy, nor to let (or cause) anyone else to be happy in her presence. In quiet truth, I doubt whether she's being unfairly treated at her office at all.

11. Rigid; inflexible; tied to little habit patterns.	11. Cheerfully adaptable, appropriately flexible.

Habits can be a strength, of course, and each of us would feel that our little habits are the intelligent ones, that our neighbor's are the comic and the spinsterly. Maybe whatever one "never" does and whatever one "always" does ought to be called into question sometimes.

12. Doesn't really like, or love, people — except as topics of gossip. Inquisitive about people — but not to help them. Sees other people as objects, governed by social rules.	12. Cares. Cares terribly. Respects privacies. Takes caring action. Asks about people — to care and to pray and to help.

"Tsk, tsk," said Spinster Sally. "Had you heard that the little Smith girl is pregnant? Such a disgrace. . . ." Sophie Single got some information to the Smiths about local clinic procedures.

Sally says cutting things about the smudged clothes and untidy hair of all the Jones' children; Sophie volunteered to babysit for the five while Mrs. Jones took her washing to the laundromat last Friday evening.

Sally thinks it's dreadful, just dreadful, that her neighbor's boy is failing in math and Spanish. Sophie took her neighbor's daughters to a concert the other night, and loaned them books for their term papers in history.

Sally wonders if it is true that Mrs. Smith is actually dating again so soon after her husband's death. Sophie invited Mrs. Smith over for tea last Sunday afternoon.

Obvious? Trite? Implausible? Oh, but there are the Sally-people all around us; I've known them. And (thank God!) I've known the Sophie-people too. I've known Dr. Mary Alice Tenney. What a wonderful "Sophie" she was! I have known Dr. Elva Kinney, our dean of women when I was in college. One of the campus legends says that a faculty family once had car trouble, away out on a country road somewhere, and their small son suggested, in all seriousness, that somebody go to telephone Miss Kinney. "She will know what to do." In many circumstances for many of us, she did know what to do. I've known Dr. Ruby Dare, a housemate of the other two. "What can I do about it?" was almost a life-motto for her.

The Sally people. Gwendolyn was one. Her job kept her making decisions about eligibility for college, and she made her decisions promptly, harshly, by the rule books. One mother, almost crying, said to me one time with bitter edges in her voice, "Well, maybe Miss Gwendolyn *doesn't* have ice water in her veins instead of blood, but I have no way of being sure." Gwendolyn's harsh efficiency, that mother felt, had nearly (and needlessly) crippled a life; I am afraid the mother was right.

Maybe, in truth, this item #12 is the root and center of them all; maybe the essential difference between the spinster and the single is the difference in a capacity for loving, and for putting love into action.

A few more genus and species indentifiers, however?

13. Foolishly devoted to pets.	13. Balanced in affection, to pets and other wise.

Agree?

14. Limited social contacts. Uncomfortable, really, except with other spinsters, or with relatives.	14. Constantly broadening contacts. Enjoys being with families, or couples or opposite-sex singles.

In another chapter, we'll be thinking more about the entire matter of the social life of the single.

15. A cheated attitude, a constant feeling of being unable to live a full life. Negative approaches.	15. Creativity, New endeavors. New skills. Happy hobbies. Positive approaches.

16. Waspish. Unable to accept criticism. Easily hurt, and brooding over hurts.

    Agree?

16. Eager to grow, to learn, to improve. Sensitive, but sensible.

17. Unable, or unwilling, to share friends and experiences with other people. Over-possessive.

17. Loves to share, and plans how to do it.

Some people are like the Dead Sea: water flows in, and flows in, and nothing flows out. They're brackish; salt-flats stretch out all around them. They're spinsters. Some people are like the Sea of Galilee. Water flows in, water flows out. Orchards adjoin them, and water is gratefully dipped out from them. They're not spinsters.

18. Intimidated by others' intellects or skills.

18. Challenged by other minds; eager to learn from them. Questioning, appreciative.

Jean and Jessie are high school math teachers. When the art gallery in their town has an opeing, Jean says, "Oh, I don't know anything about modern art," and firmly declines to go. Jessie goes, meets the artists, asks question, lingers in a lively conversation, gets invited out for coffee with a young sculptor. Which is the spinster? Not Jessie.

Martha, a nurse, moves to a new town. The church she starts attending has three different Bible classes she considers. One is taught by a university professor, and he frightens her a little. One is attended by several university staff couples, and they frighten her quite a lot. She settles for the third, a comfortable little group of quiet housewives and single office girls. And spinsterdom calcifies a little more each week in her arthritic soul.

19. Competitive. Afraid of being excelled.

19. Self-stimulated; holds himself accountable to his own skills.

20. A repository of grudges, resentments, bitternesses.

20. Forgiving, and forgiven.

Well, what else would you put on a list? I think I'll stop for now — first uttering a solemn vow and a prayer. I am single, indeed, but, heaven helping me, I will not be a spinster! And, heaven will have to help me. What I have been struggling to define as the spinster type is the character that can harden and calcify, apart from grace. What I have watched in other human beings and tried to describe here as the wholesome single is the personality that can be when Grace is flowing through it. The personality that God has touched, and is using.

Will you join me in the vow, in the prayer? "I am a single, indeed, but, heaven helping me, I will not be a spinster!"

Amen.

Amen.

Unclaimed Jewels?
Not on Your Life! 8

One year we had, at the college where I was working, some half a dozen single women on the staff, and three or four single men, and assorted couples from each decade in age brackets, the twenties through the sixties. Once during the year one of the single women stopped me to say she was planning a supper party at her home, and could I please come? "I'm having the 'unclaimed jewels' over," Diane explained laughingly. And the half dozen of us, the single women, arrived at her home.

Well, it was a nice party, a merry and sociable occasion which I enjoyed. But a small blue-purple flame was glowing inside me from the moment of her invitation, and it still ignites and re-kindles now and then: a small flame of dismay and indignation, with a few orange tones of anger.

If you are a Christian, if you have asked God to direct your life, if you are constantly living in Proverbs 3:5-6 and Matthew 6:33 and Romans 8:28 and other promises like them, then it seems to me it is getting over toward a blasphemy to call yourself an "unclaimed jewel." Jewel, yes, but not unclaimed! Not when he has claimed you for his very own, and has placed you in the setting you now occupy. He is the jeweler. If he puts you in a tiara, fine; if he puts you in a necklace for a queen, fine; if he chips you into bits and puts you into the mechanism of fine watches, that is his prerogative. He is sovereign. He is the designer.

The locution is obviously a carry-over from the generations before us, which found it harder to believe that any woman could be a person at all, other than in a husband-completing way. The Emily Brontës, the Emily Dickinsons, the Florence Nightingales were few. Jael and Miriam of the Old Testament were exceptions to the usual pattern, and so was Lydia of the New Testament.

Our own society often continues to push singles — teasingly or seriously, consciously or unconsciously — toward marriage as the one and only doorway into joy, as I have mentioned together in other segments of our conversation.

It wasn't just Diane's use of a weary metaphor that bothered me. It seems to me that anyone who (even laughingly) calls herself an unclaimed jewel, or lets anyone else in this wide world get away with dubbing her "unclaimed," either has a poor self-image or is on the way toward one. And that is not a good state of affairs. Maybe Diane needed to stand in front of her mirror day by day and say, "You're great, Diane, you're really great. God loves you! God himself is guiding your life. God values you! You are helping people in important ways. . . ."

There are stereotypes in many minds which need to be evicted by sunny humor and persistent courage. (No, not to evict the minds; just to evict the stereotypes!) Just yesterday I saw a new example of the stereotype; having lengthy minutes in a waiting room equipped with popular magazines, I picked up one journal and read a short story. Ugh. By several different criteria, it was not a good story. I decided afterward that the editors, assuming most of their readers to be housewives, thought it would be subtle propaganda toward self-satisfaction on the part of the housewives. ("See what a sad and frustrated woman this main character is?" the story said by implication. "She's middle-aged, and she has never been married, and isn't she ridiculous? Now *you,* you are married. Goody goody gumdrops. And what a fine person you are." I repeat: ugh.)

Have you noticed that, in spite of all the merry fun in them, the Gilbert and Sullivan operettas have done their part in perpetuating the stereotype? Sir W. S. Gilbert obviously found the spinsterly Spinster to be a comic type which brought the laughter he wanted to bring. Pick up, for instance, the libretto of *The Mikado.* Natisha, the ridiculous, is introduced as "an elderly Lady in love with Nanki-Poo," and the curtains swirl down after Ko-Ko insults Natisha while he proposes:

> "There is beauty in extreme old age—
> > Do you fancy you are elderly enough?
> > Information I'm requesting
> > On a subject interesting:
> Is a maiden all the better when she's tough?
> Are you old enough to marry, do you think?
> > Won't you wait until you are eighty in the shade?
> > There's a fascination frantic
> > In a ruin that's romantic;
> Do you think you are sufficiently decayed?"

Gilbert laughed irreverently at everything else on the horizon, of course, so that we should perhaps not wish too hard to malign his taste in humor. But the stereotype still needs to be dealt with.

When we face the clichés and their causes, sometimes there is a fine line between a healthy realism, with its due candor, and a self-demeaning attitude, self-deprecating, self-pitying. Realism must be. There's no point in being like Miss Havisham, of Dickens' *Great Expectation,* and continuing to wear a wedding gown when the wedding isn't going to happen. There's no point in evading any truth. But neither is there any point (nor mental health) in whining and saying "poor me, poor me" while one speaks the truth.

I wondered about that fine line between realism and self-pity one day when I parked near Madge's home in order to do an errand close by. Madge had been pruning the big shrubs in her yard and had accumulated quite a pile of cuttings. She was obviously muscle-weary and dripping with perspiration. There was almost a fierceness in her voice, I thought, as she greeted me. "No woman ought to live alone," she declared. When I didn't comment on that viewpoint she said it again, maybe with a shade less of realism and a shade more of self-commiseration.

Madge didn't need easy or saccharine reassurances that day, but I'm not sure it helped her mood to verbalize it. She seemed as self-depreciating as any speaker who might make jokes about "unclaimed jewels."

Another sort of realism, which would not be destructive, ever, is to verbalize the realism of grace. How strengthening the recognition that we belong to God, the acknowledging of who he is and of what he has done, both in our own lives and in other lives! The book of Acts resounds with accounts of God at work in and through human beings. He is still at work, in and through human beings, and as we publicize his doing, I'm very sure, we will be less inclined to speak demeaningly of any human being.

Catherine Marshall tells us that her husband, Peter Marshall, liked to talk about "spiritual research unlimited," and such "research" is the texture of her own books. There's a lot more zing and potential in "spiritual research," surely, than allowing one's self to be thought a misfit, an imperfection, a not-belonging identity. For the Christian single, there is "spiritual research unlimited" yet ahead: Who am I? Who is God? What is he doing with me and for me and through me? What is he doing in my world?

If you have a shelf full of inspirational books, perhaps it would be good to reach past Catherine Marshall to Eugenia Price and *The Burden Is Light.* (Or half a dozen of her other titles), or to Ann Kiemel's *I'm Out to Change My World.*

Do you know Ann Kiemel? She's one of a kind; it wouldn't do for anyone else to try to be an Ann Kiemel. But she is a person of a splendid and radiant faith. She has a particular flair for bubbling her way into conversations about God with airplane seatmates or neighbor kids, or anyone else. Ann Kiemel, I'd say, might be called a diamond at the cutting edge of a precision tool. Maybe she's part of the Diamond-Cutter's own set of tools, used in finding the flashing blue-white fire of other diamonds when they come from the mines in their unshaped ugliness.

Unclaimed jewels? Not on your life! Not, because of God's life in our lives. Not, and not, and not. And halleluiah. Let us praise him!

Single, and Singing   9

Sometimes, in the providences that come to us, to be single can mean rare and shining opportunities, and with the opportunities may come splendid and incredible joys.

I close my eyes for a moment and remember. It is 1969 again; I am driving across the international boundary from Detroit, Michigan, into Windsor, Ontario. As I swerve into the right lane on the 401 cross-Canada freeway (oh, immensely right, this right lane!), I break into song: "Praise God from whom all blessings flow." Single, indubitably. Singing, jubilantly.

The Canadian border officer had looked curiously at the row of my garments hanging from a rod over the back seat of my Plymouth Fury III, at the absence of any other occupant in the car. Alone? Oh, yes. Though I didn't try to tell him how utterly glad the aloneness was.

It had been a very strenuous year for me, the 1968-69 academic year, with extra committee work that had battered my spirits and strained all my inner resources. During the year I had thought hard and prayed hard — earnestly; eagerly; with expectation — and had come to a very deep sense of rightness. I would drive up to Prince Edward Island, up beyond the borders of Maine, for a summer of writing.

First, I had an obligation for a series of devotional talks in northern Indiana, at an international convocation of Free Methodist women. Working on the talks and praying about them and giving them helped, I'm sure, to tune my spirit and quicken my eagerness for the writing project. I didn't know what I would write. Something, something, as the Lord would direct.

The last talk over, there was a great lifting of joy, like gull wings beating inside me, as I tossed my suitcases into the Fury. They joined the portable record player, a few of my favorite records, a few durably inspirational books that I had selected before I left Greenville.

And I was on my way.

The gull wings soared and lifted as I drove through Michigan, and when Michigan road signs gave way to the Canadian 401, the response was instantaneous: it had to be the doxology. Never, in all my singings of the doxology, have I meant it more utterly. Praise God, praise God, praise God. Never have I more deeply desired for the heavenly hosts to join in a praising I uttered.

Alone.

Alone, in my Plymouth.

Alone, exploring the Canadian roads.

Alone, with expectations. With awe. With God's guidings that had prepared the way. With him.

A part of my utter gladness, let me note, was the practical gladness of having made it safely through the highways of the Detroit area. I was still a novice at the wheel; that Fury was my very first car, and I had owned it for less than two years. During the summer of '67, most tardily for an American, I had taken instruction from the Drivers' Education students at Greenville College, had warily driven my way to a license, had taken deep breaths and looked at cars. And bought.

And now, jubilantly alone.

For some five days, I watched landscapes and exclaimed to myself about them. I wandered off the 401 to find other scenery, to find lodgings. I paused to look at the site of the Canadian Shakespeare Festival, and was happily surprised to find a ticket for Hamlet easily available. On a leisurely afternoon, I sat for a while on a blanket looking out over the St. Lawrence, watching the current, watching the wild flowers, watching ideas.

The attendants at service stations were like successive guardian angels, I thought. I savored the names of places. My favorite of all: tiny St. Louis du Ha Ha, on highway 2, after I had swerved down from the St. Lawrence Seaway and was nearing New Brunswick. Within New Brunswick, I reveled in the hills that sloped down toward the St. John River, and the masses of lilac blossoms around the sites of former dwellings, and the sense of strange new distances. Day by day I delighted in choosing a motel when I was weary, and I thanked the Lord for the graces offered, successively, by each one.

Then, too soon and yet not too soon, Shediac on the eastern edge, overlooking Northumberland Strait, and then the Cape Tormentine car ferry over to Prince Edward Island. And again, the image of angels: the ferry attendants, in their bright orange coveralls, were surely like welcoming angels greeting newest newcomers into Forever.

On the Island, that metaphor continued and expanded, for late June on Prince Edward Island kept bringing throughts of paradise to my delighted mind. Shimmering blue sea surrounding it, incredibly colorful red cliffs and sands edging it, lush green of cultivated fields upon it, and flowers everywhere. Especially lupine: tall spikes of lupine, multi-colored, which the local residents had encouraged to grow along roadsides. And the evergreen woods, and the winging herons, and the other discoveries that I kept discovering.

For the first week, I found a pleasant room in a rustic old family hotel near Brackley Beach, where lobster suppers seemed to be as ordinary as hamburgers.

But all that was fringe benefit. I was there to write. And within hours after I settled into the old hotel, the first paragraphs of what was to become my fiction book *Strettam* were actually moving through the Olympia portable. Before the week was out, another resident asked deferentially in the dining room what I was up to, and then beamed in self-congratulation. "That's just what I told my wife," he said confidently. "I said, she's either a writer or an executive secretary."

Later, through the good offices of a professional acquaintance at the local university who had assured me that Prince Edward Island would be great for a writing summer, I had a room for three weeks in a wonderfully hospitable farm home which sometimes took paying guests. My typewriter clacked and clacked. Day by day I hiked the quiet beaches of the Island as I thought through the next chapters of *Strettam*. Day by day I gloried in the solitudes.

On other occasions, on many occasions, I am a very gregarious person. But sometimes — and certainly for those weeks in 1969 — solitude can be — well, heavenly. I say it reverently, and very intensely, and not as a flippant adjective! Those weeks were heavenly.

After the farmhouse time, I was urged not to miss the chance, while I was so near, of seeing Cape Breton Island, on Nova Scotia. I thought, and prayed, and the inner guidance gave a sense of rightness. And the Fury and I took the car ferry from Port Wood, and circled up to Cape North. My pulses quicken again today as I drive that road in recollection: Margaree Harbour, Grant Etang, Ingonish, Skir Dhu. From Cape North, at the very northern tip of Nova Scotia, I sent a postcard back to Jackson Motors in Mulberry Grove, Illinois, where I had bought the Fury III in 1967. I knew they'd be interested. Whenever Mr. Jackson serviced the car, his paternal kindness was always mixed with incredulity, that I had lived so long in a car-less estate and then had driven so blithely. And the distance from my residence in Greenville, Illinois, to the university campus in Charlottetown, Prince Edward Island, had been precisely 2,000 miles. Two thousand miles of solo driving. Two thousand miles of glorious gladness. Two thousand miles that were solo and yet not solo; I was accompanied by a Presence.

I still smile when I remember the incredulous looks I got as I drove that Nova Scotia loop; it's a drive that is highly favored, I was told, as a honeymoon trip for P.E.I. residents. Obviously it was also favored as a family vacation area. A car bearing an Illinois license plate and occupied by one lone female was stared upon. Courteously, but definitely, it was stared upon. But such joy as I was knowing was not evicted nor even diminished by the stares.

Sometimes, to be sure, the wistfulnesses popped up during that summer. Such great scenery — it would be nice to have someone to exclaim to; it would be good to come back to Nova Scotia sometime with another driver along so that I could do even more observing from the car, even more photographing. If someone else were here, I'd do thus-and-so in Charlottetown this evening, instead of thus-and-so.

But the chapters of *Strettam* mounded higher on my successive desks, and the reachings of spirit that can only come in solitude were with me.

After the Nova Scotia bit, there was a week in Mrs. Somebody's Garden Cottages. I had a hotplate to use for meals, and an orchard to write in, and a splendid blue-brilliant prong of sea to look toward, beyond the lower edge of the garden, and flowerbeds which stirred me to write new poetry about what Eden must have been like.

Then some other wanderings around P.E.I., and suddenly late June had become August, and goldenrod was blossoming. (Acres of it, along one edge of one little bay.) Brilliant, more golden than golden.

And time for sociability again. Now, as previously arranged, I blithely put aside the solitude and the typewriter and met a bus. A friend and I had planned that she would join me on the Island and help me drive home. I was ready to show her my explorings, my favorite nooks. I was ready now to patronize the one elegant restaurant I had kept in reserve as the place to go with aloud-exclaimings rather than inner-exclaimings. I was ready for some duo-driving. Yet I was utterly glad for all that I had experienced alone, and the gladness continues within me: a rare and special gladness.

When the occasion is right, when the circumstances are right, it is a great privilege to be alone.

To be single, and singing.

part two

THE LIVING OF A LIFE

The Lifestyle of the Christian Single   10

An interesting word, "lifestyle." A neologism, not even listed in moderately recent dictionaries, but quite useful.

What is your "lifestyle"? What might it be ten years from now? If Grace is really at work within you, what might it be? If you succumb to the patterns flaunted in TV programs and described in lurid news releases, if you become conformed to this world (as Romans 12:2 lets us know we easily may do), what might your lifestyle become? To focus the querying on the present, since the present is where we live our lives: if a skilled realistic novelist were to do a book about a main character who is very, very much like the present you, how would he describe the lifestyle of that person?

Lifestyle: vocation, residence, use of free time, clothing, cars, hobbies, clubs, meetings, associates, home furnishings, things read, things seen on TV or on cinema screens, things eaten or imbibed, magazines taken, letters written, sports, travelings, collectings, conversings. All of the manifestations of the inner self.

If someone gave you a $1,000 bonus, with the one provision that it must be spent soon and not put into savings, what would you spend it for? Would your choosings give some clue to your "lifestyle"? Would you buy a Tiffany lamp, or go to Las Vegas, or send the money to a Christian college, or get a new camera, or — or what? Even tentative thoughts on such a query might show some of the trendlines of your "lifestyle," in the present chapter of your life. "Getting and spending, we lay waste our powers," mourned Wordsworth, and he spoke a truth, but also in "getting and spending" we may be building up the Kingdom of God, contributing to the strengths of a community, becoming more fully his servants.

In this discussion, I am not about to issue specific counselings

about the job you take, or the auto you buy, or the use you will make
of next Friday evening from seven until eleven. I would like us to
probe toward some principles, as we think together, and to pull
some ideas out into daylight in order to examine them. Beyond that,
in the hundreds of interlinking little decisions of every day which,
together, constitute the style of one's life, each of us will have to
"work out his own salvation, with fear and trembling," as St. Paul
admonished (Philippians 2:12). But before we go on, we should
note — and note very gladly — the balancing assertion of Philippians
2:13. "For it is God that worketh in you both to will and to do of his
good pleasure." Like the sculptor who said his task was to find the
statue already present in the big block of marble, the Christian's task
is to "work out" what God is already working, has already worked.

Let's think, then, about some assertions of principles. Ready?

● We ought often to review our whole way of living in terms of
our desire to make Jesus Christ known to this desperate planet full
of desperate human beings. We are not our own; we are bought with
a price. "How is my life counting for Christ?" is a continuing yard-
stick, for New Year evaluations, and birthday-pause evaluations,
and week-by-habitual-week evaluations.

● We need good role models.
After a silly TV comedy which has implied the excellence of the
sybaritic, the sensual, the materialistic, we may especially need role
models. Last night I re-read Ann Kiemel's little volume, *I'm Out to
Change My World,* and I felt both chastened and inspired. Here at
my fingertips is Elisabeth Elliot's *Through Gates of Splendor.* Here
at my fingertips are Dr. Mary A. Tenney's two excellent books on
the way of life among the early Methodists, *Blueprint for a Christian
World* and *Living in Two Worlds.* Here, too, the *Letters of C. S.
Lewis.* And Elton Trueblood's *Company of the Committed.*
We are not to go about trying to imitate other human beings, but
we can wholesomely remind ourselves often of what they are, or
were. Thinking about the valor which other Christians have exhibited
can help to keep the options open. And that is important! It is, in
fact, my next observation.

● We need to keep thinking about potential change.
This seems to me especially important for the single person who is
moving toward middle years. An undercurrent of "what has been, will
be" can pervade our thought until we calcify and become as inflex-
ible as a stalagmite. Until, masculine or feminine, we are spinsters —
a consummation, to twist Hamlet's line out of context, most devoutly

not to be wished. (Just minutes ago I twinkled inside when I heard a radio voice on the FM station quoting Ogden Nash between classical records, and I caught Nash's rhyme about the face of the "spinster" which causes us to know we're "against 'er.")

"I've always taken vacations in Wisconsin." Well, why? Mexico awaits, or Idaho, or Hong Kong, or a village in Missouri. "But I've never audited a university course." Oh. Why not? "Oh, I couldn't possibly sponsor the teens trip." No? Are you quite, quite sure? "*Me* review a book? *Me* sing in the choir? *Me*. . . ." Maybe. Maybe *me* needs somehow to be ripped up, turned inside out, stitched together in a new ways.

● The single years are opportunity years.

This may apply especially to some of the teens and twenties, who need to gather the flowers and foliage of singledom while they may; some things will be less feasible, less likely if marriage complicates the later decidings. I think of a fellow who made a motorcycle trip to Canada after an early engagement splintered; he knew something, having come near to marriage, of how marriage would probably alter both his inclinations and his opportunities. And he's glad now for those motorcycle miles, as he drives his station wagon miles. I think of Peace Corps volunteers from among the singles, of recruits for short-term missionary projects, of employees in national parks.

But the single years may also be opportunity years for the older single, whether retired and released from other commitments, or single again. For example: intrepid Mildred Silver, a brisk and sprightly professor of English at McKendree College, who went off to Japan to teach for a while in mission schools after she had retired from her college job.

Often the single can buy, choose, shop, decide, go, do, be, with a freedom of choice that his married friends cannot possibly exercise. It can be an exciting freedom.

● Whatever the alternatives, we can sprinkle humor over them.

Maybe a humorless person cannot will himself into being a comedian, but we don't need just throngs of comedians around. We do need people with gusto and zest and an ability to see fun, to share fun, to bring the ripple of mirth into tense situations. The book jacket of C. S. Lewis's letters tells us that St. Clive had "a large talent for friendship, fun, and foolery," and the depth of his seriousness and wisdom was heartily seasoned by his "foolery." Very recently, when I was rereading some of his letters for a while before I turned off my reading lamp, my laughter shook the pillows and mattress and blankets while I savored his description to this brother of an

episode from Oxford when a singularly unpleasant man (whom
Lewis calls "ape-face") was the hapless victim of a hot match flung
toward a fireplace but falling accidentally between the collar and
neck of "ape-face." (A letter dated 20 March 1932, if you want to
join the merriment.)[1]

Near the conclusion of his little volume, *For God's Sake Laugh!*,
Nelvin Vos has some good words for singles to hear, as well as for
anyone else: "Laughter is both self-critical (in its sacrificial element
of laughing at one's own pretentiousness) and self-confident (in its
festive enjoyment and its restoration and renewal of one's vitality).
It helps us to learn not to take ourselves so seriously that the world
would collapse without our presence. It perceptively informs us that
we trust that not everything is left for us to do, but that we are sustained by the love of others and of God. . . . Laughter, most of all,
heals us, for it confirms the idea that we are forgiven."[2]

Laughter is a good part of the Christian's lifestyle.

● Selfishness can become a besetting sin of the single.

It's a built-in possibility. A thousand times a day, the single must
be making I-responsible decisions: I will, I must, I should, I may,
I might. The single woman does not go through the daily demand
for self-sacrifice that her married sister knows; no small voices
waken her crying, "Mommy, I need a drink of water." Her evening
schedules are not being juggled around chauffering Boy Scouts, Girl
Scouts, municipal band tooters, and Little League games. Her days
are not patterned around a husband's shirts and dental appointments
and pork chops and coffee. The single man is not disciplined toward
selflessness of soul by his responses to unending requests of "Daddy,
would you . . ." and "Honey, did you . . ." and "Shall we. . . ."

Always deciding "I" and not "we," the single can become very
centripetal and more and more selfish. The Christian single's lifestyle, then, will keep alert for opportunities to think with the heart,
to think "you" sentences, to ask "you" inquiries.

In one of my enterprises I had an associate of whom I thought
sometimes, with chuckles inside myself, that she seemed to believe
she was the only one in the building who ever experienced a weekend, or a vacation. On a Monday morning she was often very quick
to give the rest of us full accounts of her trips or her visitors, her
meals or her pets, but she didn't seem to be able even to frame a
question like, "Well, how was *your* weekend?" For the Christian
single, James' admonition would hold good about a preoccupation
like hers: "My brethren, these things ought not so to be."

And often they aren't. Many singles are wonderfully other-
oriented. Remembering the weekender, I remember Maria in con-

trast; she was not one to pry nor to be inquisitive, but whenever I visited her, there was a glowing warmth of "tell me about you" to match the warmth of the tea she would pour or the fire she would kindle in her fireplace.

• Singleness can offer a special vocation: to transmit love to persons all around us.

It is a love-starved world that we live in, whether we live in village or metropolitan center, whether we move among people of poverty or of affluence. For the present, at least, we are singles, not responsible to the emotional hungers of spouse or of offspring. And that leaves us free, if we will, for a real destiny of giving out *Agapé*-love. "I can practise Agapé to God, Angels, Man and Beast," wrote C. S. Lewis to an unnamed lady among his correspondents, "to the good and the bad, the old and the young, the far and the near. You see Agapé is all giving, not getting."[3]

In her book *Who Walk Alone: A Consideration of the Single Life,* Margaret Evening recounts very movingly how she came, by way of a character in a novel, to her own commitment of loving as a vocation. In reading *The Dean's Watch* by Elizabeth Goudge, Miss Evening read about a crippled girl, Mary Montague, who decided that "loving" would be a life work. "God spoke to me through Mary Montague that afternoon, in the pages of Elizabeth Goudge's novel. For me it was also a moment of awakening. . . . Loving could be a vocation in itself, loving on a wider scale than that of a family, loving in a kind of reckless outpouring that is not worried as to whether or not it will be loved in return." Her immediate response was to put love in action on that very afternoon, to give up a planned weekend of solitude and "fetch a young colleague who lived in a very dingy bed-sit" as a weekend guest. And on from there to new possibilities, she says, "if one worked at loving, as people have to work at their marriage if it is to grow and deepen."[4]

Miss Evening's affirmation would seem to echo very closely the attitudes of generosity and open-heartedness that Paul was urging toward in 2 Corinthians 9:6-15. "While by the experiment of this ministration they glorify God," he said (9:13 KJV). For all of us, the Christian life can be "the experiment of this ministration." One thinks, too, of 1 Corinthians 13, and one thinks of the tremendous description, in chapter XII of *The Great Divorce,* of how C. S. Lewis imagined the arrival in heaven of Sarah Smith, from Golders Green:

"Every young man or boy that met her became her son — even if it was only the boy that brought the meat to her back door. Every girl that met her was her daughter. . . . Few men looked

*on her without becoming, in a certain fashion, her lovers. But it
was the kind of love that made them not less true, but truer, to
their own wives. . . . In her they became themselves. And now
the abundance of life she has in Christ from the Father flows
over them."* [5]

● One of the tools for a vocation to Christian love can be correspondence.

A truism? No doubt. But worth the mentioning. For some of us,
love will work itself out more often in cookies baked or tea poured
or listenings listened. Sometimes, the encouraging word spoken, the
solicitude expressed. Sometimes, the letter written.

A few of Edna St. Vincent Millay's words in "Renascence" could
apply to our letter-writing selves. As she saw it,

> "East and West will pinch the heart
>   That can not keep them pushed apart;
>   And he whose soul is flat — the sky
>   Will cave in on him by and by." [6]

Beyond the benefit that the loving letter may convey to someone
else, it can keep the writer's soul from going flat, and keep the sky
from caving in!

● Good talk is part of a good lifestyle.

The life of the mind, the life of the spirit — how much conversation contributes to them! If one lives alone, he can come from his
quietudes and meditations with a mellow ripeness to offer to conver-
sational feasts when they occur. And conversation can be feast
indeed when opinion is challenged or reinforced, when the thought
of various authors is adduced; when "Do you think . . ." or "Have
you ever considered that . . ." moves the conversation along, rather
than the fact-only "Did you know . . ."; when mind really greets
mind, and soul really challenges soul.

The merest conventions of greeting have their place, of course;
"Good morning" should not be deleted from our use, and factual
information needs to be conveyed. But those are beginning points.
How much more satisfying when thought builds upon thought, like
an organist improvising chords!

Often, it seems to me, the resourceful single person is the one in
a group who lifts topics for discussion, steers attention away from
gossipy fact, encourages thought to be answered by thought, deters
the monologue artist and the lecturer. Maybe single minds have a
useful detachment, sometimes, from other preoccupations. Maybe

single people care about the people in the group, sometimes, and try to bring them out.

If we aren't skilled conversationalists, are we becoming so?

Once while I was teaching at Seattle Pacific College, genial Mendal B. Miller, a professor of economics, met me on the campus. "I want to talk to you sometime," he said a little solemnly. Then he grinned his delightful rogue-merry grin, and went on, "I don't know what I want to talk to you about; I just want to talk." It was, I think, one of the nicer things I've ever had spoken into these two ears!

● Lifestyle, for the Christian, is the constant choosing of duty.

It is a choosing of joy, too; that is the splendid paradox of Christian experience. But one doesn't begin by choosing joy; joy comes as the by-product, the inevitable concomitant.

To the Christian, duty comes with a sense of special endowment and of special opportunity. Whoever I am, there is only one of me in God's sight, and I am responsible to him. I am also being guided by him, in big decisions and in little decisions, as I let him guide me.

"The one secret of life and development," wrote George Mac-Donald, "is not to devise and plan but to fall in with the forces at work — to do every moment's duty aright — that being the part in the process allowed to us; and let come — not what will, for there is no such thing — but what the eternal thought wills for each of us, has intended in each of us from the first."[7]

If we can translate MacDonald's vision into the daily practicalities of buying groceries and using utensils, attending committees and writing poems, taking trips and wielding brushes, we shall be living a lifestyle that is indeed Christian, for now and for the eternities to view.

Notes to Chapter 10

1. *Lettters of C. S. Lewis,* ed. W. H. Lewis (New York: Harcourt, Brace, and World, 1966), pp. 149-50.
2. Nelvin Vos, *For God's Sake Laugh!* (Richmond, Virginia: John Knox Press, 1967), p. 69.
3. *Letters of C. S. Lewis,* pp. 255-6.
4. Margaret Evening, *Who Walk Alone: A Consideration of the Single Life* (Downers Grove, Illinois: Inter-Varsity Press, 1974), pp. 200-02.
5. C. S. Lewis, *The Great Divorce* (New York: The Macmillan Company, 1955), pp. 110-11.
6. Edna St. Vincent Millay, "Renascence," in *Collected Poems,* ed. Norma Millay (New York: Harper and Row, 1956), p. 13.
7. C. S. Lewis, ed., *George MacDonald: An Anthology* (New York: The Macmillan Company, 1960), pp. 117-18.

To Share a Dwelling? **11**

From the time you first pack a suitcase or duffel bag and leave your parents' home until you are taken to a hospital during your final illness, you will be making decisions about where to stay, where to live. Sometimes the decisions will be outside your hands. Sometimes they will change again quickly. Often one deciding will tie into a whole network of other decisions, more than you will realize at the moment.

Recurrently, while you are single, you may have occasion to ask someone else, or someone else will ask you, about sharing a dwelling.

What about it?

Well, naturally, one step at a time. And for the Christian, each step to be taken with prayerful thought, and with as much intelligent judgment as can be brought into action. "What are the alternatives?" is often a useful question in looking at any decision: college courses, jobs, majors; apartments; apartmentmates.

Several years ago I heard Dr. Dwight H. Small of Westmont College give a very wise talk at a retreat for a faculty women's club. Remember, he urged the women, that life is lived in chapters; some things that are a great annoyance or a great stress to you now are part of this chapter, but there will be other chapters. Live the present chapter fully, and be ready for the next chapter when it comes along. His perceptive comments could apply to a great many housing-for-us-singles decisions as well as to other sorts of experience.

Usually graduate school or first-employment-years dwellings will have a natural and useful sense of transience. A congenial room-mate can be a great help with the household budget as well as in sociabilities. Having a friend to share the experiences of the day at supper time, to join you for concerts and plays, to entertain with you, can be helpful and satisfying. "Emotional support," as the

sociologists call it, is no small thing. Learning to adjust to a roommate's demands in brand of coffee or standard of housekeeping can
be a good training ground in flexibility, a growth experience. Many
married persons would report that the give and take of college dormitories and of apartment-sharing gave valuable apprenticeship for
the ultimate give-and-take of marriage.

Obviously, though, if you find yourselves too disparate, apartment-
sharing can be like unto Chinese water torture. If Flossie wants
every magazine neatly aligned and you fling them into casual piles,
if Flossie wants the kitchen floor washed three times a week and you
seldom wash the dishes more than once a week, if Flossie wants
Bach and the Metropolitan Opera on the FM station and you can't
stand either — well, you'll soon be wondering who thought it was
a good idea to share the rent, anyway. I hope that one of you can
move without permanent scars to either ego. Maybe the experience
will have been a useful kind of marriage counseling for you both, in
a negative way, about some of the adjustments that you cannot make,
or are not yet willing to make.

Naturally, it will take some common sense and good humor for
the sharers of an apartment to work out their ground rules and stick
with them. Who cooks when? Who does the laundry? Who shops
for groceries? Who cleans, in what rotations? Who feeds the kitty,
and who pays the bills?

Looking back, I realize how immensely fortunate I was in my first
post-college year when four of us from Greenville College worked
out questions such as I have just been naming while we shared a drab
apartment at the University of Illinois. Anna Belle Laughbaum, who
was starting a doctoral program in English, helped to guide the rest
of us with her calm good sense. Claudine Crozier, our journalism
major, kept us amused and stimulated; her humor sparkled and
bubbled, even when she had been studying all night. (Once, though,
the rest of us were less than enthusiastic, I recall, when she merrily
decided to honor us with pancakes at 5:30 A.M.) Dola Sanders was
kindness itself, and her work in business education gave her some
practicalities, and she was a good cook. Liver and onions was her
super-specialty.

We soon christened ourselves The House of Four Gabbles, each
with her own Gabble Family name. Claudine was "Goofy"; Dola's
beautiful eyes made her "Goo-Goo"; Anna's surname made an
obvious label, "Giggle"; and I, who simply could not gain an ounce
while the others dieted and exercised, was dubbed "Gobble." I still
may get a letter from any one of them signed "G. G. G."

We laughed immoderately, studied rigorously, had friends in now
and then, shared ideas with each other from church or from Inter-
Varsity Christian Fellowship. We lived on an incredibly slim budget.

(Miss Tenney, our professor back at Greenville whom we called our Aunt Grace, and to whom we sent roses for her birthday, once asked me quietly how often we were managing to have meat, with *that* small an expenditure.) We took turns sleeping in the frigid porch-bedroom, with the two out there wearing bathrobes and head scarves and socks to bed, night by night.

It was a great year.

Looking back, I am sure that one of the reasons it was great was that we did try to work out a clear set of ground rules, and to live by the rules. We all tried for fair play and real cooperation. Beyond that, there was a strong sense of something that would not last, a now to be savored, a chapter to be lived for then.

It's quite a different thing when two or three professional people, at ages 37 or 43 or 51, think about buying a house together, or when Ruth and Zelma get a bigger apartment, after three years together in a small one, and start buying "our" furniture.

Before you sign the lease, Ruth and Zelma, have you thought enough about the implications? Before you go to a real estate office together, have you thought enough about the implications?

Companionship. Investment, rather than the constant payment of rent. Someone to worry with you about practicalities like plumbing and painting and a new roof. Those are major considerations. On the other hand, each of you may lose something of "I" in becoming so permanently "we." Each of you may do less reaching out to new contacts, new friendships, new interests. You will increasingly entertain together, if at all, and be invited together, if at all. You will tend to vacation together, to travel together. "When your friends are my friends and my friends are your friends" is fine in the old party song, but for two professional women, it can be another step into provincialism, into — well, into spinsterliness. (Not always, but it can be.)

Maybe Zelma has always been more active socially — dates more, goes to more events. Will this be an awkwardness, eventually? Will Ruth find a subtle tension either in staying at home while Zelma goes out, or in tagging along to Zelma's events? Suppose Zelma falls in love one of these times. Or suppose that Ruth's new boss is a widower who takes a fancy to her. Will the shared furniture and the jointly-owned house make a high barrier that old Cupid simply will not be able to shoot across?

After due thought, and candid thought, certainly Ruth and Zelma should reach some clear understandings with each other. Some of the understandings should be written into the legal contracts, and into their respective wills.

Beyond that, Ruth and Zelma (or Clifton and George, over in their apartment, or Sue and Beth and Toni, in theirs) should certainly, certainly work at keeping lines of communication open between themselves. One of Browning's more hideous imagined characters is the Duke in "My Last Duchess," who explains to his listener that he could not lower himself to talk over with his wife what he found amiss in her impetuous young conduct:

> "E'en then would be some stooping; and I choose
> Never to stoop."

Let it not be so between housemates! Rather than bottling in the annoyance until one day it splashes over everything like a fizzing coke, Zelma can initiate the frequent discussions of "Shall we . . ." and "Hadn't we better. . . ." Rather than never mentioning her dislike of a cluttered bathroom and gritting her teeth about it, Ruth can tease a little and urge a little, and keep the frictional topic out in the open.

"You always . . ." and "you never . . ." can leave their scars on housemates, as well as in other sorts of human relationships.

Sometimes the differences in taste and lifestyle just won't disappear. Clifton really likes to give big noisy dinner parties with grilled hot dogs and barbershop singing; George is a gourmet cook and plays baroque records softly. Clifton wants to redecorate, and George hates the new wallpaper. Et cetera, et cetera, et cetera. Well, they may compromise. Or they may decide, like Paul and Barnabas once upon a day, that the contention is so sharp it should not continue. Or George may decide, as he thinks and prays about it, that his Christian character will grow by a great deal of giving in and giving up — a little as C. S. Lewis apparently decided in the course of his residence during most of his mature years with the cantankerous and empty-minded woman who was his surrogate mother.

Sometimes housemate relationships seem so wonderfully complementary that everyone murmurs, "Providential," and sings the doxology. In her autobiography, the novelist Elizabeth Goudge pays high tribute to Jessie Monroe, whom a mutual friend (and the Lord) sent to her after the death of Miss Goudge's adored mother. Eugenia Price has told in her autobiography, *The Burden Is Light,* how very much Ellen Riley meant to her as housemate, for Eugenia's early years as a Christian, after Ellen had helped her to become a Christian. Emily Dickinson had a housemate in her sister Vinnie, as everyone who has seen Julie Harris in the splendid *Belle of Amherst* dramatization.

If it's good, it's good. And thank the Lord, and blessings upon them.

Yet, another word should be spoken.

The great elm tree out in the fields between here and Vandalia did grow to its present circumference by standing alone.

If Providence and opportunity should lead you to a residence alone, for some chapter or chapters of your life, there can be very great joy and blessing in having decided *not* to share a dwelling. I speak from years of experience, as I say it.

When I moved from Seattle to Greenville, the best-for-me residence then available (after various inquiries, various prayers) was a smallish apartment. It had no roommate potential, really. And that was better for me than I might have guessed. Being alone gave me chances to grow, toward God and toward other people, as I might never otherwise have done. My two Moody Press volumes, *Echoes from Intercession* and *Here and Now,* were the fruitage from alone-time meditations. Scores and scores of students came and went from my apartment (waffle parties, conferrings, prayer times) who might not have come had my life belonged partly to a housemate and not so fully to them.

Eventually the house containing that apartment was sold, and I needed to move. A small town doesn't always offer easy choices. I cried and prayed and searched, cried and prayed and searched. And wondered, and wondered. One day I murmured to a real estate agent that I had wished for a fireplace, and he mentioned that a house on Beaumont Avenue might come into the market, fireplace and all. Ellis File might decide to sell. Ellis File did, indeed, decide to sell, and I moved just around the corner. I live so near the campus that I can have classes in my living room to hear my records of Byron's "Manfred," to see my slides of the English Lake District, for writing labs, to sip hot punch from my collection of bone china cups.

For this chapter of my life, living alone has in many ways been a veritable refuge and an opportunity.

For another chapter — what next, God? I hope that I will listen rightly to your instruction.

And that, precisely that, is what I would wish for you, and for you, and for you, and for you. You, Zelma. You, Ruth. You, Clifton. You, George.

How Do You Handle Their Heckling? **12**

No, they wouldn't call it heckling. They're just kidding. They know you're a good joe, and you can take a joke. They're just trying to be friendly. (That's what they would say, if they were challenged.) Or, after all, it's the sort of humor that emcees always use, isn't it?

But they are heckling, for all that.

And your spirit shrivels, if you let it, and takes a while to unshrivel again.

How do you handle their heckling?

Badly, sometimes. But if you fumble, the fumbling may become a learning experience for you, and for them.

Several years ago, for example, a former colleague wrote to me about the newest chapter of her life: about her recent marriage to a widower, and about her adult stepchildren. When I was chatting amiably with Louise, a warm-hearted and impulsive matron, about our friend Marie's new state of affairs, Louise twinkled archly and made exuberant comments about how, with Marie's example before me, I might decide to get married too.

Well, I bristled inside, and bristled badly. With more time and more courage to verbalize, I might have sputtered aloud, at length. But what does one say to words like those? "My dear lady, you don't just 'decide' to get married! You know that. Not in our society. Not if you're a Christian. I might 'decide' to sell a house, or to buy a house, or to go to Alaska, or to become a vegetarian. But I'm not about to 'decide,' willy-nilly, to get married!"

As it was, while I moved with the traffic along the side aisle of our church, and watched Louise's face watching my face for a quick reaction to her quick witticism, I heard myself blurting a curt and gauche response. "Well," I said stiffly, "I certainly don't want Marie's husband." And I still don't, but I hope that now I'd be able to cope with her heckling a little more graciously; I think I learned something about the soft answer. I hope, too, that Louise may have learned a wee something from my small explosion, and have become a little more sparing with personal remarks that have to seem barbed to the recipient.

How does one cope with their heckling?

Like everything else in mortal affairs, it all depends: on time, place, person, circumstance.

In general, though, it's often good to meet flippancy with flippancy. A merry heart still doeth good like a medicine, and most human gatherings need the merry hearts. Alumni reunions, family gatherings, office parties need the truly merry hearts. QUERY: "Not hitched yet, George? When are you going to quit running around and find a wife and settle down?" ANSWER: "I'll be receiving applications next Tuesday from four to six P.M. Want to pass the word along?" QUERY: "Don't you have a husband yet, Susie?" ANSWER: "Yup, six of 'em. I keep them in cages in the backyard and feed them ripe bananas."

My friend Beth says she had her standard reply; when her relatives used to tell her, "Beth, you ought to find a husband," she would regularly retort, "Whose?" And that, she reports, would give them pause. As she intended. Beth's relatives would have said, of course, that they weren't heckling; they were advising kindly, and for her own welfare, they would have said. But the reaction inside Beth was a heckled response.

Sometimes, then, to meet flippancy with flippancy.

Sometimes, the firm but gentle turning of the topic. Aunt Eliza bustles into your new apartment, surveys your new décor, pinches your drapery fabrics, eats your bran muffins. "A cook like you are," Aunt Eliza announces, "ought to have a man to cook for all the time. A woman with your skills in homemaking — it's just a shame you aren't making a real home for someone."

"Aunt Eliza," you ask earnestly, "do you *really* think that beige fabric is right for the draperies? I've thought about getting something in turquoise, that would highlight the hassock — you remember the hassock that Uncle Vincent gave me, from Grandma's things. . . ." Very earnestly, you say it.

Or maybe you don't.

Maybe Aunt Eliza is, instead, your cousin Jackie, and maybe you take a long, slow breath before you start the next chapter of her education. Maybe you are as firm and gentle and earnest as with Aunt Eliza, but maybe you point out to Jackie that she is being insufferable, that she is assuming her own lifestyle to be the superior lifestyle, that your choices are your own choices.

Sometimes you may feel a responsibility to an offender, and to all the persons whom he will encounter in his future, to have a quiet word with him in private for offences he has spoken in public. An emcee for an Inter-Varsity Christian Fellowship banquet, let's say, might deserve to have a word of brotherly admonition: "Bill, I wish you'd do a little thinking about that Most Eligible Bachelor routine before you use it again; Ike laughed tonight, but he was hurting, man, he was hurting. . . ."

Or you may sit down at your Underwood Portable and write some vigorous words to a celebrity:

> "My dear Dr. Bluff,
>
> "When you spoke to our Bible study group last Sunday evening, you used some opening humor to gain the attention of the audience. I think you should know that a number of us were deeply grieved, and even angered, that you chose to use silly old clichés about 'old maids' in your repertoire of jokes. Such humor, we think, would be in bad taste from any comedian, and is quite out of place from a member of the body of Christ. . . ."

Maybe you will meet flippancy with flippancy. Maybe you will quietly change the topic. Maybe you will help to educate offenders who have been thinking in stereotypes and have been wounding feelings egregiously.

Maybe, sometimes, you will have an opportunity through the heckling process for joyously ackowledging Christ in yet more of your ways, as you continue to live out Proverbs 3:5. Maybe one of your tormenting friends will discover, in ways he has really never known, that being a Christian can be a full-time, full-life, all-the-way-of-every-day sort of gladness and faith. Keith claps you on the shoulder at the 10th anniversary of your high school graduation. "Well, Pete, old man," he says, "by yourself, huh? No woman in your life, yet, huh? Or just too many of 'em, huh?" You grin, as he gibes on about what a Lothario you were back in high school. Look, you tell him finally, you're a Christian now, see? And that means for you that all of life is under the direction of the Lord Jesus Christ. See? Got that? And therefore your love life is something that you pray about, and for right now there's no leading lady in your life, and life is good. Okay? Okay. And maybe, afterward, Keith will be starting the beginnings of a quest he didn't know existed. It may be.

So far, so good. But there's another word to be said, underlying all the rest.

Whether it's a pinprick wound to the ego, or a gash left by a flailing axe, it's to be offered up — as is any tribulation the Christian ever encounters — to our Lord Christ.

Little grievances, or larger ones, aren't to be kept and fondled. They become evil pits. They gnaw inside a heart, and make it a very den of stenches.

It's a marvel: that our Lord would want ugliness to be given to him as a part of our worship. But he does want it, and he's the only one who can handle it.

In the moment, then, of hearing what sounds like a taunt, one can perform an act of worship and give the taunt to Christ. At evening devotions as one reckons up the transgressions and blunders of the day, one can experience the catharsis of confession. Sometimes, looking back across months or years to a conversation that still twinges, still suppurates, one can let Christ touch the old wound. And he will, he surely will.

Now let's think about a different slant on all this heckling. Sometimes when your acquaintances speak their teasing words or ask their prying questions, it may help your poise if you can give some eyeblink-rapid thought to why they are saying their sandbur-textured sentences. How you handle their quips may change a good deal when you hear what else is being said behind and underneath the spoken words.

Maybe Uncle George is really only wanting rapport with you when he stops you at your little sister's wedding reception and asks you jovially, loudly, when it will be your turn for the wedding gifts. Maybe, under his teasing, what he is really saying is, "I'm fond of you, Mike." And rather than telling him flatly that your singleness is your own business, maybe your deft response would be, "Oh, hi, Uncle George! Say, how is that big John Deere tractor behaving these days?"

Sometimes your friends are genuinely curious about your intimate life. You're like a TV serial happening right in front of them, like a chapter from a good novel. The same sort of curiosity that keeps all of us attentive to Shakespeare's people or Thackeray's people may nudge them toward questions that are, yes, intolerably personal in real life. Maybe they find you so interesting, so exciting, so different from themselves that their askings are a kind of compliment. Well, you are free to confide if you wish, or to parry as you wish. Maybe you will open wide eyes, assume a British accent, and pretend you are responding to a news correspondent. One of my friends tells me how she coped one time when a university colleague asked her with blunt seriousness why she had never married. "Oh, I don't know," she replied thoughtfully. "I was just lucky, I guess."

Sometimes you will recognize, even as you are being amused and annoyed by their tactics, that your friends are really saying, "We like you, and we want happiness for you." Happy in marriage themselves and seeing you as capable of unusually great felicity in matrimony, they nudge and prod and suggest. Your first reactions may be toward vexation or angry sarcasm over their attempts to run your life, over their smug superiorities. If you can listen beyond the teasing to hear the real affection behind it, you will know better what to say. Perhaps you will talk, after a moment, about how much you value Jan and Jerry; about things you have done with them; about new and joyous episodes in your life which you want to describe to them.

Sometimes you will feel strongly that the quippings come, at least in part, from their deep unwillingness to accept the idea of a single life as good and right and chosen, or divinely appointed, for anyone. Then it may be that you will respond, with earnestness or with humor, in a way that declares the Christian person's freedom to be single. Suppose you're a youngish lawyer, back at your alma mater to give a convocation address. The dean, chatting with you before you go to the platform, learns that your three sisters all met their husbands here. "Well, well," says the dean in patronizing tones, after a quick glance at your left hand, "and why did Matchbox College fail with *you,* my dear?" And you may look at him, with as much attentiveness as you give any witness you ever question, for several very durable seconds before you ask him to define "failure." Or maybe you will say, "I beg your pardon" in slow tones that will cause him to seek the pardon of other single alumnae for quite a while to come.

For various conversations, back at Matchbox College and beyond it, you may want to borrow a line from Tim Stafford. Here's his report: "When well-meaning people ask me, 'What's a nice guy like you doing without a wife?' I sometimes answer, with a grin, 'I'm just hoping to be more like Jesus!' "[1]

Beyond quipping, that is what all Christians want, isn't it? — to be more like Jesus. And ultimately that is what we will desire in our handling of the hecklings, as well as in everything else we do. "Like Jesus" is not a simple formula, though. If we read the Gospels more often and more deeply, we will know more definitely how his own traits are to be expressed through us.

Because we are his, we will want to handle the hecklings — and everything else — in his ways.

Note to Chapter 12

1. Tim Stafford, *A Love Story: Questions and Answers on Sex* (Grand Rapids: Zondervan, 1977), p. 92.

Other People's Children 13

On December 9, 1973, a very memorable concert was retelevised in Nebraska: a concert honoring the centennial of novelist Willa Cather. Because Willa Cather had been their deeply valued friend when they were children, violinist Yehudi Menuhin and his sisters, pianists Hephzibah and Yaltah, came from England to take part in the concert. They knew her from 1930 until her death in 1947. Through the good graces of Channel 9 in St. Louis, I saw the concert in January of 1978, and it stirred me profoundly; I shall remember it for a long, long time.

In the intermission interviews, Hephzibah spoke of "feeling loved, safe, comforted" in Miss Cather's presence. Yaltah reminisced about going with her to visit the Frick Art Gallery. "What a complete human being she was!" exclaimed Yehudi. "We could be natural with her, just as if she were of our age." He remembered the books she had given him — the works of Heine and of Goethe — and her influence toward beauty and rightness.

Watching Channel 9, I exclaimed within myself: Yes, oh, yes! That's one of the bright, bright strands in the tapestry of life that we are weaving. Other people's children.

Not always is the weaving so richly colored as in the Cather-Menuhin friendships, nor so durable, but the same sort of thing happens often and everywhere, among the single persons who live life fully and joyfully. Willa Cather could not have known that her three young comrades would fly halfway around a world, later on, to pay tribute to her, and we can be quite sure she was not out to earn any tributes — that the friendship itself was her full reward, that it meant as much to her as it did to the eloquent rememberers.

For many of us who are single, even a quick and cursory counting of our many blessings would include the glad, glad moments when other people's children have cherished us, and when we have cherished them. The infants, the toddlers, the bouncing school children, the long-legged adolescents, the young professional people — who seem to have been toddlers just about three years ago. Do you flick the switches in your memory? I flick some switches in mine: niece Nancy chortling on a blanket in the yard when she was six months old. The little pink-painted high chair for dolls that I took to Kansas once by bus, at a Christmas season. Picnicking with three bundles of energy on a beach near Seattle, while their mother was in the hospital with their new sister, and their vigorous praise of the potato salad I made for the occasion. Niece Claudia, age 2½, helping me bring laundry from a clothesline; Claudia, a senior in med school, bouncing under my car to diagnose a hideous mechanical noise. Emphatic young voices at dining tables: "I want to sit with Aunt Elva." Karyn at 15, touring the Boston Museum of Fine Arts with me.

Now I'm in California, a speaker at a writers' conference, and a small friend is slipping a piece of costume jewelry from her choicest treasures on my wrist while her father handles conference arrangements.

I'm hiking with niece Nanette or niece Charnell around Whidbey Island lanes.

I'm hearing a young neighbor play his Beethoven piece from his current lesson book for me.

I'm being introduced to a teen-age lad who is in deep trouble; he already knows me through correspondence, and flings his arms around me.

I'm opening a letter from a third grader, telling me about her family's trip "by fairy" across the Mississippi River.

I'm hearing long distance telephoned voices: college plans, job plans, wedding plans.

The brightnesses. Thank God for the brightnesses, from other people's children! Of such, said our Lord, is the Kingdom of Heaven. As we are like Christ, we other singles, often and often parents will come to us, too (in their own ways that are right for them and for now), bringing their children for our blessing. As we are like him, surely we will often (in our ways, that are right for us and for now) be giving our blessings. Of such is the Kingdom, still.

In primitive communities, the kraal or tent or cave or camp would contain old and young, adults and children. Everyone needed everyone. Everyone still needs everyone, but in our present segregated activities and segregated residences, singles may not always realize how much they need children and how much children need them.

My good friend Dorothy Docking realizes more than most persons do. Dorothy is a brisk, blithe, wonderfully alive little British woman who taught for a time at Westmont College in California. When retirement decisions were being made, she thought carefully about moving back to England; she loves her country and misses some aspects of British life very much indeed. But having weighed many things, including her deep desire to be in a situation that would afford many natural contacts with children, she settled upon retirement in Santa Barbara, with the faculty families of Westmont College as her own extended family. "To be with little children" was, she felt, a primary necessity for her. For of such, she knows, is the Kingdom.

Contacts will need planning and contriving and arranging, but the efforts are worth making. Grace and tact and courtesy and initiative can make the single person a valued contributor to the lives of other people's children: a strength to their strengths, a joy to their joys, a widener of their horizons, an enrichment to their experiences.

Initiative. Let's think about it for a minute. Sometimes a relationship with children is ready-made: you are their aunt, you are their uncle, you are their neighbor or their cousin. Sometimes the parents know how to include you warmly in the family circle, and continuingly let the children know that you are a person to be valued. Even so, there will be the initiatives for you to take. Sometimes the relationship is not ready-made; sometimes the parents are not easily and naturally the facilitators of trans-generation friendships. Then, more definitely, there will be initiatives for you to take.

How? When?

Well, not in the same measure and degree with everyone. In our contacts with toddler-size people as well as with our contemporaries and with our seniors, the Holy Spirit will instruct us, I believe, about special commissions that he will appoint for us. If we paid more attention to his monitions, we would more often, and in more ways, have the children being brought to us for our blessing; I'm quite sure of that. If we are alert, he will bring into our lives the children to whom we can minister.

How? When?

For some of us, vocationally. Donna Saylor's expressive, vibrant face leaps to my mind, and I think of her last letter. Donna is an inner-city missionary in Brooklyn. Trained as an elementary teacher, she works now among youngsters who are blighted by their environments; the limited and longing, the deprived and depraved. Other people's children. She touches many, many lives, and touches them for Christ. Among the singles, some of us are nurses, elementary school teachers, recreational leaders, Christian Education directors, social workers. Because we are his and because we are single, we have a very special enablement for his work, through us, among other people's children.

For some of us, through adoption or foster care. It is happening
with greater frequency, we're told, as patterns are changing in our
society; with more and more divorced persons all around us who
are "parents without partners" by necessity, courts and communities
are more ready to accept the idea of the single person's becoming an
adoptive parent. To adopt is a huge decision, obviously; if your
courage is right for it, and your circumstances, and your sense of
inner leading, blessings to you! And a hearty salute. I admire you,
and wish you well. And I think now of my friend Lana, whose
vivacious adopted Susie has been such a comrade, such a gratifi-
cation to her. Lana found it a more possible venture because her
parents were living with her when Susie became her daughter; their
babysitting assistance and grandparently affection help Lana through
the transitions. I think of Marian, whose adopted son has changed
all the dimensions of her life.

For some of us, by giving foster care from half a world away.
Through church boards and other agencies, programs are becoming
more and more widely available through which an American adult
can sponsor the care and support of a child in some famine-touched
nation, some poverty-bare nation. And I think now of Mara; she's
a brilliant and loving educator whose work keeps her in touch with
many, many American children, yet her foster child in Bangladesh
is dear and special to Mara as no other child on earth is dear and
special.

*For some of us, in loving outreach to neighbors and relatives and
personal friends,* more nearly like the young Menuhins in the life of
"complete human being" Willa Cather.

And for all of us, the continuing initiative, the small serendipity,
the impulse which gives gladness if we will follow it. Of her own
mother, the poet Louise Bogan wrote in her journals that on occasion
there were "truly loving moods" when "affection rayed out from her
like light."[1]

Among other people's children, the single person can be one from
whom affection continually will, similarly, just ray out like light. (As
I tell you that, do you think — again — of C. S. Lewis's most memorable Sarah Smith from Golders Green, in the opening part of
Chapter XII of *The Great Divorce*? She deserves the thought!
"Every young man or boy that met her became her son — even if it
was only the boy that brought the meat to her back door. Every girl
that met her was her daughter."[2]

"Well, how? How does one take good initiatives?" someone asks.
"Let's get specific."

All right. Let's get specific.

Some single people travel quite a lot. They tend to be free to travel, and they often have jobs that require travel or incomes that permit travel, or both. When you send postcards back from Paris or Honolulu or Haifa or Edinburgh, or from a fishing weekend in the next county, do you sometimes send postcards addressed to small Johnnie Neighbor or wee Cindi Neighbor, and not just to the J. A. Neighbor family collectively? Probably few pieces of mail that have come to me in my whole career of writing to editors and hearing from editors have been more valued than a postcard that came when I was eleven, from the woman who had been my teacher in a little yellow-painted country schoolhouse during the previous winter. I remember, I remember. And it helped to mold my life.

When the occasion is right, do you sometimes borrow a child (for your own joy, and for his) as Willa Cather borrowed Yaltah Menuhin for an afternoon of friendship with great art, at the Frick Art Museum in New York City?

My own memory flicks again. It's Easter of a year when there were three young teen nieces in a Kansas home and I, there on vacation took them over to Lindsborg. We "did" the antiques, the Swedish pancakes, the museums, two concerts — and it was a day that I shall always treasure.

And now memory retrieves an August evening, and three nieces are on a four-mile hike with me, exclaiming with me over crimson clouds (brightening, glowing, changing, softening, darkening) in one of the most glorious sunsets, surely, that western Kansas has ever produced.

Do you sometimes lend your books, even as Willa Cather put Heine and Goethe into the hands of young Yehudi Menuhin? Books, or records, or tools, or other extensions of you?

Do you put yourself in touch with children by volunteering where you are needed in the program of your church? For everyone, that isn't a rightness. If you work in an elementary school all through the week, perhaps you should not be a Sunday school teacher also; perhaps, though, the Sundays will give you some shining-splendid chances to touch lives you would never touch otherwise. If you work with adults during your earning-the-living hours, maybe you can have, and give, very special joy in Children's Church on a Sunday morning or a Wednesday evening.

Let me tell you about a college executive I know; call her Catherine. All through the week Catherine is busy with hirings, interviewings, scheduling her various employees, budgets, computer work. She doesn't feel she has a flair for Sunday school teaching, but she is often on the staff for baby-sitting in the toddlers' room during a church service. Dolls and blocks and stuffed animals and a low rocking chair are a rejuvenation to Catherine; in getting to know other people's children, she finds a joyous outpouring for and renewal of her affections. And she likes the involvement with church families that she finds; there's a new closeness with the Browns, the Smiths, the Nelsons and the Olsons, after Catherine has calmed their Johnnie and Katie and Beth and Susie and Billy. (Calmed, caressed, rocked, read to, played with.)

Or let me tell you about Julia. Julia has been a college teacher now for — um — well, for some twenty years. Julia has no relatives for many, many miles from the campus where she works. But Julia has musical skills, and delights in using them, and a part of her week is spent (joyfully, lovingly) with the other people's children of her church. The church is stronger for it, and so are the children, and so is Julia.

Or there's Nell. She's the kind of person friends describe as someone who likes to go places and do things. Her church has an active program in competitive Bible quizzing, and Nell's doing includes coaching young teens with their Bible lessons; her "going places" has included chauffeuring kids across several different states, in taking them to Bible quiz tournaments. And, believe me, Nell sparkles more because of it; she has deep friendships with numbers of her former quizzers, and their continuing careers are a source of unending interest to her.

But the initiatives aren't always so structured as the sponsoring of a youth group, or directing a cherub choir.

My executive friend Catherine told me with a cheery glee, one time, of a small bartering of labor she had just worked out; one of her business associates had promised to bring his tools and do a tricky piece of carpentry work on her apartment, and in return she would do a stint of baby-sitting for him and his wife. Her "I. O. U." is one that the young parents will find very useful, and Catherine (being Catherine) will enjoy getting to know their wee and cuddlesome Ruthie in newer ways and deeper depths. Initiative. Serendipity. More singles ought to be more like Catherine! For their own sakes, for the benefit of all the cuddlesome little Ruthies, for all the assistance-needing young parents, more singles out to be more like Catherine!

Let me add another word about Catherine. We were doing a bit of last-minute Christmas shopping together, once upon a Yuletime, and I was interested in the way her eyes (and purse) kept going toward diminutive toys. I knew she had no niece or nephew near at hand, and it was too late to be shipping parcels away. Then she explained, with a blitheness and a sparkle that gave an extra glow to that whole Christmas season for me. One of her part-time staff members was a young woman with a tiny son — as well as a tiny income. The baby had been with his grandparents for months, but was coming home for Christmas. "I'm filling a stocking for Davy," Catherine explained as she picked up another little toy.

Sometimes the initiatives will need to be of a quite other sort, when the other people's children grow taller and put away, in their turn, the childish things. Then it may be the cheery note to a mail-hungry freshman away at college; the telephone call to say "I'm praying for you" when final exams are grinding down a college senior's morale; the listening ear when a romance is going through its throes, or when job decisions are being made, or when applications are going out to graduate schools.

Since almost my entire working life has been spent on college campuses, I am deeply, deeply aware that other people's children need some "significant other" adult in their lives, beyond their own parents. Parents do what parents can do, but even when they have done their utmost, there is still need for the "significant other." The single person who is sensitive and aware can have an immense usefulness.

Sometimes (heaven help us!) it's the role model that is needed. Kids watch us. Kids evaluate us. Kids want to know why we chose the careers we chose, what we believe, what we have experienced, who we are. Who we really are.

Sometimes they need an outsider to whom they can talk about the growing-up tensions with Mom and Dad. The confidante needs huge measures of grace and wisdom, to be a listener and a prober and a fair-minded counselor, when the time is right for the counselings. Not to take sides in prejudiced and bungling ways. Not to scold, and close the door to further confidings. To give trust. To receive trust. "My parents say. . . ." "My parents don't understand that. . . ." "My father hasn't ever said. . . ." "My mom is a wonderful person, but. . . ."

They talk, and they talk. And we listen, and love them, and listen yet more, whether the topic is Mom-and-Dad, or anything else under the shining sun. Sometimes the telephone rings at odd hours. (Once, in my home, at something past one in the morning, and a voice saying, "Dr. Mac, would you please pray hard, right now?" And I prayed, very hard, and cited Scriptures to him, and talked, and listened, until something past three. How I thank God that he called!) Sometimes, one's dinner is postponed or the day's appointments are juggled because of an unexpected ringing of a doorbell, an unexpected tap on an office door. And thank God for the postponing, for the juggling!

Sometimes they will say to you, if you're the significant other, what they might not say to any other human being. What they need to say to someone. Memory flicks again. Now I am leaving a funeral home. The coffin is long and bronze-colored. It is the coffin of a former student of mine, and I have just had a part in his funeral.

A parent hand grips mine, and a parent voice thanks me for my part in the dead boy's questing after God. "He didn't share with us in those ways," says the grief-quiet voice. "Sometimes it takes someone from outside. . . ." Yes, sometimes it does. They had loved him, dearly and desperately, and they had loved God, but an outsider was the tool. Thank God that I was near at hand, to be the tool! Thank God he had nudged me to take some initiatives, to say, "If you want to talk, you know I'm here." Thank God!

You may feel veritably pulled in two, sometimes, in being fair to the parents when they're absent, and fair to the turbulent youngster when he's absent, and fair to them all when all are present, but the pain of the pulling and the tugging are worth it. Believe me, they are worth it.

During the last few years, I have had to think over and over again of a particular ministry the single person can have in our divorce-torn America. Kids whose homes are splintering need most especially to know a sustaining "significant other." The aches will be different if the child is three or seven when divorce happens than the aches of thirteen or seventeen, but they are terrible aches, whatever the age. When the whole world is debris and disaster to a child or to a teen-ager, a parent-age person who is not a part of the storm can be shelter and stability.

I realized it with a new clarity during one recent semester when a freshman boy telephoned to ask about bringing a theme to my home. I was a little puzzled, since he could easily have handed the paper to me at class the next day, but after I received the theme he lingered to talk, and to talk, and to talk; I heard about Mom's departure from the family, and about a lot of other things. The theme was incidental; he needed a stand-in Mom that night. I'm glad I was here!

Several years ago a mother telephoned me from a distant part of the nation. Her divorce was about to become final, and she knew that her Karen was fond of me, and would I please break the news to Karen? Karen could handle it better, she thought, if I would tell Karen.

As I think about Karen's mother, I think of how, maybe more than they know, parents also need the singles among their associates to be the "significant other."

Parents can help other parents, but the detached and separate person, the single, can also be a very important part of the family relationship. Parents need someone to hear about their hopes and fears for their children. Psychologically, sometimes they need someone who doesn't instantly counter their news about Mary Jane and Bobby with similar news about the listener's Betty June and Rob. Parents also need role models, inspirers, stimulators. It's scary to have that kind of modeling thrust upon one, but scariness should not make us run from it.

Again, the flicking of memory. After I had signed the contract for my fiction book, *Strettam,* but before it came from the press, I was invited to dinner in a home where parenting is taken very seriously. A lovely home, thoroughly Christian and always aspiring. The invitation was made very specific; "I want my children to know the author of *Strettam,*" my host told me with a brisk, blithe grin. At the dinner table he shaped the conversation into a bit of informal interviewing, so that when the book appeared its publication would be an event of significance to the children.

Sometimes (or often? or always?), parents need prayer support in their great task of rearing their children. Do singles give the support of intercessory prayer as often as they might? Cathy is in a romance that we are concerned about, they say. Would you have Cathy in your prayers? Jimmy is studying college catalogs; help us pray about Jimmy's decision. Keith has started smoking; we wish he weren't, but he is. Pray for our Keith? Trisha is all confused about her vocational plans; would you have Trisha in your prayers? Johnny — Johnny — Yes, our Johnny was arrested last week. . . . Will you pray. . . .

And I name them over as I turn on my pillow during wakeful minutes: Cathy. Jimmy. Keith. Trisha. Johnny. Oh God, deal with Johnny now. Cathy. Jimmy. Keith. Trisha. It's a great trust, when a parent says, "Please pray." It's a greater trust, when the Holy Spirit lifts out one prayer topic from among the many and impels a prayer.

And, yet again, the flick of memory. I'm in a hotel room in Lucerne, in Switzerland. Usual devotions are changed as a strange, deep intensity of prayer for a certain lad grips me. There is a physical problem in his life, and I wonder if God is leading me to pray the kind of prayer that could transmit a miracle of healing.

Afterward, there was no word of a sudden change, of any obvious miracle. But just two days ago now I was telling a colleague of the continuing miracle of grace in that young man's life, of the Christian witness he carries wherever he goes. Thank God for all that the young man's parents ever shared with me of their prayer requestings, for all Christ ever instructed of prayer respondings. Thank God for the prayers in a hotel room in Lucerne.

It's a Saturday in March, a quiet Saturday with campus dormitories silenced by spring break. I watch March winds toss the boughs of the big maples in the little woods beyond my study, and my eyes trace the gray-white peninsulas of thin little snowdrifts melting into the winter-brown leaves and grasses. While I watch, events of recent weeks skitter with the March winds. Many things have brightened

January and February and March for me this year; some of the brightest, surely, have been the episodes of the Other People's Children.

Last Sunday, when a tiny blonde detoured her post-Sunday-school skippings to skip over and hug me. She didn't say a word, but her eyes said many words. A letter from one of those divorce-scarred kids, with exciting new job plans and a "please pray" paragraph. A long distance call to a high school sophomore whom I value deeply, to be sure he knew about a Shelley program on TV. (No, he hadn't known, and thanks. Thanks very much!) An eighth grader's warm greeting from among snowdrifts, when he saw me arriving for lunch with his mother. The same eighth grader's poised and pleasant conversation when he was out earning money — to my gladness — as a shoveler of drifts.

A long distance telephone talk, and, yes, I'd pray about whether his alienated daughter would attend the special church event next Sunday.

The box of Snoopy valentines I bought on an impulse when I was in a stationery store, and sent off in a whole series of merry impulses. (One went to a girl in med school. One I saw on a dormitory door two days ago when I was erranding in a college residence hall.)

A letter from Jeannie, with new photos of her children and "please pray" and "please pray" and "please pray." Living beyond the divorce is hard for Jeannie, very hard. In a way, hearing from her couldn't be called brightness at all, but how glad I am that she wrote, that she trusts me enough to write.

A glittery brightness: Susie's happy chatter about taking her fiancé home to meet her family during spring break.

A different kind of brightness: shopping for an Easter something I could send along for Susie's little sister. (If you want to know, I settled on a demitasse cup from the college bookstore, with the college seal on it. Susie's little sister, in junior high, is thinking eagerly about colleges.)

And there was one evening at a college basketball game. After the JV game, I hopped down the bleachers to chat with two colleagues before the varsity squad took the floor. "Checking up on your son," I told one of them. "He's been talking with Connie, over there, for twenty minutes; is something developing?"

"Timing him, are you?" teased the second colleague. But he added very quickly, thinking of his own teen-agers, "I just hope you'll care that way about *my* children when they come on to college." (The Significant Other.) We talked a little about the game, and I mentioned that I had made a point of coming because of my nephews on the varsity team.

"Do you really have nephews here?" asked the second colleague with quick interest. Oh, no, I told him. Fellows I've had in class, or in the campus writing club. "I've sometimes said I have about a thousand nephews," I told him, chuckling.

The telephone rings. I talk with a woman in another state about reading material that might be good for her teen-age granddaughter, and suggest *Campus Life* magazine. She's delighted with the thought, and thanks me warmly. Other people's children, other people's grandchildren. Returning, I study the peninsulas of snow again, and notice how they have diminished during this morning. They're a very parable about how things change all around us — how things change in children's lives. What thou doest, do quickly. Work, for the night is coming. Opportunity knocks. If serendipity brings us a chance, with the other people's children, we may need to catch it very quickly, before it is away and away, like a bright-winged butterfly dipping off into the forest.

Alacrity, then, as a premise and a promise when we are in contact with the small ones?

A few other premises might be mentioned.

Keeping *their* needs in mind and not *our own,* for instance. As I've been indicating in this whole discussion, the single person may derive great joy from association with toddlers and teens. But the principle must be to give joy, not to seek it, or we may turn into exploiters rather than agents of gladness and grace. Love toward children may be a shallow sentimentality. It may become a greedy need-love. Or it may be a true *agapé* love, which gives and gives and gives.

Some time ago I read a truly pathetic letter in an "Ann Landers" sort of column. The questioner was feeling very doleful and self-pitying because she and her husband, childless themselves, never received gifts or greetings from the nephews and nieces whom they always remembered at holiday times and birthday times. "Level with them," advised the adviser; "tell them if they don't start giving you some gifts, you're going to stop giving to them." Well, that's one approach: we give to get. Lacking love received, delete love given. The more joyful way, one would think, is to give and give and give: because one loves, and because God loves. A Sunday school song is whistling itself, now, through the March winds: ". . . not for reward, not for the praise of man but for the Lord." Maybe the "other-people's-children" relationship, more than most others on earth, gives opportunity for the affection that does not need reciprocities to nourish it.

Alacrity.

Agapé love.

What about a practicality like this? We must not, must not, try to usurp the parenting of the parents. The single person visiting in a home is not usually the one to administer the discipline, to speak the scoldings, to verbalize the principles of behavior. It's up to us to reinforce parent-child affection and respect, not to replace or threaten it. If a child visits us, travels with us, goes on a picnic with us, we should send him back more loyal, loving and responsive to his parents than he was before. We are to bring strength to the home, not to compete with it. Not at all, at all, at all.

And the urge to spoil a child may need its guardings, too. Delighting in the child whom one sees occasionally, the visitor (aunt or uncle or friend) may be as prone as the traditional doting grandparent to put momentary indulgence above the disciplines of growth.

Common sense and Grace are not at odds in relationships like these, I'm sure. To obey the Lord and love children in ways that are for their good will be a harmony, a unity.

One professional woman I know has various diplomas tucked away in boxes or trunks, and various citations of honor on plaques or certificates. I don't know how many *Who's Who* sorts of reference books carry her name. But, she values more a word her sister once wrote to her: "I'm so *glad* that my children have had an aunt *like you* while they were growing up." I don't know that Alice ever sat down to talk with herself, when she was twenty or thirty, about how to go about aunt-ing; I'm sure she thanks God now for what he has enabled her to do and be as she groped and experimented, while her sister was groping and experimenting with the mothering processes.

Perhaps in her own ways Alice was to her sister's children what Willa Cather was to the Menuhin family; what more of us could be to more of the other people's children, if we would. If we will.

Notes to Chapter 13

1. *The New Yorker,* January 30, 1978, p. 40.
2. C. S. Lewis, *The Great Divorce* (New York: The Macmillan Company, 1946), p. 110.

Given to Hospitality **14**

St. Paul, that tough-minded, sweet-spirited, gallant admonisher, has set before us a shining ideal and a firm command: we are to be "given to hospitality" (Romans 12:13). His injunction flows out, naturally enough, from the rest of the chapter, from all the rest of his life and thought. We are to be "kindly affectioned one to another with brotherly love," he had just said in verse 10; love is to characterize us — love without dissimulation (verse 9); we will be "distributing to the necessity of saints" (verse 13).

In the midst of all the daily practicalities and pressures of our twentieth century America, do Christians need to think continually renewed thoughts about the implications of being "given to hospitality"? I am sure that we do. I am very, very, very sure!

Our hospitality is to be one of the tools for building the Kingdom of God in our local environment. Our hospitality should bring joy to other persons. And, in the wonderful chemistry that Grace is always using in grace-full lives, the extending of hospitality can bring joy to the extender. Joy, and the other fragrances in the fruitbowl of the graces that St. Paul described in Galatians 5: love, joy, peace, long-suffering, gentleness, goodness, faith, meekness, temperance. Show me hospitality-hearted singles (deeply; genuinely; at the heart of the heart) and I will show you singles who give and receive gladness, who are at peace with themselves and with God.

But, you say, I don't have the facilities. . . . My living arrangements. . . . I know, I know. I know what it is to live in a tiny, shabby grad school apartment, and I know what it is to exist so near to the brinks of physical depletion that I have even had to turn down pleas from hostess committees who were lining up casseroles or desserts for neighbors in an emergency. But the principles of hospitality are

109

still there, and ideas about hospitality still tumble around in the head. Let's skim through a list, a rather random serendipity list. Let's pause to talk now and then as we move along. Okay? And how about checking some ideas that you want to come back to, to think about, and talk with someone about, and pray about?

1. A basic tenet: my present home is not my own. It belongs to God, and is mine to use for him.

Whether it's a fourth floor walk-up utility apartment or a country estate, it's his.

2. Essential hospitality is heart-hospitality. It will find many different expressions, with differing opportunities, but true hospitality is always heart-hospitality. It may be warmth and inflection in a telephoned voice; it will not be, let's say, a voice like that of Mim the Grim! She was a spinster-woman I knew whose aorta was said to be a conduit for ice water. When I had occasions to telephone Mim for information from her business firm, or in connection with Christian groups we both belonged to, her voice regularly seemed to say, "I'm busy; I don't like you; I wish you hadn't called; I hope you'll stay out of my way after this."

Hospitality may be deep-smile eyes and smile-lingering lips which say more than they say. Yesterday I talked for a few minutes with three or four junior high school students who were crossing our campus. One lad greeted me with such animation and sincerity that I walked on up Spruce Street feeling as though I had been at some royal garden party. (Well, almost.) He is hospitality in action, in an eighth grade version.

Hospitality may be the greeting hand in a Sunday narthex, the touch of encouragement on a drooping shoulder, the brisk, firm pat on a deserving back.

3. The open doors. Would it be useful if you would get out a pencil and think for a while about the past six months? Wherever you live, to whom has your door opened? Why? Whom have you had over, for what events?

Now, would it be useful if you would keep the list before you while you read Luke 14:12-14 and translate it into the colloquial idioms of your town? "Call not thy friends, nor thy brethren, neither thy kinsmen . . . call the poor, the maimed, the lame, the blind . . . ." Have you invited some of the persons who couldn't possibly, possibly return your hospitality? Do most of us follow Emily Post, and our own inclinations, much more closely than we follow our Lord's commandings?

4. Variety is good. Sameness stifles. Ruts are ruts. What are the implications for you? If you are single and about 39 and feminine, have most (or all) of your guests in the past six months been single

and about 39 and feminine? Then it's time for some new thought and new experimenting! A retired couple from your church might love you for adopting them for a Sunday supper; a bride might be delighted not to cook next Saturday evening; a fourth grade Sunday school class might love to have their next party in a new location.

5. Happy people take initiatives. Some opportunities will come to you, ready-made. Cousin Susie may telephone and ask if she can spend the night with you on her way to San Diego, or a college classmate may come to town for a convention and look you up. But if you wait for Cousin Susie and Cassandra Classmate to turn up, you'll be missing a very great deal. The supper you could plan, the dessert party you could give, the gracious breakfast you could serve — they will continue to be like paintings unpainted or symphonies unwritten.

6. Do you keep a guest book? It's up to you. Maybe you'd rather not. Sometimes I have, sometimes I haven't. Often a guest book is a useful tool. It can help you remember happy times. It can serve as a prayer list for devotions, sometimes. To review events of a year ago or a decade ago can help stimulate new ideas for new hospitalities. Just a few evenings ago, some curiosity or another sent me to a shelf in my living room and I pulled out guest books going back and back, far back, across events and events and events. The clock ticked away past my usual "lights out" time as I relived the days and thought about the people. Looking and remembering, I could wish now that I had been even more regular in pulling out the guest book, event by event, and in collecting the autographs. I could wish, too, that I had done a little more of inserting notations to help my own recollections. Here and there, I see, I penned in a heading: "English 101 Class," or "Alumni Falconettes," or "Open House." Now, those notations help the luster of the rememberings, and I wish there were more of them.

A few minutes with a guest book can stir up thoughts of some sins of omission. "My word," you may say to yourself, "I've never had the Does over, not once, and they have been working with me for three years now!"

7. Spontaneity, sometimes. Some events you will plan with love and care and precise detail. Fine. Other events will never happen unless they are caught on the wing — like hummingbirds or butterflies past a camera lens. Like a day some weeks ago when I planned my supper, realized that what I was concocting would easily serve two persons, and picked up the telephone. Yes, friend Elise would be free to join me; yet, she'd *love* to come over when she got off work. Or like the Easter morning when I went to a sunrise service without the rest of my day fully planned, greeted there a young preacher-woman whom I value very much, and brought her home

with me to share further "He-is-risen!" fellowship at breakfast. And he was indeed present with us. Or like the time when a former student brought a stack of his poems to show me on a Sunday afternoon, and lingered with such evident need to talk that we continued the conversation over an impromptu snack supper. Exceedingly impromptu; exceedingly valued.

8. Candles. Do you have an assortment of interesting candle holders? Do you keep adding to your supply of candles? Maybe a tall one, scented with lily-of-the-valley; a fat one, with cranberry odor and cranberry color; a deep brown one that fills the room with black walnut fragrances.

If you're a candle person, the touch of a match to a wick and a teakettle on the burner can say "Welcome, welcome, welcome" within moments when a friend drops by unexpectedly. Daytime candles, too? Well, why not?

9. Some party napkins ready between the planned parties? To make a prairie, Emily Dickinson said with her lovely whimsicality, requires one clover and one bee. To make a party, one candle and one teapot? That's quite enough. But gaily printed paper napkins may add to the warmth and sparkle of "I'm glad, glad you dropped in today; do come again."

10. China, silver, linens, glassware: an investment in caring.

Do you have dishes that you really, really delight in using and sharing?

Do you like your silver?

Do you have placemats that make you want to set a table and invite someone over whenever you look at them?

I'm not pleading for lavish expenditures; Christian stewardship applies in home furnishings, as in everything else. But too often, I think, the single person postpones and postpones, thinking vaguely of a sometime that may come, and makes do with oddments provided by a landlady or accumulated without much thought or care.

I have been very grateful that one Christmas my sister gave me a jelly server in the "Daffodil" pattern of Rogers 1847 silverplate. At a time when I had no cooking facilities at all, she watched me admire daffodil-graceful silver in a shop window and heard me say a "maybe, sometime" comment. She nudged me, then, by giving me that one piece, and not long afterward I bought a set, and later other pieces joined it. And what a gladness, continuingly, to prepare a table with Daffodil silver!

I have been very glad that some impulse led me to start collecting bone china cups; on a first trip to the East Coast years ago I wanted practical souvenirs and brought back several little demitasse cups. Since then cups from Venice, Greece, Switzerland and the Netherlands have joined them, and gifts have come from many nooks of America. My students know it's a tradition of my home, when the living room and library and study are buzzing with study groups, that each person will choose his own cup to use, and the warmth of "glad you're here" is warmer when hot spiced punch is being poured into the chosen cup.

11. Remember, life is lived in chapters. Last year isn't here. You can do some preparing for next year or for your retirement, with good thoughts and good hopes, but now is now. This chapter for now, and the next chapter when it comes, and the next when it comes.

The vague "maybe someday" attitude often haunts, to their loss, the younger singles who keep telling themselves semiconsciously, "Some day I will marry, and then −" The "someday" attitude can also be a daily demon who heckles the single with a too-small apartment, a too busy social calendar, a too-demanding job, a lack of confidence with recipes. But the present chapter is always the one for present living, and not the "maybe someday" one!

12. Those Joneses: to learn from them is fine; to try to keep up with them is silly, and a needless frustration.

So Martha of the Manor does have sit-down dinners for thirty-five people? You're not Martha. So Catherine has people in every Sunday night after church. (Every, every, every.) Well, you're not Catherine − but you might like to ask Catherine if she would share her recipe for cherry nectar.

13. The scope of invitations. A good many considerations will enter in. Basically, as you are God's tool, will the invitations be going both to people who need you, for one reason or another, and to persons whom you need in order to keep you a good strong tool?

Everyone needs some form of love, care, attention, fellowship, solicitude. Often you can provide it for others. You, yourself, need interaction of mind with mind, of spirit with spirit. You need the people you will invite over.

14. The hospitality of the restaurants. The facilities available in your city or your village will determine your decidings − the facilities, and your own inclinations, and your budgetings, and your time, and some other et ceteras. Some guests might really prefer a peanut butter sandwich at your kitchen counter to an elegant steak at an elegant inn. Sometimes for you and for your friends the restaurants will be happy adventuring. Sometimes Dutch treat is right and good. Sometimes you'll do the hosting, firmly and gladly; sometimes you will be the initiator of ideas, and your spark of leadership will be the hospitality you provide.

When they're right for the time and the people − thank God for restaurants!

When your emotional energy flickers very low and any cooking for any guests seems far beyond you, thank God (doubly and triply and deeply and verily) for restaurants! They will make possible some good socializings that just couldn't otherwise happen.

15. To set some goals? Do you, sometimes? Have you, sometimes, given yourself some explicit aspirations?

By way of illustration: several years ago, when I was the faculty sponsor of a senior class at Greenville College, I knew that class sponsors at Greenville had traditionally done a good deal of entertaining seniors in their homes. I talked it over with myself and made a definite plan: I would try to have every senior in my apartment for some special event at some time during the year. I made a card file for the class — some 140, plus several spouses — and made notations on cards as I circulated invitations and received replies for waffle breakfasts, or for after-concert parties or for suppers. Their schedules were busy, but only two or three, as I recall, were not able to join one of the invited groups. It was a richly rewarding year for me, and the students were most, most appreciative.

What might your goal be?

To invite over, seriatim, each of the persons who have been on current civic committees with you? To use your church directory as a working list, and select certain pages from it for your invitings? Your employees? Your employers?

I think of my friend Judy, and wonder about goals for her; she attends a church which many college or university students attend, but she doesn't have much way of getting to know them, and she is very wistful. Terribly, achingly wistful. I wonder. Judy was an English major in college, and she is a charming person with many interests now; if she were to start a project of trying to invite each of the English majors who attend her church to come to her home at some time during a new semester, it might be a great thing for Judy and for the students.

16. Do you have a specialty? We shouldn't get into ruts; I've already noted that. And the chapters change. But sometimes it is a good thing to develop a specialty with which you are especially comfortable, so that the entertaining more easily does itself.

One exuberant professional man whom I know likes to put on spaghetti suppers.

For you, chili suppers? Buffet luncheons, with salads and cold cuts?

As I look back through the old guest books, I think about how very much glee I have had with waffle breakfasts. College students have exclaimed and exclaimed about leisurely Sunday mornings around a waffle iron. And as I have served up the pecan waffles or black-walnut-sprinkled waffles, I have often told my guests that they were really indebted to my Greek professor, Miss Ruby Dare. When I was her student, Miss Dare lived in a dormitory room and her hospitable impulses were rigidly constrained, but she would set up a card table in her room from time to time and ask a few of us to share waffles with her.

Sunday mornings have been especially pleasant for me, since Saturdays usually gave a chance for certain dustings and polishings, and I could prepare the table and set out ingredients on Saturday evening. The single person, entertaining alone, thinks about practicalities like that.

17. Accepting help? Why not, if you are comfortable with it, and your guests are comfortable with it? Sometimes sociability becomes very special when dish towels are in hand. But don't give someone a task with which you don't really trust him. And his question about "anything I can do?" may be more of a courteous sociability than a real impulse toward the tossing of a salad.

18. A temporary host? Amy Vanderbilt says, in her big book of etiquette, that a woman entertaining alone should appoint some relative or close friend to be her "host" — to greet guests at the door, help with coats, help with seatings and pourings and so on. I wonder how often Amy's counsel is followed in most circles. Not often, I suspect, in informal circles. But I have often laughingly asked first-arriving guests to make themselves at home in the living room and to serve as "butlers" for the next arrivers while I went back to the kitchen stove.

19. Living room sipping? If you are hostess, cook, maid and butler all at once and it's a dinner party, do you often serve a first course in the living room? I have enjoyed using the demitasse cups from my collection; they're conversation pieces as well as containers for hot lemon-tinged tomato juice, or warm apple juice touched with nutmeg, or bouillon, or whatever. And using those cups informally has certainly helped me move from role to role in a more relaxed fashion.

20. The friends of friends? For some "at home" events, a definite guest list is useful. For some others, "come and bring someone" can be a pleasant experience. With the waffle parties, I have sometimes asked a student I knew well, "Would you like to come, and bring some friends? The table seats six — bring whomever you like."

Once recently I was the invitee, in a thoroughly delightful episode which I shall remember pleasantly for a long time. When our campus writing club members assembled at my home one evening, lively Chad arrived with wry annoyance all over his face. He was invited to a dinner party and was supposed to bring a feminine guest, and his plans hadn't worked out, and now he had to go straight from Scriblerus to the dinner. The other students chuckled with him and at him, and all the girls started asking each other whether they had already been to the Dining Commons. Yes, this one had and yes, that one had. "What about you, Dr. Mac?" someone inquired. "Have you already eaten?" Well, no, not I. Wanta go? asked Chad. Surely, why not? The hostess and the other guests seemed to think it a rather Providential circumstance, since they were having a dinner-and-discussion session, to talk about singles in today's world, and they thought me a useful resource person. (And Chad felt nobly chivalrous, he said, in having rescued me from the TV dinner which I told him I had promised myself after Scriblerus!) A happy occasion.

21. The definite invitation. "Come and see me sometime," is a pleasantry. We mean it — to a certain extent — when we say it. But it usually conveys general suffusion of good will, and no more.

If you really want to enrich other lives by your hospitality, and to be enriched in your own life by their coming to you, why not plan toward the definite invitation?

I could wish Olga would think about the definite invitation. Olga is a very lonely person, a divorcée whose wounds still bleed. She needs friends. Probably she needs friends more than she would ever admit. When I was last in her town and at her church, Olga spoke quite urgently: "Come to see me! Come *any* time! Do come!" But I haven't gone to see her, and, realistically, I doubt that I shall. Life hurries along. Appointment pushes against appointment. The books I should study and the professional magazines I should read are always there. If Olga were to telephone and say she's having a few people in for supper on Saturday, and wants me, I would probably clear Saturday evening and go.

In contrast with Olga, I think again of Dr. Mary Alice Tenney, the saintly and gracious scholar who gave so many of us so much inspiration. It was the habit of her mind to say, "I *do* want to get to know the young Smiths; I think I'll have them up for tea sometime soon." And a few weeks later I would hear from her how much she had enjoyed getting to know Sam and Susie Smith, when they had come for tea on Thursday.

22. Hospitality is solicitude. While I'm reminiscing about Miss Tenney, let me mention one specific episode. While she was in the hospital during her final illness, when she was past eighty, I stopped in to see her one day. She greeted me warmly and we talked quietly for a bit. It had not been a good day, she said. And in a tone of real self-reproach, she confessed ruefully, "I wasn't able to be a very good hostess when Harriette was here." I gasped a little, inside my-

self, and I have not forgotten it; from the very pillow that Death was standing beside, she wanted to be a good hostess! For her on that hospital day, as in all of her days, hospitality was solicitude: the comfort and ease and happy welfare of her guests was important to her. And we were guests in her presence, whether we were in her home or on a street corner or anywhere else!

22. Hospitality is to give someone your full attention, even for a few moments.

Would you agree?

Right now I am, retrospectively, at a lavish party I once attended at a West Coast hacienda. The food was elegant and the hostess had a whole staff of assistants in the kitchen, but the strong recollection I carried away was not of all that, but of how little anyone knew or cared about my real identity. A group of people had been invited to a big home, and I was part of that group, and the host wanted general good will. But he didn't really care about who I was, nor why I was there, nor what I thought on any topic under the shining sun.

In contrast, that eighth grade boy who greeted me yesterday was the more hospitable; he gave me his full attention for the moments while we spoke together.

23. Hospitality with a special purpose: Counseling. Counseling can happen almost anywhere and almost any time, I presume. Sometimes there is a particular ease and naturalness in the situation if the counseling happens beside a fireplace or across a coffee table. When one is deeply involved in the lives of young people, it's one of the real advantages of living alone: Wherever you are can become a counseling area at a moment's notice.

And I smile, and remember a time a few years ago when a senior girl who was using my front porch as a haven while she wrote term papers came in to chat with me for a while; I was reading in bed, and some of the big issues of her life got talked about from my very pillows. Or the time, longer ago, when a fellow told me he wished I'd have a chat with his good friend Marge; she was terribly edgy and weepy, he said. I telephoned to ask if Marge would like to come over for a TV dinner; (I knew I could manage that menu on short notice.) She came, tearfully grateful, and talked on and on about how her fiancé had ceased to love her — which he had not, obviously, from the evidence she cited. Courage, my dear, I urged her: faith, and hope and charity. And her marriage has been solid and good.

24. Hospitality with a special purpose: Consolation. We could do a lot more of it, couldn't we? — the inviting over of bereaved friends, who need to talk, who need not to be left alone, who need to feel tangible love.

And their need persists much, much longer than anyone not really close to them might ever guess. It's one of the things that recent specialized studies of "death education" have been stressing: the durability of grief. Within that durability, the love that you make tangible in sandwiches served or coffee poured may do more than you know. Your willingness to listen may do more than you know.

The hospitality of consolation may often be spontaneous and certainly need not be lavish. "I care, I care, I care" can be said in a great many different ways. A few weeks ago, the form it took was for me to assure a student that, certainly, she could watch a Metropolitan Opera telecast with me. She knew, and I knew, that an hour of opera was not her real need; she was reaching out for stabilities after a death message had overwhelmed her.

Mary Grace, a friend of mine who is now a widow, tells me that she has dreadful guilt feelings when she thinks back to a time when she, not yet married, shared a duplex with recently-widowed Alice. "I could have done so much," says Mary Grace, penitently, "to help her through that time in her life; I just didn't realize. . . ."

As we realize, and realize, can we often provide the hospitality which is also Consolation?

25. Hospitality with a purpose: Evangelism. Does it happen often among us? Groups of housewives in many churches are talking about "coffee cup evangelism." We hear about families reaching out toward their pagan neighbors. Do we hear also about singles who let their homes be frontier encampments of the colonies of heaven? "I came to his door, not a Christian; I went from his door, on my way to becoming a Christian." How often can it be said about our doors, as they swing and swing on their hinges?

26. Hospitality with a purpose: For minds to grow! Just now, I'm looking back through the years. I'm in graduate school again, and the telephone rings in my residence hall. "Hi. This is Betty," I hear. "We're having another Shakespeare party on Friday night. *Hamlet*, this time. Can you bring your book and come over?" Betty and her apartment-mate, Julia, were energetic and comradely and deeply dedicated to Christ. They were also splendidly purposeful in the uses of their apartment, and of their time. They liked sociability, and they liked to be learning. So, from time to time, they would designate a play and an evening. Arriving, we would have parts assigned to us: "You be Polonius, Bill, and Cathy can be Ophelia, and who wants to be King Claudius? Okay, Jerry. And Laertes? Horatio?" And we would read through the play, or parts of it, with lively asides interspersed. Then Betty and Julia would set refreshments before us, and we would go gladly on our ways, each a little more educated, each feeling valued and cherished.

Among Christians, any social event may have its opportunities for "high civilization, sweet reason, and the life of the mind." (The phrase is Sheldon Vanauken's, from *A Severe Mercy*.) Yet why should not some events be deliberately planned around "the life of the mind," as Betty and Julia liked to plan?

Have you recently given a dinner party for which the real main course was a recent issue of *Christianity Today* or *Saturday Review* or *The Other Side,* with each guest bringing his pre-marked copy of the magazine? Why not?

27. Hospitality with a purpose: Christian fellowship. Someone blinks. Isn't that what we're talking about all the time? What else?

Yes, it may well be our intended purpose, underneath, but sometimes can the purpose become more explicit, more overt? A college Sunday school class I was teaching once did some vigorous and constructive thinking about this assertion: "Every get-together of Christians is not necessarily a Christian get-together." Sometimes, the pointedly and purposely "Christian" event?

A regular Bible study, maybe?

A group like the early Methodists' "Class Meeting," established for mutual reportings of Christian progress and practice?

One single man of my acquaintance made a tremendous contribution to his community when he opened his spacious, gracious home for a singles' Bible study after church on Sunday evenings. His friends took turn and turn about in bringing refreshments, and some of them drove for miles to join in the fellowship which he made available; it was really "fellowship."

28. Hospitality with a purpose: Healing of relationships. It takes tact, diplomacy, courage, love, and grace — but those commodities are available to us.

Suppose Greg and George have clashed so many times at building committee meetings that each grits his teeth when the other clears his throat. Suppose they have never seen each other in a close, intimate, friendly situation, away from the committee rooms. Suppose you were to have them both over, among others, for your next chili supper. Love and prayer might season much more than a pot of chili for Greg and George.

"Can you come for dinner on Thursday?" Roberta asked me once. Yes, I could. The invitation did not surprise me; Roberta was a dear person who did many invitings without explicit purposes. On Thursday, she went on, Willa would be coming also. Fine. I was neither particularly pleased nor displeased; I hardly knew Willa. Looking back to that Thursday evening, however, I am very, very grateful — and now I know something of what it cost Roberta in emotional risk. I realized, through other contacts later on, that a promotion I had just received had, through complicated circumstances, led Willa into some harsh and bitter feelings toward me. Roberta's lovely dinner table held more love than I knew; the evening helped Willa, and helped me.

Healing. Therapy. Reconciliation. If we were more responsive to the Holy Spirit's guidings, would they happen more often on our patios, around our fireplaces, at our kitchen tables?

29. The hospitality of any empty house. Circumstances vary. Sometimes your room or your house may be hospitality itself when you are not even around!

Trustful Rosella Wilson left her house key and her car key in my custody one summer while she went off to Europe; the blossoming trees and sandy beaches of her California town for those weeks were one of the immense blessings of my whole life.

On a smaller scale: days ago, our campus writing club planned a party at my home and then, unexpectedly, I was summoned out of town for long and arduous committee work. Be at home, I told them in advance; if you light candles, be sure to blow them out when you go. When I got back, ping-pong balls were pinging and ponging in my basement, and records were thrumming from the stereo. I chatted a bit, yawned, and said quietly to the club president, "I've had a long day; I'm going to bed. Be sure to blow out the candles when you go?" She nodded across the Scrabble board. During the night I awakened and realized that the TV was quiet. They had gone. And I smiled with a happy gladness: the house had extended its hospitality without any help from me.

30. Hospitality in the casual encounter. If your eyes care, and your smiles care, and your heart cares, the hospitality may be within very casual encounters. Maybe you will extend "hospitality" to someone next to you on a plane, or at an elevator landing in a hotel, or in an office corridor.

The casual encounter.

Like Milly's, a few days ago, when she went to a buffet luncheon for her office staff. When she saw two people whom she did not recognize, "I'm Milly; you're new here?" was a natural query. (New, yes. Actually, visitors. En route. Invited to the luncheon by an executive because of interviews with him.) Milly learned all that, and more, after they gratefully joined her at a table, after she made some introductions. No one had appointed Milly to be a hostess, but she has a hostess heart — and she made the day smoother and brighter for several people around her.

Once, I recall, I stood waiting for the elevator (there, called the lift) at the Russell Square subway stop (there, the Underground) in London. When several people, obviously American tourists, were debating whether to wait for the elevator or to take the stairs, I tossed them a small amused comment about what a long hike they would find it to be. And one of them, thinking me British, made a pleasant little speech about our useful and efficient British subway trains. A casual encounter, a tiny encounter — but I was actually privileged to extend the hospitality of one nation toward another!

31. Hospitality for a quick change of a dark mood. The dark moods come. For some singles, the dark moods may be very dark indeed, as all the blues and blahs in the world seem to settle in at once. (More of that circumstance in another conversation.) Sometimes the dark dark blueness is a symptom of too much me-centered thought; sometimes, to cook a steak or pour hot chocolate for someone else is useful therapy. And the hospitality can serve a good many other purposes simultaneously: deepening friendships, stirring up minds, opening avenues for evangelism.

Recently the TV guide told me that a lecture was to be given at 6:30 on Sunday morning about singles in our society. After I pried my eyes open, I watched and listened as a lecturer talked about the grim games that people play in trying for attention at the singles bars. Sometimes he goes, he admitted; he knows they are the very worst places to meet people, but he can't stand looking at the walls of his apartment any longer. Well, that's his solution: the further bruising of his psyche in a singles bar. I wonder how often he thinks of counteracting the walls by bringing some people inside them. Planning, inviting, serving, cleaning up, remembering: five steps in hospitality, five big steps away from a "poor me" mood!

32. Man-sized hospitality. What works for one man doesn't work for another. (How's that for the platitude of the week?) Some men seem to be innate hosts. Some men have been coddled by their mothers and kept out of the kitchen by the other women in their lives until they feel total ineptitude at any entertaining. But man-sized hospitality can be a great blessing, to Sir Host and to the people lucky enough to receive his invitations.

One of the brightest and most memorable evenings of my graduate school years, I recall, came when a very eminent bachelor professor told our evening seminar class to come to his home next week for an informal meeting. Cokes and potato chips; Gilbert and Sullivan records; lively conversation; and a high sense of privilege.

One single man I know is a gourmet cook. He thoroughly enjoys amazing his friends with his complicated French recipes.

Another is holiday-minded; acquiring Christmas goodies is one of his great joys, and dispensing them to hordes of young people, from his job contacts or from his church, is a further joy.

Another has a happy knack for cooperative parties; his friends appreciate his big living room, and enjoy bringing brownies and nut breads and lemonades to it.

Another is a robust, hearty man with a great guffaw when he is amused — surely some descendant from old English innkeepers. He likes to induce some housewife of his acquaintance or some caterer to roast a ham or a turkey for a feast of his hosting, while he stirs and bakes and brews things to go with it.

Another — well, he's the reluctant one, and I'm sorry. Jerry has lived in his present apartment for three years, and has not had one person in to sip or sup with him. Not one, not ever. The loss is his, but not his only.

33. Hospitality in off-beat ways. Sonia has a good idea. She belongs to a diner's club, of the sort that affords dinners for two for reduced prices at certain restaurants. Within a year, she can invite guest after guest to join her in successive pleasant evenings, and having the membership keeps her more alert about ways to use it.

One year when I was car-less, I looked wistfully at the announcements of a special concert series. (Very special indeed.) I looked and thought, looked and thought. And, having thought, I purchased three tickets. As the concerts came around, I talked with various car-owning friends and made a friendly deal: I'll provide the tickets, you provide the transportation. Okay? It was a good year for some overtures in friendship that I might not have had courage to make without those tickets.

34. The "come-along-with-me" hospitality. It comes in many kinds of packages. It's valuable!

Once when I was studying in Switzerland, a young woman who lived at my *pension* thought I should see the August 1 fireworks — on their Independence Day — from a good vantage point. Although my German was fragile and her English was fragile, we managed the train trip and the viewing in a blithe way. I was grateful for her hospitality.

Once when a Swiss teacher, Fräulein Erika Sadu, visited me in America, a loyal friend who knows St. Louis like the back of her hand took both of us on a tour of the city. Fräulein Sadu was delighted, and so was I. A special hospitality.

Once I asked a British friend at our residence hall in London if she would like to go out to see the Keats house in suburban Hampstead on a shiny October afternoon. We paid our fares on the big double-decker bus, the #46 bus, and she thanked me over and over again.

Times without number I have led friends on little hikes. ("I'm going to hike out to Hickey's restaurant for breakfast; want to go along?" "I'm going to walk around Greenville Lake this afternoon;

want to go along?") And that, too, in a possible-for-then and happy-hearted way, has been, I think, a kind of fulfillment of St. Paul's admonition: "Given to hospitality." Of his Father's world, of any nook in it, or of the particular nook on which he pays utility costs, the Christian can say to other persons, "Welcome! Welcome! Do make yourself at home in my home! I'm glad you are here!"

One other observation, one other idea:

35. Christian hospitality doesn't keep close balancing of its ledgers. "I can't invite Nancy. She has been here five times, at least, since she had me over once." Well, and what if she has? If Nancy needs you, or if you need Nancy, if the Holy Spirit seems to be prompting you to pick up the telephone and dial Nancy's number, then do as love directs you! Three singles, we understand, lived in a home in the ancient village of Bethany; another single, our Lord himself, was apparently the frequent guest of the three. One cannot imagine their hesitating about an invitation while Martha or Mary or Lazarus reckoned up who owed whom the next measure of hospitality. And if we are Christ's, then any guest we invite, ever, is also Christ himself. When we light candles and pour cups of hot wassail and ladle bowls of chili, we do it for him. We do it in his name.

About Dating Widowers **15**

Not everyone will want to sign up for this seminar. If you don't, fine; run along and balance your checkbook or buy some new shoes or do your hair while the rest of us talk it over. If you are the one who asked for the seminar to be scheduled – here, have another cup of tea while we talk. And let me make the music softer in the background; Sibelius is asking for attention a little too stridently right now.

Comfortable?

"Except about George!" murmurs someone. Well, let's not ask her right now about her George and his ardors, or lack of them. Let's think about a few principles.

First of all, dating widowers is not outside the whole province of things we pray about, and ask God's definite guidance about. Sounds obvious, but it may need reiteration and reiteration as the days (and the widowers) come and go. Proverbs 3:5-6 still applies, as it did when you were considering colleges during your senior year in high school, as it did when you applied for your first summer job. "Trust in the Lord with all thine heart" (all; not an occasional trust impulse) "and lean not unto thine own understanding. In all thy ways acknowledge him," (all; all, all, quasi-dates, non-dates, semi-dates; all) "and he shall direct thy paths." Or, in the gently archaic but very valid words of Hannah Whitall Smith, "Take each little step as He makes it plain to thee. Bring all thy life in each of its details to Him to regulate and guide. Follow gladly and quickly the sweet suggestions of His Spirit in thy soul."[1]

"Yes, but. . . ."

I know. How to translate that idealism into what you're going to say to George the next time he telephones and wants to take you out to dinner.

Well, we can't generalize too far. Widowers are, after all, very diverse mortals, each from the other, and what is true for one certainly isn't true for all. And you are you. You will have to decide your own decidings.

Often, anyone would notice, widowers can move very quickly — very quickly indeed — from casual dating to serious courtship to a proposal. For some, there has been no "casual dating" at all. Deeply happy in marriage and intolerably lonely without it, they have been trying on ideas about another marriage from Date One with you. And before that. I remember one fine and worthy individual who had an occasion to talk with me only hours after the funeral of his wife, and I, startled, couldn't help knowing that at conscious or subconscious levels he was saying "What if?" to himself about me. Well, no, I don't have any tangible proof of what I'm saying; I certainly didn't ask him for an affidavit! But there was a subtle difference in his intonations, a subtle difference in his manner, and I knew; I knew clearly enough so that I had to ask myself, in turn, "What if?" And, realizing he could not be a rightness for me, I carefully put some restraints on ordinary cordialities while he was in social groups.

And I remember. (Hmmm. These seminars pull episodes out of memory that I haven't glanced upon for years!) I remember a curious paragraph of conversation when a handsome textbook salesman, recently a widower, took me out for coffee or for a lunch once in Seattle. When I made some small allusion to the house I had started to buy, his murmured reply was approximately, "Oh. You own your own house? Well, that would be okay." And I had to understand that, though we were hardly even on a first-name basis, his mind was saying, "That would be okay, if our lives were to merge."

Of course life still moves a step at a time, even when they are very rapidly taken and consequential steps. But you take them with a care, or there may be some very tangled emotions later on, and some guilt feelings about having "led him on."

Maybe you are at least a little interested, already, in him as a suitor. Maybe you're very much interested. Then what?

Well, then, have in mind (but not too much in mind) that all the Mrs. Grundys in your town, and for three counties around, may talk if he starts seeing you very, very soon after his loss. If you like being with him and he likes being with you, you needn't give Mrs. Grundy more than a gentle-happy smile when you meet her on the street. Let her be aware that you are aware that she is aware, and be quite calm about her twitterings.

If you like him and love him and trust him, if he likes you and loves you and trusts you — our felicitations! I hope you will be wonderfully happy, and it's likely that you will. Many a widower,

when he turns again to love, is so gallant and gracious and so trans-
parently enraptured that everyone around him (and everyone around
her) is gladdened. If that is your story, blessings to you both! But if
it *is*, you aren't sitting here fingering a teacup during this thoughtful
seminar, are you? You're out playing golf with him, or choosing the
wedding music, or selecting the new draperies for his dining room,
or buying your trousseau.

So, back to the seminar.

Back to the people who are struggling to see just how Romans
8:28 and Philippians 4:11 and all the rest of our Father's promisings
apply within a still-puzzling relationship.

Maybe as things progress you will discover that you and your
George are not likely to become more than friends. Well, fine. You
may be a great strength to him as he moves through the darker shadows of grief, as he copes with and recuperates from the greatest loss
of his life. Your tact and gentleness and sensitivity may be a medication to his spirit that no one else is giving, or could give. And he
may be a strength and stimulus to your mind and personality.

Maybe George will eventually ask you to marry him, but you will
know (and he will know) that it isn't a whole-souled proposal; you
will know that it could not be a whole-souled marriage. Whether he
says it in eloquent Victorian rhetoric or not, you will know that his
heart is in her grave. His children need a mother, he needs someone
to help him manage a home and his personal affairs, he needs some
affectionate solicitude. Are you interested, and willing? Well, you
will have to decide. Would his mild affection and the care of his
home be God's leading for you, or would it be a fourth-best, from
which God will protect you if you let him?

Speaking of Victorian rhetoric: they tell us that the great lover
Robert Browning actually did propose to a Lady Ashburton, after
the death of Elizabeth Barrett Browning, in just about the terms I
have been describing. Probably with wisdom, Lady Ashburton continued to be Ashburton, and Robert Browning continued to be the
widower. He did not cut himself off from feminine friendships, however. One of his important later poems, *La Saisiaz,* was in part a
tribute to his loyal platonic friendship for Miss Anne Egerton Smith;
the poem records some of his profound thoughts about life, death,
and immortality after Miss Egerton Smith died suddenly while they
were vacationing, along with his sister, at a chalet in Switzerland.

Robert Browning would have said, in Browningesque phrases, as
C. S. Lewis said in more recent times, that he could not imagine Eros
coming twice in a lifetime.[2] If George is a man like to Browning and
Lewis, then surely you can date him easily, joyfully, and naturally,
as often as you like. His friendship can be one of the great blessings

of your life. Knowing a widower like that can be a little like a good fraternal comradeship with a Roman Catholic priest. You can talk with candor and trust about anything under the shining sun: scenery; travel; Malcolm Muggeridge on television; economics; theology; iambic pentameter; the poverty in Calcutta. You can be a stronger person because there is masculinity in him, and he can be a stronger person because there is femininity in you. The Holy Spirit can be your continuing chaperon, and elements that threaten some other friendships are simply not present.

Another factor. Marriage to Robert Browning would have been less than a total marriage, but friendships with him were surely brightened by the shining recollections he always wore like a nimbus. But maybe you will not find it so. Can you handle Ethel's memory as a companion in the car with you and George, and at the concerts and in the restaurants?

It could be that you will like George enough to find yourself giving up other friendships for his, and that his lack of interest in a new marriage will close a door against some other proposals that might wait down one of those untrodden paths of friendship. You will keep that possibility in mind. It can happen; it happened for a woman I knew — call her Winifred — who became a partner in some business ventures with a widower who lived next door, and her friends said that his home became her home for most of her waking hours. Only waking; she didn't spend any nights with him. But she cooked for Wilbert, baked for him, washed his clothes, did landscapings in Wilbert's yard as well as in her own. Well, that's one sort of lifestyle; I doubt whether many of us would ever opt for Winifred's way.

When you go out with George, do have in mind that he is a wounded person, a scarred person. The death of a spouse is, obviously, one of the most immense cataclysms that can ever come to a human life. (Have you read *A Grief Observed,* by C. S. Lewis, or *When You're a Widow*, by Clarissa Start, or *A Severe Mercy*, by Sheldon Vanauken?) For some persons, the healings come very, very slowly. For some, the healing may be more difficult and more delicate because the marriage was ill-matched, painful, traumatic. For some, the "grief work," as the counselors call it, may have been very imperfectly completed when dating happens, and the widower may be endeavoring to hide from or to assuage his grief more than he, or you, would guess when he asks you out.

Remembering. Now I'm remembering Vince. We had been moderately good friends — Vince and his wife Lucy and I. A few months after her sudden death, Vince found himself not many miles from my then-location, and he telephoned eagerly about seeing me. It was a curious experience. He didn't seem to need or want to talk about Lucy — it might have been good therapy if he had — but he didn't really seem to know who he was. He made me think of a jig saw puzzle strewn out on a table. And, not knowing his own new identity, he seemed to find it hard to identify who I was. Not that he was disoriented or psychotic; not that, at all. But he was not far enough along in recuperation for the roles he wanted to be taking. If your George is at Vince's approximate point, and you go out with him many times, you will need quantities of patience and tact and of being strong emotionally for two people. And maybe that will prove to be the great joy of your life, and the beginning of other joys. If so, blessings and benedictions!

Now the query you've been waiting for me to make. His children. Does George have children? And if he has, will you be able to cope?

If he has toddlers and you adore toddlers, maybe his children are a big part of his fascination for you. But before you let things go very far between you and George, you might do well to ask yourself whether you are really ready for taking on all that the mothering of those charming toddlers will involve. Are you confident? Are you eager? Then blessings to you, and love and courage!

If he has pre-teens and teens in his home, it may take some hundreds of interviews with yourself (and with him, and with some of your friends who are experienced in step-parenting) before you feel the green lights going on inside yourself. Can you adapt? Can you learn to chauffeur the children around, to shop for them, do laundry for them, listen to their music, get them to tennis lessons and to dentists and to textbooks? Can you devise disciplines? Only utter fools ignore obvious realities. But please don't just assume that the traffic lights are all stuck on "Caution"! They may be about to turn to a very bright green. Maybe life with George is indeed God's best plan for you, and maybe his teen-agers need *your* steadying hands instead of any other hands in the whole wide world.

If George is a notch older and has away-from-home children, busy with their own careers and their own homes, you will still want to do some consulting with yourself and with him. Will you be able to accept, and enhance, his love for his children? Or will you be a possessive-jealous second wife, who will both threaten and be threatened by the paternal part of him? Can you easily start wearing the role of a grandmother to his children's children?

If he's yet a notch older, there could be some frictions if his children have been expecting his houses and lands and stocks and bonds, his silver and china and oil paintings, to come to them and to their offspring. Then you intervene. You might become his sole heir. You might produce squalling infants, to compete with their own infants for Grandpa's goods. If I sound as though I have been reading a lot of fiction by Thackeray and Henry James and the other novelists who talk about "marriage settlements" — well, I have read a lot of fiction. Also newspapers, and letters. And I hear conversations. And I am a people-watcher. Maybe for you and George this paragraph is utterly, utterly irrelevant; if so, thank the Lord and keep on thinking what you will wear to the symphony with him next Tuesday. Or maybe any risk is worth the taking, and the relationship with his family will be part of what you will be praying your way through day by day, telephone call by telephone call, family reunion by family reunion.

Somebody stirs a little, over there in the corner, and starts to ask a question. Let's have some hot tea first. Okay? Here's a fresh pot of Earl Gray blend, and here's another of cinnamon stick tea. And neither is required. Now. Now, on with your question.

Very well.

What one does on dates, and how far is too far, and all that.

Well, wouldn't you think that all the things you have thought or heard or read about dating and sex would still apply, only more so? In the book which I mentioned a while ago, Clarissa Start talks realistically about the difference she found when she started dating again after her husband's death. For the young girl, she says, a good-night kiss is an ending point, a culmination of dreams; for the widow, whose body and emotions are conditioned by her married years, the kiss is a beginning point.[3] Obviously, widower George's emotional reflexes and his nervous system are not those of an adolescent. His body knows its needs.

Which means? Well, doing some of the getting acquainted in social groups and not just in his car or your apartment. Some discretion about trips taken together, about where you will go after the symphony next Tuesday, about the maintaining of your sense of humor. Thoughts about the supportiveness you can give to his whole-person needs, his ego needs. Some common sense in what you wear. If you put on a dinner dress that looks like a negligee — well, there is a proverb in some communities about a person who doesn't have the sense that God gave a goose. Human sense, common sense, Christian sense, feminine sense: use them.

Yes. The mores of secular America as shown in Hollywood and TV comedies would hoot. But you and George, I'd assume, are not from Hollywood's less admirable scripts. Since you are here in this seminar, I take it you are convinced of the resolute biblical standard: absolute chastity before marriage; absolute fidelity after marriage.

Now, look. How much do you and George really have in common? Is he good husband material? Can he adapt to you, and can you adapt to him? Habits of a lifetime are pretty deeply ingrained for you; habits of a household are pretty deeply ingrained for him. Are you both flexible enough to adventure together in building a newness that has never, never been before? Can you handle without undue stress the comparisons that may come? — your housekeeping and Ethel's?

But those are secondary questions. The big one is still there, underneath all the rest. Is he the one who holds within his two hands God's will for you? If you are convinced and he is convinced, felicitations from the rest of us are pretty superficial, but you will have them, believe me!

And you might like to be reminded of what you surely know already: that the second marriages of many, many widowers have been blithe, and serene and full of blessings. How often have you seen an older man, in the third or fourth year of his second honeymoon, fondling his wife's hands as though hands had just been invented yesterday?

I glance at my watch.

Look, friends, this seminar must end. Sorry about that, but I have a commitment....

Oh, one other thing. If George is wrong for you, there can be a particular and special sort of joy when you hear about his engagement to Susie or Betty or June or Mary or Beth. And on the day of his wedding, you can sing new and jubilant doxologies, that God has guided you away from a blunder that would have marred your life. Go, singing. Go with God. Go, under the Mercy.

Notes to Chapter 15

1. Hannah Whitall Smith, as cited in the March 23 reading in *Joy and Strength,* ed. by Mary W. Tileston. (New York: Grosset and Dunlap, 1901), p. 83.
2. C. S. Lewis to Sheldon Vanauken, in a letter dated 23 September 1960: "Like you, I can't imagine real Eros coming twice. I still feel married to Joy." Sheldon Vanauken, *A Severe Mercy* (New York: Harper and Row, 1977), p. 229.
3. Clarissa Start, *When You're a Widow* (St. Louis: Concordia Publishing House, 1968), p. 123.

The Appearance of Evil 16

You are to abstain, Paul wrote to the new Christians in pagan Thessalonica, from all appearance of evil. (1 Thessalonians 5:22.) He spoke a wise word for the Christian single in pagan America.

We are not to be timorous and apologetic and super-sanctimonious people who do not take any action lest someone misconstrue it. As Paul himself said in another context (1 Corinthians 5:10b), "for then must ye needs go out of the world." We are to be exuberant, warm, outgoing people, loving everyone for Christ and making that love known. We are not to withdraw and withdraw, but to have life, and to have it "more abundantly" (John 10:10). One who lives with verve, with impetuous zest may, now and again, blunder with full innocence into an action or circumstance which he wishes had gone otherwise. Yet the Christian life is surely to be the life of minimum regrets. (That phrase was a coining of Professor Burton Beegle, a rare and saintly man who taught mathematics — and Christian principles — to many young people at Seattle Pacific College: minimum regrets; my gratefulness to his memory.)

Without undue concern for the Mrs. Grundys of our environment, then, let us not forget the Mrs. Grundys either. Let's remember also the younger people who watch and wonder and evaluate and check us out. Let's remember self-respect. And it's worth keeping in mind that we all walk, all the time, just about three steps from the precipices of moral disaster. (That epigram isn't from Mr. Beegle; it's from me — a coining formed in the crucibles of experience a while back, when I realized something of how close I had been to cliff edges while I stood, actually, on the slightly tilting deck of a ship; while a ship's officer said — well said some intense words into my greatly startled left ear.)

Avoid the appearance of evil. And, as Romans 14:6 commands, "Let not then your good be evil spoken of."

That will mean some invitations declined. ("Oh, come on, be my guest," he says. "My wife wouldn't mind. I know she wouldn't.) But you know that in these circumstances she would mind, and she should mind.

It will mean some discretion from singles who are counselors and preachers and teachers about when and where they meet with their counselees. Remember Catherine Marshall's amused description, in *A Man Called Peter,* about how Peter Marshall had to avoid the wiles of women who didn't seem to mind the appearance of evil, and wouldn't have minded the evil itself?[1]

It will mean some discretion about the administering of "the holy kiss of Christian greeting" — which in some contemporary Christian groups seems to move over toward the facile kisses of old Roman orgies, or of any other orgies.

It will mean care, of one sort and another, on all sorts of occasions. And probably the care, at best, will be punctuated now and again with a scorching awareness that one has failed, that an appearance of evil has indeed occurred and cannot be recalled. Do illustrations tumble into your mind? My own mind winces to remember a time in New England. I had been fortunate enough to attend a national writers' conference, a very sociable and stimulating event. On the last evening, I was chatting with a genial man from New York City, and he mentioned that he might miss breakfast; his neighbors in the hotel were checking out early, and he didn't have an alarm clock. "Look," he said, "why don't you just step into my corridor and yell, to be sure I'm up? Would you mind?" Not at all, I said; glad to be useful. So I yelled in the corridor at the appointed time, heard an answering shout, and went on back to my room. As I turned from his corridor into the main hall, though, I noticed a very odd look on the face of a woman who was just walking past. She must have thought, I realized later, that I was coming from inside a room and not from speaking outside it, to be leaving his corridor at that hour. By then, I couldn't run after her with protestations of my innocence, but the recollection of her cynical face has perhaps reinforced my decorum on some other occasions.

Like decorum when a youngish college executive from another state, a close friend of mine, was able to visit our campus, and I made a point of having chaperon guests around while he was my house guest.

Sometimes "the appearance of evil" is only verbal, the consequence of an awkward tongue. Sometimes to think twice before speaking is a good thing. There was a time — how I shudder to recall it. I was telling various people, most enthusiastically, about a particular concert and drumming up a crowd to attend it. After I had talked with one young wife, I was puzzled by the seeming curtness in her voice. As I did a mental replay of our conversation, though, I became less puzzled and more horrified. My burbled sentence had come out sounding as though her husband were being invited to go, he only, and not the two of them. Oh dear, oh dear, oh dear.

If we listen, if we pay attention — as in that dismal episode I had not paid attention — the Holy Spirit is protector, guide, instructor for the Christian. Of that I am sure.

Thoughtful men, gracious men, have a particular care about avoiding the appearance; that's a reason to call them gentle men. Like gentle Chuck. I had been helping him with a project for most of a morning and he wanted to reward me with a luncheon of his own preparing — which he did; but first he telephoned Lou and asked her to join us at his castle. Or I think about Danny Cade's habit of asking the blessing aloud in a restaurant. During the last six months of his life, Danny was often at my home for counseling times or for prayer times or to talk about poetry. At other times I would join him at the Holiday Inn where he worked, and we would spread a Bible or a notebook of poems or Thomas Kelly's *Testament of Devotion* or other such fare on the table before us while we ate. Danny always wanted grace to be said, and he wanted to say it aloud. I was glad he had that inclination, there among all his employees, who might have daunted someone else in his situation. Looking back, I think Danny's praying aloud had chivalry and discretion as well as Christian affirmation in it; I think he wanted an appearance of evil not to touch my comings and goings, not with any breath.

The single who is a guest in a home needs, obviously, to have alert wits and sensitive discretion. Arrivals, departures, lingerings, activities shared and not shared will all need common sense and good judgment, as well as mutual faith and trust, if fellowship is not to be shadowed by the unwholesome. If Tom has been at Jim and Mary's home over and over and over, he still may think with some caution about the impressions he creates if he keeps on dropping in just as freely when Jim is off on a speaking tour.

The girl who works with men always needs discretion, both when wives are present and when they are not. (Of course! you mutter. How obvious can we get?) But it isn't all that obvious when you're living it a day at a time. To talk shop with a husband at a church picnic and seem to ignore his wife may be a fine and efficient thing, or it may be a stupidity. (It may be.) Granted, some wives are suspicious when they needn't be; let their edginess cause you to have a care. I remember a day when I was teaching freshman "Rhet" (otherwise, Rhetoric and Composition) at the University of Illinois, and several of us had to work late in marking placement tests. Well, Cleanth and I happened to leave Lincoln Hall just at the same time, and both of us were going in the direction of the Union. Naturally

I didn't fall ten paces behind him nor linger at a drinking fountain until he disappeared; I knew him around the English offices, but he didn't mean any more to me than — than the drinking fountain itself. Just as we got to the Broadwalk, talking about the papers we had been grading (I suppose) and probably laughing about some of the freshman ineptitudes, a witch-faced young woman was suddenly hurrying toward us. Cleanth's wife. Dinner was ready, and she was worried about him, and where had he been all this time? I have never forgotten the dark look of suspicion and dislike she flung toward me. Her declaration of ownership was sad and pathetic. I went on my way marveling. Me! She was actually jealous of me. I wanted never, ever, to cause any wife such a flash of pain again. The Christian single should not be a flash of pain to any marriage, but a benediction.

I think I may have been a benediction, a year or two ago, to another university man's wife. She was a benediction to me. Professor X came from his university (it would be an impertinence in me to address him by a first name, even a fictitious one) to get some materials from me which he wanted to use in a special project he was directing. As he shuffled papers, and rose, at the end of a lengthy conferring, he looked at his watch. "I may take you to lunch, may I not?" he asked. "My wife would count me most remiss if I didn't take you to lunch." At her invitation, so to speak, I went, and he told me about her, about their travels, about the university. Even though I had not met her, it became a good and gracious three-way friendship.

Sometimes to avoid the appearance will have a bearing on letters one writes, or receives. One came a while back, long and newsy, from Professor Y, whose wife I know, and I found myself reviewing it and wishing that it had contained some tiny allusion, at least, to Mrs. Y. The appearance, the appearance.

Maybe I should breathe a prayer for Professor Y, that the Holy Spirit will educate his alertnesses.

"The Love of God," wrote George MacDonald, "is the perfecting of every love."[2] What an insight! The perfecting, and the protecting. Let God's love be our wisdom, our enabling, always, as we avoid the appearance of evil.

Notes to Chapter 16

1. Catherine Marshall, *A Man Called Peter* (New York: McGraw Hill Book Co., Inc., 1951), pp. 47-51.
2. C. S. Lewis, ed., *George MacDonald: An Anthology* (New York: The Macmillan Company, 1960), p. 90.

Single and Sensitive 17

When I was in junior college, I had an instructor in English (Mr. Keith E. Case, bless him) who believed firmly in the merits of outlining as an intellectual discipline. We worked with Roman-numbered divisions and sub-dividings and sub-sub-dividings. We outlined essays that we read. We outlined and outlined.

Just now, reminiscing about the redoubtable Mr. Case, I have been formulating, with a bit of mild amusement, an outline to encompass all of humanity:

    I. Married persons
        A. Insensitive individuals
        B. Sensitive individuals
            1. Touchy-sensitive
            2. Graciously-sensitive
    II. Single persons
        A. Insensitive individuals
        B. Sensitive individuals
            1. Touchy-sensitive
            2. Graciously-sensitive

Well, Mr. Keith E. Case, what do you think of that one? Whatever he'd say, suppose the rest of us talk about it for a while. Part I we can ignore, or almost ignore, in the present discussion. I might just mention, though: it has sometimes seemed to me that the fraction of "sensitives" is rather higher among married persons than among singles. Have you found it to be so? Maybe sometimes the marrieds are trained in looking out for the welfare of a spouse and of their children, and sensitivity reaches on out to others beyond their own hearth. Maybe sometimes sensitivity has been one of gifts of personality which attracted a mate, like the subtle odors which attract mates among exotic butterflies, so that sensitive individuals have gravitated toward the "married persons" bin in this particular sorting of mortals.

And maybe my tentative generalization is quite wrong; maybe more singles tend toward more sensitivity. Do they?

At any rate, we're responsible for ourselves and not for the people over in the other bin, so let's talk about us.

Actually, we ought to be the super-sensitive, creatively sensitive persons. We have gifts of personality to spend in looking after the welfare of everyone around us, rather than limiting our primary aletrness to spouse and offspring — as 1 Corinthians 7 should keep reminding us.

Mr. Case — or any other good teacher of freshman English — would quickly point out that my small outline is quite faulty, inasmuch as outline categories should be mutually exclusive. In actual fact, within hours any one of us may be a very klutz of insensitivity, and also a touchy-sensitive victim of gripes and grouchings, and also a graciously sensitive human being. But the groupings do tend to exist, and of the mixings we would have to acknowledge with St. James, "My brethren, these things ought not so to be. Doth a fountain send forth at the same place sweet water and bitter? Can the fig tree, my brethren, bear olive berries? either a vine figs? so can no fountain both yield salt water and fresh." We ought, all of us, to be more consistently examples of II, B, 2: *graciously sensitive*. Ought we not?

I am indebted to Eugenia Price, and some splendidly thoughtful talks she gave at Seattle Pacific College, for the "touchy-sensitive" label. As Eugenia talked about it, "touchy" is what one becomes when the self is demanding its rights rather than being obedient to the calls of Christian discipleship. *I. What I want. What offends me. What annoys and embarrasses me in someone else's behavior*. That is the language of touchiness. And too often, I'm afraid, it is the very language of spinsterliness among us. Touchiness gets its feelings hurt when someone else is recognized. Touchiness needs lots of apologies offered to it. Touchiness resents a colleague's promotion. Touchiness harbors grudges. Touchiness says "tsk, tsk" about the neighbors, and the neighbor's children, and the preacher, and the choir, and the secretaries. (But touchiness never finds time to *help* the neighbor, nor the neighbor's children, nor the preacher, nor the choir, nor the secretaries.)

Touchiness is, in very fact, the exact opposite of 1 Corinthians 13, while gracious sensitivity lives right in the midst and being of 1 Corinthians 13. And it's both interesting and frightening to realize what a thin, thin line may separate one from the other. Touchiness, for example, may go home crying when the boss scolds, while sensitivity may reach for extra Kleenex when the boss praises!

Somewhere at the back of my brain I hear the wise, thoughtful voice of Dr. Mary A. Tenney speaking carefully, years ago, to one of her counselees at Greenville College. "Your sensitivity can be your genius," she was saying, "if you can direct it. . . ." Knowing Miss Tenney as I did, I am sure that the texture of her further counseling conveyed a larger "if": *If* you will be obedient to the Holy Spirit, and let him direct you.

When I think of Spirit-guided sensitivity in action I think of Ann. She is a walking exemplification of 1 Corinthians 7:32, it seems to me; St. Paul would approve of her freedom, "without carefulness," to give her attention to "the things that belong to the Lord." A friend spoke her biography to me once, in one terse sentence: "Ann gives herself to people who need her." Ann is a professional person, and her job often carries evening and weekend duties, but within any typical six months the recording angels might note that she had taken a young widow on a shopping trip; had written notes of appreciation that no one else in her community thought to write; had spent some evenings with a solitary and very lonely older friend; had written lively, cheering letters to several missionaries; had arranged a luncheon for a handicapped person; had visited hospital rooms. Let me add quickly: I'm only guessing and extrapolating from bits of knowledge that I have acquired; Ann doesn't go around beating any cymbals to announce her latest self-givings, believe me!

The Christian single person with open eyes can find many, many opportunities to use the gracious sensitivity that hurts in someone else's hurt, and does something about it; that rejoices in someone else's gladness, and does something about it.

Have you read Ann Kiemel's books? Some of her ancedotes would give example after example of what sensitivity can be and can do, if it is willing to be the gracious kind and not the touchy kind!

Or try these for size.

There's Jim; several years ago I had a merry-hearted and very learned colleague, Jim Moody, who had a very real flair for brotherly sensitivity. When friends exclaimed admiringly about my new coiffure one autumn, I told them merrily — if they were close enough friends to want the background bit — that I was indebted to Jim. He had said to me, along about Commencement time of that year, "Elva, you've *got* to do something about your hair! The kids are guessing you to be in the age bracket of Professor X and Professor Y." (And he named two distinguished gentlemen who were some 20 years my senior.) Touchiness might, I think, have winced at hearing the unflattering guesses; touchiness might have said "Tsk, tsk" to mutual friends, and discussed my hair when it wasn't around. Jim was more sensitive and more valiant than that!

There's Alice. Alice did some extra shopping at a recent holiday time and sent some gifts off to children in a family she doesn't usually include on her lists. The family is now a divorce-splintered family, and Alice knew it would be a difficult holiday season for all of them. And she guessed a guess about what she could do to help.

There's Mary, who knew that her colleague Donald was having cyclones and hurricanes inside himself when a job change had promoted someone else in a way that seemed grossly unfair. Mary didn't know Donald very well, but well enough to send him a note, very prayerfully composed, to assure him that he and his career were in her thoughts.

There's Lena, who picked up a telephone when George (who attended her church) had been fired from employment he really liked, and the job-hunting process was very intimidating. "How about dinner out somewhere tonight?" Lena asked. "Well, okay," said George. He would probably tell you that he needed Lena's attentive listening far more than he needed any calories that evening. And Lena is a good listener, he says.

In fact, to be a good listener is often a fairly big part of sensitivity in action, isn't it? One warmly responsive and personable woman I know has observed with wry amusement that men are more interested in her ears than in any other feature she has. And she doesn't have pretty little shell-shaped ears, nor does she have a collection of exotic earrings. But she listens, and listens, and listens. Actually, men like having her around, I think, because she listens with her eyes and eyebrows and smile muscles and expressive hands, as well as with those ears that the men pour their concerns into.

Might I mention one or two episodes in which, if I perceive truly, the Holy Spirit enabled me to be one of his sensitive ones? I thank him and thank him, as I remember.

On one occasion, mine was a participating voice at a funeral. During the other parts of the service, my eyes caught (and caught again) the eyes of a young lad, maybe 12 or 13 years old, in the audience; I already knew that his grief was very great, and I thought I was receiving small telegrams. After the benediction I was able to move over to where he was seated and to say quietly to the relatives seated beside him, "I want to speak to Kenny." My arm went around his shoulder — where my arm knew it belonged for that moment — and I spoke a few sentences, and his intense response made it a moment I shall never forget.

Once during a summer I heard that a young faculty wife, new in

our town, had gone to the hospital to await (and await) the arrival
of her new baby. No relatives here, I told myself. Maybe. . . . When
I arrived at the hospital the nurses were not welcoming; the maternity ward wanted only immediate family. But finally they said well,
all right, and brought her out to an alcove where we could talk. Afterward, times of Christian fellowship in her home were very special to
me, and the little guy whom she was waiting for on that summer day
is still very special to me. And I thank God that he nudged me to go,
when I might have counted myself both too shy and too busy to go.

Our goal of gracious sensitivity is what the Emily Post books talk
about, but it is a great deal deeper, isn't it? Sometimes it's love in
blue jeans. Sometimes it's love with cookie sheets in hand, or casseroles. Sometimes it's the word that alerts someone else, that makes
a referral.

Like Dave, whom I was fortunate enough to have in classes several years ago. "I wish you'd have a talk with Marge," he said to me
one day. "She keeps dropping things in chem lab. She isn't herself
at all. Something's bothering her." I made some gentle inquiries,
and found that Marge wanted very much to talk with someone about
her troubled romance. Dave thought — rightly, I'd guess — that he
wasn't the one to be Marge's confidante, but he was sensitivity in
action, definitely.

Often sensitivity is a gift for vicarious experience. It's a gift that
everyone needs, even to be a good conversationalist. Especially, it's
a gift single persons need, and can develop: vicarious joy in another's
engagement and wedding showers, in the wedding itself, in the arrival
of children. Vicarious joy in all the chapters of parenthood.

Vicarious sharing, too, in the pains and stresses and grief of
others. The sensitive one may not say in explicit words, "I know just
how you feel." He probably shouldn't, in fact. Those pat words can
make the listener flinch, and protest inwardly that no one else could
possibly know just how he feels; no one. But the sensitive one can
walk the dark valley of grief or disappointment with another, can ask
the quiet question, can speak the word of love and faith and reassur-
ance.

I have known singles who lacked the gift of vicarious experience
so totally that they regularly avoided weddings. What a loss for
them! I have known singles who seemed quite unable to offer congratulations for games won or honors received or promotions announced, unable to glean joy for someone else's travel or study or
vacationing. What a loss for them! And I have known singles who
would walk across the street rather than meet a recently-bereaved
young widow, or older widow, because they were so unable to enter
vicariously into her grief that they hadn't any notion of what to say

or do upon meeting. What a loss for them! To enter into suffering with and for another is, strangely and paradoxically, a significant part of the joy of being human.

I write these words on the evening of Good Friday. Earlier today, the St. John Passion was on my stereo in my living room (in the presence of an Easter lily, in the presence of half a dozen glowing candles). Afterward, I joined with other believers in a service of commemoration. And I think I understand a little more today than I ever have before of the ultimate in sensitivity. He was the completely vicarious one. He, who was without sin, knew sin in the utter, utter dregs. He, very God of very God, endured the full reaches of humanity. He had been sensitivity in action at a well in Samaria, at market places up around Galilee, at a tomb in Bethany; he had been sensitivity in action to children and lepers, to prostitutes and despised quisling tax-collectors. But on the cross he was sensitivity in its final and complete intensity.

And we are his disciples.

In spite of the distance we are accustomed to placing between our comfortable routines of life and the demands of sensitivity, we are his disciples.

Single, and sensitive.

The Blues and The Blahs 18

It is a Friday evening.

You get home late from the chem lab where you work and open a tin of Campbell's tomato soup for your dinner, with a tuna sandwich for your entree.

There's a symphony on downtown, but you haven't quite wanted to go alone and haven't recruited someone else to go. You look through the TV guide. Dullsville.

Suddenly, it seems to you that it's been ten light years, at least, since you have had an interesting date. You are thirty-four years old, and a cold wind of loneliness is blowing across the North Pole and right into your apartment.

The books on your shelves repel you.

The house creaks with quiet. Five other apartments, and everybody else must be out tonight.

Lonely. Lonely. Lonely.

You think about the lab reports you will have to write next week, and about the rising rent, and about getting your car worked on. A deep malaise shudders through you, a feeling of not being able to cope, ever, with anything.

You put a gospel music record on the stereo, and realize, appalled, that it isn't speaking to you. Not at all. The phrases seem ethereal, distant, quite unrelated to your existential now.

Helpless tears well up, and you brush them away, and other tears follow them and drip off your face and spatter against the soup bowl.

"Oh God, what's the matter with me?" you tremble. "Oh God, oh God, oh God, oh God. . . ."

Maybe you're nineteen and a clerk in a bank. Maybe you are

twenty-seven and a medical doctor. Maybe you are fifty-seven, a divorcée who sells lingerie. Maybe you are a widow, sixty-seven and not employed. But the mood is yours, your very own.

Sometimes they come, the blues and the blahs.

When they come, you may feel as though they have never been away. But they have been away, and (thank God!) they will go again. You may feel as though you're the only miserable person in the entire world. Well, you aren't. You may start accumulating a dark pile of guilt feelings. Don't; there are better things to do with your emotions!

Try these for size? For shape, and fit, and color?

What about physical causes for emotional catastrophes? Are you still recuperating from flu, or from months-ago surgery? Have you been reading late for too many nights in a row? Are you at the downward side of the menstrual cycle? Maybe you need a very hot bath and three extra hours of sleep more than you need any counselings about your soul.

Is there anything specific you can identify which started a downward spiral of dark and darkening mood? If you are a sensitive person (and thank God for it, if you are; the sensitivity can be the enabling for special creativities, special aptitudes), then a very small reproof from an employer, or some contretemps with a colleague, can quiver inside you for hours or days, and fester in the quivering. To identify it and then laugh at it, or write an apology note about it, or apply an unguent of prayer to it, or talk with some objective person about it (or any combination of these therapies) may bring healing very quickly.

You will need to recognize — we all need to recognize — that there are high tides and neap tides for the human spirit. We're not made to live at one sustained and unchanging level. If the ebb goes too far down on the sands, and if it stays at ebb for undue amounts of time, then one may need to see someone who knows a great deal about tide levels — a minister, a counselor. But often there are the high tides of euphoric creativity and the balancing low tides which prepare for them to happen again. Meantime, while the tide is low: maybe extra sleep, as I've already suggested?

Or maybe something edible will be therapeutic. Maybe you should wash up that tear-dribbled soupbowl and prepare a really luscious dessert, or some other specialty. Several years ago I had one standing prescription when I was unutterably weary and would feel the threatening proximity of tears; I would prepare myself a plate of crispy brown french fried onion rings. And they had to be accompanied by a pot of steaming hot tea, with nutmeg in it. (Hmm-mmm; it's ages since I cooked onion rings. Maybe I should reward myself soon for something or other, and not wait for the prescription use!) What about contact with other human beings? Pick up the telephone and talk with cousin Susie in Denver, or your former roommate in Missoula. Call half a dozen older people from your church who may not know about the special meeting on Sunday evening. Call a shut-in and ask about running over for a game of Scrabble, since you know she loves Scrabble. Or get out the stationery boxes and write half a dozen letters to people who need a word of cheer from you.

Yes, I said *cheer*. It is a deep, deep principle of human experience: you may not always *have* happiness, but you can always *give* happiness.

Actually, it's a point of common sense to pour out beakers of cheer, rather than of loneliness and woe and morose gloom. If you tell people how moping and melancholy you are, they will be very loyal friends indeed if they don't start avoiding you — and, besides, you will have made yourself more melancholy in the process of telling. Maybe that goes for letters even more than for conversations, since the letter-getter may feel real frustration in trying to know how to respond to you by remote control. I'm thinking now of a letter I once received from a missionary, who had apparently seen my stories and poems in various publications and decided that I would have a listening ear. Mostly, as I recall, she talked about how dreadfully, dreadfully lonely she was, since the other missionaries on her station were all couples who had each other, and she had no one. I tried to respond, but I didn't find it easy, (I wonder now what I said) and I didn't hear from her again. If she had just chattered about the little happenings of the day and had asked my opinion on some issues of interest, rather than wailing to me, I might have become a pen pal who could have really sustained her through the dreadfuls. And a newsy, chattery letter would probably have been a better form of therapy for her to write.

If you don't make direct contact with someone on this rainy Friday evening, think about doing something for someone. When you yourself are wretched, *yourself* may need to be heartily ignored, or put to action for another mortal. Make a pan of sugar cookies to take to your elderly aunt, or to somebody else's elderly aunt. Start making a doll's quilt for a Christmas gift.

Speaking of Christmas: one prescription would be to work on definite planning toward some future event — your vacation, Christmas, someone's approaching birthday, a dinner party you will give, a missions conference you're going to attend. When the glooms engulf *now,* tomorrow can be important to think about, and the day after tomorrow, and beyond.

Maybe it will be helpful to put some little part of your life in order. Unwelcome tasks, thought Alexander MacLaren, are grim little personages while we evade them; "Accomplished, they are full of blessing and there is a smile on their faces as they leave us. Undone, they stand threatening and disturbing our tranquility, and hindering our communion with God."[1] To clean a desk drawer, to straighten the towels on their shelves, to put a clothes closet in order, to label a box full of slides — any of these can be emotional therapy. To scrub a stove, to defrost a refrigerator? Well, not all those on the same evening. Maybe only to mend a skirt.

Or to make a skirt?

For some people and some moods, a making of something is a particularly good enterprise. Depending on your skills, you might write a poem or do a water color or stir up some fudge or make a recipe of granola. Or write a prayer. Do you sometimes try writing a prayer, whatever the circumstances? One need not be a professional writer to jot words into a scribble book, and to get strength from the jotting. Looking through Marjorie Holmes' books of kitchen-outcry prayers might stimulate you to pray on paper. And to God we can be utterly honest; nothing we say will startle him, and nothing is too petty to tell him. "Anything large enough for a wish to light upon, is large enough to hang a prayer upon," thought George MacDonald.[2]

Maybe by the time you have washed the soup bowl, you will decide that you do, after all, have some books which are worth your greeting.

Maybe, particularly, you will find the Book to be one to pick up. Maybe an hour with a pencil and a concordance and two or three different translations of the Bible will make it a very different evening by its ending from the way it felt at its beginning.

Be very sure that God's great love enfolds you, no matter what the glooms are or can possibly be. In Lord Tennyson's words, "Closer is He than breathing, and nearer than hands and feet." He has not gone away, and he will not.

Notes to Chapter 18

1. Alexander MacLaren, cited in the January 12 reading in *Joy and Strength,* ed. Mary W. Tileston (New York: Grosset and Dunlap, 1901).
2. *George MacDonald: An Anthology,* ed. C. S. Lewis (New York: Macmillan and Company, 1947), p. 53.

Comparisons Are Odious 19

My mother, bless her heart, had whole pocketfuls of useful aphorisms by which she endeavored to bring us all up in the ways we should go. One of them was "Comparisons are odious." We heard it often, in a great many different practical circumstances of the sort that can happen with six vocal and energetic siblings tumulting through childhood on a depression-era farm. One of my brothers did his own translations when he was an eighth grader or thereabouts; "odious" became "odorous," and then, the rest of us would be admonished, with vigor and laughter, "Ah-ah! Comparisons stink!"

Well, inside the psyche, comparisons sometimes do carry their fetid odors. Sometimes, truly, they may stink.

One of the things the single person needs to face honestly and deal with carefully is the temptation toward comparisons that are less than useful, comparisons that buzz like attacking wasps, and leave waspy stings in the soul. Comparisons that stink!

I think we would say quite safely that any single person who hasn't had to grapple with the grumbly comparison is — well is not fully alive and aware. Even St. Paul had his stormy moment of it: "Have we not power to lead about a sister, a wife, as well as other apostles, and as the brethren of the Lord, and Cephas?" (1 Corinthians 9:5). If he hadn't named Cephas, it would sound more like general and impersonal rhetoric; as it stands, we can assume that we are surely hearing echoes of other outcries: "Why, Lord, why? Old Peter has a wife to comfort him, to cook his meals, to mend his cloaks; why, why don't I?"

A very little thing, unpredictably, may make you feel as though you have just walked on a piece of broken glass. Once when I was visiting Susie she, amiably garrulous, was talking cheerily about old clothes and new clothes and related topics. "I had this pair of shoes," she said, "that I really liked, but they did need to be fixed, and Ron just told me to throw them away and get some new ones. . . ." Something inside me twisted and stirred and started chewing, and I knew it for a green-eyed little monster named jealousy. To have someone make the sticky decisions for me like that, so crisply and wisely and well. . . . To have someone care whether I wore old shoes, whether my shoes needed repairing again. . . . (Why, God, why? Oh, it isn't fair! I wish, I wish. . . .) On a thousand other days Susie's remark wouldn't have registered with me at all, to make me compare my state with hers, but that day some malicious imp was right at my elbow, and his green-eyed malevolent ally was quickly ready to dive right inside my aorta, and dive fiercely.

Once at a family reunion the pervasive general always-awareness, "They all are, and I'm not" flickered into a little forest fire. I don't quite know why it did. It singed and charred, and the room I was in became a temporary extension of Dante's purgatory.

Or maybe a letter comes from a friend about her utterly adorable grandchildren, and some relative of Beelzebub starts beating on your forehead with mallets, and chanting hateful rhythms about the grandchildren you don't have, won't have, can't have. Or you are coming home from a concert with friends when the married couple in the back seat beside you starts getting more and more amorous, more and more married. You stare out at the night sky, and dig your fingernails into your clenched palms, and ask the front seat rather inane questions about the concert, and almost feel an arm around you like that, like that. . . .

In candor, I'd have to say that the twisty-wild moments of odious comparison have been wonderfully few within my life, and I'm grateful that they have tended to shun me. But I know that they can come.

What to do about them?

Long-range, to build and maintain "the attitude of gratitude" is both prevention and treatment. If we live in a climate of constant rejoicings and praisings, those green-eyed beasts tend to get asphyxiated, or to crawl off seeking other prey. They don't thrive among doxologies. If I had been naming over joys and gladnesses on that day at Susie's, if I had offered up more thoroughgoing sacrifices of praise earlier in the day, I would have heard her little remark about the discarding of shoes with a lot more objectivity, I'm sure.

One can even give praise that he has the power to feel pain. Dead flesh doesn't feel rats nibbling off toes. If you're alive enough to know a dreadful ache, then sensitivity is present, and sensitivity can be used in new creative deeds.

Long-range, to keep developing a prevailing stance of vicarious enjoyment is both a vaccination against the virus of the odious, and a therapy for its attacks. If "I'm glad for you" is a growing habit of life, daily and always, the surprise attacks of the virus will become less frequent and less virulent. I know one person — call her Nell — who seems to find it truly hard to rejoice with anyone about anything. I haven't been with her enough to document this fully. Probably no one except her guardian angel (and maybe Screwtape's special assistant who has her in his care?) knows how constantly Nell lives in bitter comparings of her own lot with other people's circumstances. But I have seen enough shadowings of a hard joylessness to have some inkling. Once I was near her at a social event where one person in the room was receiving congratulations from everyone — but everyone — on some very happy news, and Nell's evadings of any contact with the honoree became a sad comedy.

To tell someone about the twisty pain inside?

Maybe, and sometimes.

If you're talking at deep levels with a counselor, with a pastor, with a close and trusted friend and your proximities to envy need discussing, fine. But some attitudes grow in the very process of being described widely and often, and you may be walking into more of self-pity rather than into new strength. You may become more susceptible to the disease rather than being treated for it. Besides, widely spoken comments on your hurts and aches of spirit won't, frankly, endear you to the general listener. Bitter people tend not to be the welcomed people, in any circle. (Well, maybe in the Mafia!) "Here's my grief of today; commiserate with me" may win a listening ear at first, but it's the kind of phrase that pulls heavy leather coverings over ears as it is repeated, and repeated.

Yet to deny a pain isn't always the way toward the healing of the pain, or to new and constructive attitudes. When should you find a counselor? A pastor? A trusted friend? You will have to decide.

If you are a person with creative powers, the pain may (in a trite enough image, but one that still has merit) become the sand that begins the forming of a pearl. A new painting, a new story or poem, a new piece of music may have its beginnings in a throbbing moment of "she has and I haven't" thoughts.

And there is one Friend to whom the whole thing can, and should, rightly be told. "This pain, this ugly jealousy of today, Lord Jesus," is a confiding that will not surprise him at all, and he will not use it against you to your hurt. Not ever, in all the eternities. Maybe, indeed, you should tell him now about some of the remembered odious comparings that you have been doing for years, or for decades. Ruth Carter Stapleton's instruction on "the gift of inner healing" (in her book of the same title) encourages us to invite Christ definitely and deliberately into long-past episodes of hurt and evil. Perhaps most singles have episodes hidden away which he needs now to enter with love and cleansing.

Sometimes he may have a word of very definite instruction for us. Once when Peter introduced a comparing of his lot and John's, our Lord's word was very specific: "What is that to thee? Follow thou me" (John 21:22b). In that command, ultimately, is the untying of our knots of jealousy, the release of hurtful me-compared-with-him attitudes. It is a word that transfers to all of us; it was not just for the restless Big Fisherman.

Sometimes in addition to that kind of instruction through his already-written Word, there may come a pulsing of love and reassuring and teaching for the immediate now. Maybe while you are still tense and sore from those mallets on your forehead, after your friend's innocent braggery about her grandchildren, you will hear a counsel from God about some special ministry of love he will give you, quite apart from grandmotherly care.

In any case, "Follow thou me." That is totally inclusive.

The following, let me add, will not be leading to a "sour grapes" response to the odious comparisons.

Realism, yes. Humor, yes. Contemptuousness and undue protecting of one's pride: no.

Even when someone seems to be pushing a general sort of cheer about your single state into your hands, you may feel that he is really offering you a platter of sour grapes to nibble upon, and you may need to withdraw from affirming what he says. When a woman who has been traveling to the grocery stores and to the laundromat while I have been in Europe sighs to me, "Sometimes I think you are the lucky one," I don't feel inclined to pursue the comparison. (Comparisons are odious!) I smiled with a young father when he, busily cleaning up vomit during a daughter's illness, looked up at me with a grin and said, "*Now* aren't you glad you didn't marry What's-his-name?" But I didn't feel inclined to pursue the comparison. There's his path for him (and What's-his-name's path for him), and my path for me. When another young father talked slowly, painfully, to me about the kinds of vacations he could not take, not with small children in his paternal care, I listened carefully and attentively, but I certainly didn't say anything aloud (and hardly whispered any word within myself) about how great are my freedoms.

There's a fine line, though. I'd reiterate that a general mood of constant gratitude for our estate is right and desirable.

If we are complainers and reach for "I'm-better-off-than-you-are" assertions to reassure ourselves, we may be following paths which are the other side of the envy and jealousy roads. If we're already rejoiceful and twinkle within ourselves over specific mercies, the grapes may be sweet enough, and our mirth may grow in wholesome ways. If, very weary, you put breakfast on a tray and go back to bed while you eat your toast and cereal, why not thank God that you don't have a husband and five children to make breakfast for? If shopping today for one coat and one pair of shoes has depleted your *joie de vivre* beyond believing, why not give thanks that you aren't responsible for fitting two or four or six pairs of feet? If you go to a convention in Boston or New York and suddenly decide to stay for several more days of concerts and culture, why not be joyful, very joyful, that you are free to do just that?

You will, though, have some discretion in the kind of cards you mail back from New York to your friends whose horizons are now limited to Pampers and pablum, won't you? A greeting that implies "I'm glad, and my gladness will be greater if I share it with you; may I?" will be rather more welcomed than an odious one that conveys an implicit "Nya, nya, I'm here and you're not, so there too."

Make love your aim. That's what it all comes down to, isn't it? Love for God, who has patterned your ways. Love for the other person, whose life you truly enjoy in vicarious ways. Love for the neighbor whom you do not want to taunt in subtle little ways by glorying too noisily in your advantages and freedoms. And, yet, a healthy kind of love for yourself, which will not permit destructive grumblings to kennel inside you.

Surely we suffer most from the jabs and punchings of comparison demons at those times when we are most I-centric. I, I, I, I. I want, I need. I must have. I deserve. The wanting I opens itself to many pains. In you-centric moments, we're more ready to be vicarious: to joy in the joys of others, to share their stresses, to forget our own greedy demands. And when we move (have moved, keep moving) from the I-centric life to the life that centers on God himself, what releases from the threatened and comparing ego!

To be a self, a whole and wholesome self, and yet not centered upon one's self: help us, Lord God!

The Matter of Mom **20**

It's a sunny morning in May. The maple trees beyond my study window, which wore sheathings of ice and shawls of snow when I made my Epiphany covenant with the reader, are now full of shimmer-green leaves in tented clusters. The quince bush nearer the window still has a few scarlet blossoms nestled among its lush new foliage. The tips of its new leaves are bright translucent bronze, like another kind of blossoming. Wild violets are thronging through the new grasses, and first seed-heads of dandelions are showing.

For Americans, it's the month of Mother's Day, and today I think about singles and their mothers. About you, the singles I now write to, and your mothers. All human beings need to think, continuingly and often, about their mothers; from time to time, the single needs to do a new and perceptive evaluation of this matter of Mom, if the single is to grow and obey God and "serve the present age" in right ways.

Let me say immediately: your relationship with your mother is a precious and private matter. No one but God himself knows all the episodes, all the conversations, all the emotions that have brought you to this present hour. No other human being can prescribe or dictate. More than in most of the sensitive relationships within a lifetime, you must "work out your own salvation." Yet some principles can be identified and discussed, for the strengthening of us all. Let's talk and think together. Today, while you have been shopping for a remembrance for her, while you have been collecting ideas for your Mother's Day telephone call to her, shall we talk and think?

Naturally, some of the thoughts about Mom will also be thoughts about Dad. If your father is still with you, thank God that he is with you, and extend our discussings to include him, of course — whether

your phrasing is "Father" or "Daddy" or "Dad," or some other
family-treasured nickname. Yet the connection between a mother
and her child is different from any other family relationship. Among
many singles, it has a particular significance because Mom is now a
widow, and her present singleness intensifies the parent-child relationship even more.

All right, let's think.

At the outset, we might observe that the Ten Commandments
have not been superseded by space age technologies; the moral axis
upon which our world turns still contains the Biblical principle of
Deuteronomy 5:16. Moses brought from Sinai the injunction to
honor parents, "that thy days may be prolonged, and that it may go
well with thee." It's still a basic, basic instruction for society, and
rebellious American teen-agers are not the only ones who flaunt it
to their own detriment.

Yet how to work out "honor" in specific circumstances within a
life is not immediately and easily discerned.

Where does "honor" end and a crippling overdependence begin?
Where does "honor" end and a too-passive or subservient obedience
to a motherly dictator take its place?

While we ponder about these boundary lines, let's face directly a
fact that almost any single would probably affirm: the most persistent and continuing pressure toward marriage may come from Mom.
Her earnest wishing may become a real embarrassment to you, and
may be building up unacknowledged resentments inside you. And
the pressure may well continue, with varying amounts of intensity,
as long as you both live — or as long as you are single. That's the
way things are with Candy, who wrote me after she saw a published
article of mine about serene singleness. Her Mom, said Candy almost
fiercely, is one of those persons who is absolutely sure there is a Jack
for every Jill if Jill will just keep looking, and Candy never really
escapes for her mother's nagging. Candy feels genuinely sure that she
is obeying God, step by step, but her mother has not really reached a
similar trustfulness on her behalf.

Mom's solicitudes are understandable.

She wants to see you "settled"; she wants you to be happy; she
wants to feel that someone is looking after you and protecting you;
she wants to be able to believe, at deep and subconscious levels, that
her work in rearing you has been a success. And the norms of society
that she has lived in and has known may all point toward your marriage as the answer to all those wantings.

More than she knows, perhaps, she may be wanting to live her own
courtship and marriage vicariously in watching and helping you
through the rituals. Two glances at Emily Post or Amy Vanderbilt

will make it very evident that "mother of the bride" is an exceedingly important day in a woman's life, and you are the one to permit or deny her that role. Since you were a toddler, she has probably been saying, "Now, when you are married. . . ." And all of that wanting, all of that imprinting, is a force that you and she must both face candidly.

I myself has thanked God often for the liberating attitude that my own dear mother was able to reach in her counsels to me. She was, and is, a person to whom a right relationship with God is absolutely supreme, for herself and for anyone else she can hope to influence. I was only 16 when she wrote me a letter that became a major landmark in my life, a landmark of liberation. "You know," she wrote, "that Daddy and I have no claims on you, except that you do God's will." I continued to consult and to confide, you may be sure, but I had been set free: free to be single, free to marry a missionary or not to marry a missionary (or a farmer, or a senator, or anyone else on this green earth), free to continue my studies or not to continue.

Yet even for my earnest mother with all of her marrow-deep Christian commitments, the traditional maternal solicitudes were not utterly relinquished, once and for all. More than once even she has wondered the gentle wondering, has queried or hoped or wanted to urge.

Early on in adulthood, the young person's relationship with his parents surely must move to Peter's declaration in Acts 5:29. You, too, ought to obey God rather than men — even if the "men" are dearly-loved parents, even if the command you disobey is the hinted and implicit and even subconscious desire that you marry. Honoring one's mother, then, surely does not mean either giving up or retaining your singleness just because Mom wants you to.

What does it mean? What, indeed?

All the Mother's Day sermons across the nation may be offering ideas a few days from now, both for the day itself and for all her days. Corsages? Candy? Gifts? Telephone calls? All of those? What gives her special joy?

Among the other things, let's not forget that little practical gifts she can use and use may say "honor" in curiously loud tones. My mother probably still has the hand-embroidered valentine pot-holders that my siblings and I made at our rural school when I was nine or ten. And I know that she has used for these 20 years and more, with continued loving grateful exclamations, some durable floral placemats that I once brought from Seattle to brighten farmhouse mealtimes.

But at a deeper level, to honor her is to be what she esteems, more than it is giving to her or doing for her. When you make any decision for righteousness, you honor the one who said "No, no!" and "Mustn't!" to your baby fingers. When you assume and fulfill any responsibility, you honor the one who taught you about washing dishes and finishing homework. And letting her know about some of the decisions and the responsibilities of your adult life may be a deeply valued part of the continuing honor.

To honor, though, is not to accept domination. Not at all.

Have you seen it happen in other lives? Marilee is past 50, a woman of wide experience in her vocation. Anyone in the nation would classify her as an adult. Yet her strident mother can still turn Marilee into a tearful child when she comes visiting and derides Marilee's clothes or friends, when she demands that Marilee's vacation be here and not there. Mom scolds, commands, advises — and poor Marilee doesn't know how to cope any more that she did when she was a gangly adolescent. Do you know a Marilee? Will you become a Marilee?

Biographies tell us about the Marilees, and their brothers or cousins. According to what we read, the mother of John Ruskin, for example, must have been a fearsome individual. I never read accounts of the work of that great art critic without wondering what might have been in his life, had there been more of common sense in his early home, or had he learned how to find his independence from it. The domineering Mrs. Ruskin even moved up to Oxford, we are told, in order to supervise young John more efficiently when he went to the university.

How does one grow up enough to outgrow the dominations, the supervisings, the excess advisings? Well, some singles never do — and some married people never do; all the mother-in-law jokes in the world are bitter evidence of that fact, and all too many divorce proceedings are other evidence.

A very, very important thing, certainly, is to keep the communication lines open. To bottle anger inside yourself may seem to be the way of the dutiful and affectionate son or daughter, but candor might be more cleansing. Suppose that Susan reluctantly goes home for Christmas, knowing that Mom will be full of questions about her recently broken engagement. Suppose Susan keeps biting back tears and anger. Hurt leads to more hurt, and Susan is not becoming more mature. Suppose, instead, she writes a careful and calm letter in advance: "I want to come home for Christmas, Mom, but I am not (repeat, *not*) ready to discuss anything about Bob and me. Not anything. If you will find it necessary to talk about Bob, then we had better plan that I will visit the Florida cousins this year, as they have been wanting me to do. Let me know how you feel about this, so I will know how to plan." And let's hope that Susan, having written in that vein, will carefully live by her declared plan, and will grow inches in her inner stature during the holidays.

Suppose Mom visits son Kevin once a year and tells him over and over how much she dislikes his chromium and vinyl furniture. Suppose he has always tried too hard to be discreet and dutiful, and not to let her know that her comments have hurt and angered him. Suppose that he takes her out to dinner en route from the airport next time, and levels with her: "Mom, we need to talk about something that is important to me. I like my apartment very much, and sometimes it really makes me angry for you to say harsh things about it. And being angry with you tears me up inside. I'm not sure how we're going to work this out, but you've got to know how I feel. . . ." And then what? Well, then Grace can help them both know what comes next.

Sometimes the maturings will be helped along as Marilee or Susan or Kevin talks with someone else about the Matter of Mom. Having heard Mother's Day sermons and poems all their lives, along with incomplete expositions of the fifth commandment, some people in their 20s and 30s and 40s assume too easily that their need for outgrowing Mom's domination is undutiful. They may believe too certainly that other adults — other Christian adults — do not find their own parents to be frictional. To talk in depth with a pastor, a close friend, an objective counselor, may be a step of great wisdom in understanding a complex relationship.

I'm thinking now about Ken. Ken is a very successful professional man, past 40 and highly esteemed by his associates. I had been in his home quite a few times and knew something of how he and Marie managed their schedules around the comings and goings of Ken's eccentric mother. (Are there many mothers who do not sometimes seem eccentric to a 40s-plus son? But perhaps Ken had more reason than most to wince and grit his teeth and choose the softened answers that would turn away wrath.) Once when I was talking with Ken and Marie on some deep-level topics, Ken suddenly started reminiscing brusquely about events of his early teens. I wondered afterwards if he had ever talked about those scarring memories at all, even in his prayers. It seemed to be deeply healing to him to remember, and to acknowledge the old pain, and to talk candidly about what Mom had been like when he was 14.

A next awareness.

To recognize candidly that a time has come (when the time has indeed come) for other responsibilities to take a primacy over some of the filial responsibilities may be important in defining the scope of "honor." For the person who marries, the scriptural instruction is clear; as Matthew 19:5 declares, a man is to "leave father and

mother" and cleave to his wife. For the single person, the example of
our Lord himself (Mark 3:31-35) would indicate that the time
comes also for a leaving and a cleaving. Like Christ himself, the
mature Christian single will normally "leave" the blood ties of
mother and siblings, and "cleave to" the other linkings that bind him
to other associates, people who are joined to each other in doing
God's will.

And Grace enables. The continuing adjustment within "honor,"
from babyhood until the final mortal parting with one's parents, is
surely within the scope of God's great love to us. If we let him, the
Holy Spirit will bring us constant lessons about pride and pettiness
and selfishness in ourselves which the filial relationship brings out
into daylight, as well as about those declarations of mutual independence which maturity ought to make.

Grace. Grace. I think about a man whose home I once visited.
Call him Howard Blaine. He and his wife were entertaining Howard's mother also on the day of my visit, and I'm afraid that the
older Mrs. Blaine was truly like a Dickensian caricature: opinionated, shrewish, talkative, blowsy, frumpy. Howard kept his affability,
kept his courtesy, and I saw the discipline of years in his patient face.
When a less gracious person would have argued, Howard did not
argue. Once, a less controlled person might have shouted, "Mother,
for heaven's sake, sit up straight and pull down your skirt!" Instead,
Howard quietly went over to look at a book with Mrs. Blaine and just
as quietly straightened her offending hemlines. Grace was at work in
Howard.

Throughout most of his adult single life, Grace was at work in the
famed Christian apologist, C. S. Lewis, also. Have you read in the
biographies about the dismaying woman, mother of a World War I
comrade, whom Lewis accepted as a surrogate mother? His brother
wrote later, in introducing Lewis's *Letters,* about how she interfered
constantly with his work, imposed "a heavy burden of minor domes-
tic tasks," and otherwise caused him "stress and gloom."[1] Yet from
this very tryanny, already long established when Lewis became a
Christian, and from his endurances within it must have come of his
deep understanding of what *agapé*-love can mean to the human
spirit, and some of his very sainthood.

As I think of Howard Blaine and of C. S. Lewis, I think also of
Sonia, who told me with tears about God's work in her heart, and in
that of her aged mother, and of how they came to a depth of mutual
affection during her mother's final rest-home months which they had
not known before. Grace had touched Sonia, miracle-bringing grace,
for the new harmony was very different from the years of fretfulness
and stress that had always existed inside Sonia.

Sometimes all the expressions of grace, the outworkings of 1 Corinthians 13, are harder to show towards the persons who are nearest and dearest to us than toward semi-strangers. Are they not? Sometimes we need reminding that the chance to cherish is a very precious opportunity — an opportunity we shall not always have. Sometimes, having received and received and received from motherly hands throughout childhood and teen-time years, we need to be reminded that "it is more blessed to give than to receive." Sometimes, if you are a Howard Blaine or a C. S. Lewis or a miracle-touched Sonia, or someone even a little like them, you will give a rare quality of love to your mother, not because she is lovely but because you are loving. You will give and give and give. You will forgive, 9 times and 90 times and 9 times 90 times, because God is forgiving and he is loving through you, and not because she does or doesn't deserve the forgiving. As he enables. As he enables.

We should note, in thinking through this whole topic, that even if a mother has several children and loves them all dearly, a son or daughter who is single will probably always have a special claim on Mom's affection. That's the way mothers are. And it's a fact that has to be taken into account in the complex formulas of relationships. Within the special claim, there may be domination — or cherishing; there may be mutual destruction — or mutual supportiveness.

Recently I heard my pastor, Dr. Frank Van Valin, talk to college students about finding God's will for their lives. A right relationship with your parents, he told them firmly, is absolutely basic, a prerequisite for finding God's will. What he was saying to sophomores and seniors is usually true at other levels of life also, wouldn't you think? Finding God's will for the whole of life depends upon obedience and love and common sense and grace in each part of it. Surely many people — many singles — have missed an accurate reading of his blueprints for them because they were either unduly subjugated by Mom or unduly indifferent to her.

It would seem clear, I'd think, that for many singles of middle age (and other ages too), there may be a cleansing which needs to happen through a deep forgiving of long-resented happenings, attitudes, episodes reaching back through the years.

To let the Holy Spirit work through your memory to a depth-level forgiving, then, might be a far better Mother's Day gift than any scented soaps or gloxinias could possibly be. Maybe Mom did not even know how furiously you resented the dress she made you wear when you were 10, or being grounded from high school events when you were 17, or the stern advices she gave you about your hilarious friends when you were 23. Maybe she didn't know; maybe she did. If she truly did not know then, you may not feel that you should exhume whole scenes now; maybe you will talk only with God about the details and not with her, as his Spirit gives you direction. But the remembering and the deep, deep forgiving may make a difference in all the chapters ahead. As the old memories are healed and made gentle, as you are made more loving, there will be new enablements.

Is *acceptance* another Mother's Day gift you might be shopping for? People used to chuckle about the comic strip, "Bringing Up Father," but the desire of younger persons to "bring up" and remake their parents is not altogether funny. Often it is pain and tension and dismay. Mom is what she is. What she has been for 50 years (or 60, or 70, or 80, or 90) is really not likely to change greatly, is it? Of course, some adjustments of personality to personality happen as long as one lives, and sometimes one hears of the dramatic deathbed change in a lifetime's habits. But, basically, she is what she is. You may need to grow in your own ability to accept, and accept, and accept, without tearing yourself apart.

A motion in the maple tree catches my eye, and I glance up. A female cardinal is flitting from bough to bough, her modulated red-brown feathers blending beautifully with the red-bronze of japonica leaves in the foreground. (Thank You, God, for such beauty!) And here comes her scarlet husband. I wonder where their nest will be. Cardinals, one assumes, don't know about teaching their children the Ten Commandments, nor about letting go of their children emotionally. Cardinals don't let their feathered children stay in the nest indefinitely. It's human beings who can cripple each other emotionally, or can release each other into freedom for eternal becomings.

Let's think of acceptance a little more. If it is genuine and growing, will it bring new levels of candor and honesty and clear-eyed tolerance along with it? Sometimes we try for sentimental affirmations, saying what we wish we felt, to persons as we wish they were, and we become mawkish. No, I don't mean the genuine affirmings that encourage people through gratitude, through our praise for what we appreciate. What do I mean? Well, for example, I recall a time when I was in my teens and wanting to be very noble; I wrote to my mother telling her that I myself could echo what Abraham Lincoln had said: "All I am or hope to be I owe to my angel mother." It sounded good to my adolescent pen — though I felt a little phony in writing it down, I'd admit. And my brisk mother wrote back urging me not to speak such nonsense, ever again; she was no angel, she assured me, and it was not a very good idea even to use such language!

Breezes now, in the quince bush. My eyes move from twig to twig, searching out the few jewel-scarlet blossoms remaining. Two weeks ago it was full of buds and half-open blossoms. The cycles of time.

Transitions. Whatever we are to do while we are mortal, we must do soon. Whatever you do, with or for your mother.

Postcards?

News items that she would like to know about, from your social calendar?

If she lives with you, the evening out with her sometimes when she needs it, or the evening at home with her sometimes when you cancel some other plan to read a new book to her?

The sharing of prayer topics? Perhaps she feels, much too often, that your career is very separate from her present life, and that you yourself are almost becoming a stranger. Do you confide specific concerns and ask for her prayers?

Do you tell her about some of the people in your life, until she can visualize them and your life with them?

Do you send her snapshots? Several years ago, one of my brothers found a splendid gift for our mother: a small magnetized bulletin board, with metal dividers to hold snapshots in various arrangements. Mother changes it often, and she has great times in choosing which scenic postcards, which pictures of grandchildren, which old family photos to put up next.

Do you make a point of taking things home to show her? If your next visit will be for only a few days, you may like to take along some clothes you won't even wear, just to let her see you model them. She will like to know what you are wearing to work these days — if she is like my mother. If you have slides from Jerusalem or the Hebrides or your own back yard, she will be a totally unwearying audience — if she is like my mother. (Mother's one regular criticism of my photography is that I don't get enough shots with Elva in them, amidst the scenery and the foreign cities.)

Do you find things that she can do for you? My mother fairly purrs if there's a blouse she can wash for me when I'm with her, or if I mention something I'd like to have her cook. And a few years ago she counted it a special privilege when I chose to have a bit of elective surgery in her town rather than in mine, and she was able to coddle me with post-operative soups and Jell-Os and other solicitudes.

Do you share her with your friends? When I have been in Kansas on my way to other destinations, my co-travelers have enjoyed getting to know Mother, and she has liked knowing them.

While you share your now-world and your present interests with her, do you also do your part in keeping her interests from becoming too tightly you-centered? That's important too, you know. (And I pause a moment to thank the Lord for my mother's lively interest in politics, in current events, in W.C.T.U. and her church and various missionary propects.)

Once, being in the town where my friend Monica and her mother were then living, I telephoned and then stopped by to take Monica's mother out for a drive. Monica was away at the time. I shudder a little every time I think back upon that excursion, for Monica's mother was so totally "Monica's Mother" that she almost seemed to have no other identity at all. A tape recording of our conversation that day would be substance for a writer like Sinclair Lewis or Philip Wylie to turn into quite a satire. No paragraph that I introduced seemed to have any interest at all until it gravitated back to Monica. Scenery? Monica's last trip to Banff. Politics? Monica's views. Hobbies? None, really, except waiting for Monica's next willingness to take her somewhere. Monica's boss, Monica's clothes, Monica's car. Monica, Monica, Monica.

I'm not really sure what Monica could have done or could still do. Maybe to pay Mom's dues in a senior citizen's club would be a better Mother's Day remembrance this year than anything else. Maybe Mom could be unrelentingly nominated for civic service committees. Maybe Monica could quietly give some neighbor two season tickets for a lecture or concert series. Maybe Mom could be urged into more of the activities of her church. Monica can't do it all. But it would seem as though she must be doing something, or there will be less and less of Monica for her hungering mother to prey upon.

For some of you to whom I write, trading places with Monica for a while would be a great boon. For you, this newest Mother's Day will have a very bitter flavor, because this year it means hospital room or nursing home or the darkened estrangements of senility. Yet you, too, will be sustained by the habitual patterns of honoring. Our Lord gave us a pattern when he spoke from the cross, commending Mary and St. John to each other. Although he would not be with his mother in traditional human ways through her later years, he made arrangements for her, and he cared.

For some of you, these are days of immense pressure because your home is the nursing home. Maybe you seldom get away from your mother's bedside, even to walk around the block or do her errands. Courage to you! Courage and blessings! Life is lived in chapters, and there will be other chapters in yours. Insofar as you can possibly manage, are you keeping open the friendships, the contacts, the ideas that will still be there when the next chapter comes?

For some of you, anything you have read in this whole essay has been a reluctant and yet welcomed pain because you are now going through the appalling loneliness of a world from which Mom has recently gone away. Losing her cannot be the same as any other human loss, and you may be walking through great deserts of emotion. For you, my dear, my dear: love and courage. Let the bright rememberings of other days cheer you, and let the sure sense of God's great love be rod and staff for all the hardest climbings. Grief, writes Eugenia Price, is to be *used* and not to be *wasted*;[2] maybe your grief of now can send you to someone else's mother, who needs you very much. Maybe it can send you to some task in your church which you will do in your continuing honor of her.

Now shadows are darkening through the trillions of little green tabernacles, the maple leaves beyond my window. Or is the triangular clumpy winging shape of new leaves a metaphor for trillions of angels? In the twilight, I could almost see them as Perelandra-green wings.

Hours ago, after I started talking with you, the postman arrived. An income tax refund, and a letter from Great Bend, Kansas. Shall I say to you what my mother said to me most recently? You're welcome to look over my shoulder:

> ". . . How are you? My love and greeting to
> your dear friends. May you ever push forward
> the work of the dear Christ!
>   "My love to all who are serving Him.
> May we be united in his service in this world
> and in the wonderful one to come.
>   "Now for business . . . ."

All right? For the rest of each lifetime, whatever it may bring you: Now for business.

Notes to Chapter 20

1. W. H. Lewis, "Memoir of C. S. Lewis," in *Letters of C. S. Lewis* (New York: Harcourt, Brace and World, 1966), pp. 12-13.
2. Eugenia Price, *No Pat Answers* (Grand Rapids, Michigan: Zondervan Publishing House, 1972), p. 57.

Some Thoughts About Friending 21

One of the immeasurably great privileges of human beings is to have friends. A strong and true and loyal friendship is of incalculable worth to any mortal. Of greater worth, actually, than our modern era knows how to value properly, thought C. S. Lewis in his splendid little book, *The Four Loves*. He thought friendship to be "that luminous, tranquil, rational world of relationships freely chosen,"[1] and "the sort of love that one can imagine between angels."[2]

To any single person, friendships are tremendously important, whether they are at the splendid mind-to-mind comradeship which Lewis discusses as "Friendship," or at the level of casual acquaintance and association, or somewhere between. If our lives are to be what God destines them to be, he will be at work in and through our friendships.

Some thoughts, then, about friending, and about being friended. What observations would occur to you? What statements would be brought together if 10 or 20 or 120 of us were thinking aloud together? Shall we enumerate some commands, some urgings, each to each?

● Live with gratitude!

Thank God for friends. The diversity, the encouragement, the warmth, the loyalty they bring to us. The shared events we have valued. The challengings and chidings that have come from them.

● Recognize the need, always, for God's guiding.

Friendships are not automatic; you can't order one, ready-made, for $199.95 from Sears, Roebuck! On a new job, you may be introduced to 50 new people within a day or two. Which of them will become more than a "good morning" to you? Is any one among them a "soul friend," who will keep pace with you, and incite you, on very high mountain trails of spiritual ascent? Which one will God bring closer to himself through you, if both of you obey him?

During any week, there are the multitudes of little decisions that, accumulated, shape the textures of your friendships. To answer this letter, or this, or this? To lunch here, or there, or there? Tonight, to telephone Susan or Betty or Joe or Jerry or Jim or Mary or Ken, or all, or none?

Your attitude when someone brings a task to your desk. Your caring, or not caring, about someone's broken ankle and someone else's asthma.

As you obey Christ, he is in the midst; he still comes in when doors are apparently closed.

● Allow yourself to blunder!

There is a natural human tendency to draw back from some good friendships, from some potentially great friendships, lest one's overtures not be welcomed. Sometimes the overtures are not welcomed. Sometimes you are ready to be a very Jonathan, but your harp-playing associate is not looking for a Jonathan.

And there are other blundery human tendencies: to misinterpret a conversation; to make a wrong decision. Well, so be it! "Nothing ventured, nothing gained" has been a principle in human friendships ever since the first cave men made gutteral welcoming noises to each other. If you have said an awkward thing or done a gauche deed, let God forgive you, and forgive yourself, and move on from what you have learned by the blunder! Depending on how your gaucherie affected Tim or Tom or Terri, you may need and want to say an apologizing word, in the process of forgiving yourself. Or maybe the apology would be more of a salve for your own ego than a needed healing in a relationship, and would be better lived than spoken.

● Keep yourself open to variety.

Too often all human beings limit themselves by assuming that their good friends will be approximately of their own age bracket, their socio-economic bracket, their experiences-in-life bracket. Too often single people make these kinds of assumptions — and are the losers. And that's a great loss both to their potential friends and to the singles, who are needing networks of human relationships, of what the psychologists and sociologists talk about as intimacy needs, sharing needs, continuity needs.

Several years ago when I was en route from Seattle, Washington, to Greenville, Illinois, I spent my last Seattle night at the home of the R. H. Kendricks. They took me ceremoniously to the train, and

I wore for departure a corsage Mr. Kendrick had made from his own greenhouse growings. The Kendricks were perhaps 30 years my senior — but our friendship was rich and strong and good. My next stop was in Portland, Oregon, and some of my time there was spent with Roger Wilder as my tour guide. Roger had just been one of my students and was perhaps a dozen or 15 years my junior — but our friendship was rich and strong and good. Variety can exist!

Are your friendships as inclusive as the old nursery rhyme that people used to chant when they fingered the number of buttons on your toddler-size jackets and told fortunes? ("Rich man, poor man, beggar man, thief; doctor, lawyer, merchant, chief; cowboy, sailor, tinker, tailor.") If not, are you ready to reach out, and to reach out?

• Recognize that proximity and a status-similarity do not automatically mean a close friendship.

Can you bring your associates to recognize this principles also? Joe is single and Alex is single, and they both work with the same chemical products. But Joe likes Dante, Bach, and quiet hikes in high mountain country; Alex likes rock festivals and X-rated movies. And yet their colleagues at the lab seem continually surprised to learn on Monday morning that Joe and Alex haven't spent any part of their weekend together. Well, they haven't, and they won't.

"I'm so glad to have another *young* person on the staff," cries Charlotte when she meets Anne, the new art teacher. "We'll have to do lots of things together this year!" But every day that passes leaves Anne more acutely aware of how differently she and Charlotte see students and teaching and recreation and moral principles. Charlotte keeps telephoning to suggest evening events, and Anne keeps inventing excuses. They are not friends.

"The Soul selects her own Society," wrote Emily Dickinson.[3] It was not a whole truth, but it's an important part of a truth.

• Don't worry very much about whether some particular episode is a "date."

You wouldn't, would you? Well, you might. After a faculty bachelor came to sit with me in church one time, a woman who knew us both scolded me roundly. "Had he *asked* you ahead of time? Oh, you shouldn't let him take you for granted like that!" Well, goodness me, he wasn't asking for my hand!

Some of the very happy experiences of my life have come along through blithe non-dating informalities, when one person said "Let's" and another person (or persons) said, "Yes, let's!" Since I seem to be a person with a certain amount of initiative and what our campus used to call "spizerinktum" stirred into my being, I have rather often been the one to says "Let's." And, yes, I have said it as various times to "coed" groups or to masculine buddies, as well as to women.

It has been my good fortune to have various bachelor friends who were truly friends. In C. S. Lewis's terms, *storgé* was present, and *philia,* and *agapé* — affection, and friendship, and charity — but nothing at all of Eros.

Friend Eric was a buddy like that, when he and I were both visitors on a campus for a semester. Eric would telephone me often, to ask me about his grading of a theme or to get information on local events or to report on his weekending away. We hiked together and talked theology together; I gave him advice about job-hunting, as I would have to one of my own students. Eric could say, or I could say, "Hey, there's a concert downtown. Had you noticed? Wanta go?" Later I helped him to find another job, when he was ready, and smilingly told him that he might find a wife on the new campus. He thought me some kind of a sibyl when he did indeed find Mrs. Eric there.

Probably nothing I ever did with Eric was a "date," but every conversation I ever had with him was a tonic.

Tall Richard is a friend like that.

Richard has given me advice, asked and unasked, with comradely loyalty. He helped me buy a car once. He met me at an airport more than once, when the meeting hour was weird. We have laughed together (he in a huge and mellow guffaw that fairly shook the building) when someone has asked him delicately if I weren't a bit — uh — beyond the age bracket for him to be — uh — considering. (He is maybe 15 years my junior.) Well, if Eros were on the scene, I suppose that a paltry 15 years would not impede either Richard or me. But Richard and I are friends; an appointment with me is no "date" for him. Yet my life would be more meager if Richard were not a part of it.

● Be wary about possessiveness, given or received.

Is there any single person who has not tugged against tentacles, now and again? Is there any who has not had to ask God to forgive a friendship-need that was starting to displace him, and to warp another human being?

Freedom in Christ will mean a freedom, too, from what the international treaties have called "entangling alliances."

Pride in having Louise as a "very best friend" may be natural and good for Julie when they are both in junior high school, but even then jealousy and hurt may be too prominent as ingredients of their association for friendship to be spontaneous and good and growing for both Louise and Julie. If they're both in their 20s or 30s and Julie constantly needs Louise's approval and Louise's companionship and Louise's activities, then each is probably stifling the better self of the other. When friendship is a gladness to both and each makes each more able to reach out to other persons, fine. When Julie resents any time that Louise spends with Josie or Jim or Judy, then beware, beware! When Julie goes into emotional tizzies in planning toward the events that she will or will not share with Louise, beware, beware! And if, after Julie has already been putting out tentacles of possessiveness, an opportunity comes up for the two of them to rent an apartment together, probably the "beware" should be reiterated about 15 times.

Maybe, more than she would admit, Louise enjoys wielding power over people and gets a subtle pleasure from being needed so urgently. Maybe both Louise and Julie need to talk earnestly to the Lord about their identity, both as individuals and as friends, before him.

Maybe, too, they need to have some frank conversation with each other. In general, though, one could wish better things for a friendship if "our relationship" is constantly being talked about, evaluated, analyzed. Good friends are brought together and kept traveling together by the depth of their common interest, as Lewis wisely noted in his "Friendship" essay of *The Four Loves,* rather than by a preoccupation with each other.[4]

● Singles can strengthen each other by affirming each other, praising each other, giving honest compliments to each other freely.

It's all right to love and praise and affirm everybody in your personal world, of course! I hope that affirming is a part of your Christian lifestyle. But singles do need their networks of emotional support, and John or Joe or Mary or Trina Single may need very much to have a brotherly word from you today. Brotherly, sisterly. And beyond "need" they might value the word, and be strengthened by it.

Sometimes I think the angels must shake their heads in puzzlement at our slowness to speak the commending word. Do we too often assume that other people are strong and confident, and do not need our reassurances? No one is ever that strong and that confident! Just about everyone needs encouragement, just about all the time. And so much that could be spoken is never spoken!

A tiny example? Once during a vacation I bought, with some care, a shirt in a colorful design that was very reminiscent of European sites. It stirred recollections of my travels, and I wore it with some glee. And I thought my friends would enjoy it too. Maybe they did. Nobody mentioned it, no one at all, until one day (a good while after the vacation) when I stopped in to see a retired shut-in who loves beauty of all sorts. She exclaimed and exclaimed about the shirt, wanted me to twirl before her like a model in a fashion show, and helped my morale for that whole day.

Christians, thought St. Paul, should outdo each other in giving honor to each other. Have you looked at Romans 12:10 recently, in half a dozen different translations, to catch the impact of his commanding about it?

And among Christians, singles should surely be among the ones who give honor and affection, for they know (deeply) that people really do need each other.

Some Bible-studying single persons have been intimidated needlessly by Genesis 2:18, and have thought themselves disobedient to a divine fiat because they are "alone" when God himself once said, "It is not good that the man should be alone." In our present era, existential aloneness is not to be solved by the loss of a rib, and not always by the arrival of an Eve in every Adam's life. Yet the aloneness is there, and the mutual affirmings by other human beings can deal with the "not good" element of the aloneness.

● To confide in your friends is often good. To brag to them is never good.

A tight rope to walk? Well, probably.

One of the joys of knowing someone really well, to share at deep levels of sharing, is the opportunity to confide gladnesses that are too personal to share widely. Good news cries out to be shared. Since I live around a campus, I am well aware of this fact. Someone receives a scholarship, and runs to his major professor with the letter of notification. Someone gets elected to an honor society. Some senior lands a good job. Someone receives a better grade than he had hoped for on a huge examination. And friends rejoice, and rejoice.

"May I share some good news with you?" is a question that can deepen a friendship.

But bragging, or something that sounds like it, can loosen emotional cords, can build barriers. I remember Virginia's bitter tone, when I asked her one time if she was still in touch with the X. Y. Z. family, whom we had both known in other chapters of our lives. "Oh, I get their annual brag sheet," she said. The X. Y. Z. family would have been horrified, I'm sure, to hear their lovingly written Christmas letter so described, but the principle was at work: bragging alienates.

We like our friends to be confident, poised, self-assured; we also like them to exemplify the grace of humility. Sometimes God will have to prune our prides ruthlessly in the process of making us better able to be good friends!

● Have a care about loading your friends with your gripes and your worries.

Talking anything over with a trusted confidante can, of course, be a great therapy, and we can come to clearer decisions when we discuss alternatives with an intelligent listener. Galatians 5:2 does apply to all of us; we are, indeed, to bear one another's burdens. But the command three verses later also applies, and each of us is to "bear his own burden."

Mathilda fusses and worries and consults everyone in her office about all her decisions, until the other workers want to put cotton in their ears. (Will she wear white shoes or blue shoes with her new suit? Will she drive to Denver, or fly? Will she bake brownies or coffee cake for the potluck?) Maybe Mathilda lacks self-worth and is trying to convince herself she is important. Maybe she is trying to make the other office girls into substitutes for a demanding mother, whom she tried too hard to please with her little-girl decisions. In any case, the other typists find her pretty wearisome.

Ruth has health problems, genuine health problems, but her friends find it hard to be sympathetic because her "organ recitals" are so unending.

George doesn't like his bosses, and all his friends are inviting George over less often because he spends so much of his conversation in bitter anecdotes and diatribes about his job.

If you are a good friend, a really good friend, there are probably some things you will tell God and no one else. Through his grace, you will truly bear your own burdens.

Some things, probably, you will tell your doctor and no one else. And what he says on some topics you will tell no one else. Not that your health is any huge secret, but often there are better topics, you will decide, for general conversation with friends.

Some things, probably, you will tell the person or persons involved, the persons who can take action, and no one else. If a reorganization of George's office is being planned, he may need to talk to some committee persons about politics, let's say, and he may need to tell them some unpleasant anecdotes to prove his points.

To confide is often good. To confide unduly may not be so good. Blessings to you, as you try to decide which is which!

● Respect the confidences that come to you through friendship.

Mary said. Mary said that Jane said. Mary said that Jane said that Theodore said. Sh-h-h; don't tell anyone, but Mary said. . . .

No.

The trusted friend respects the trust.

I remember warmly how another colleague at Seattle Pacific College once paid tribute to Mabel Shipley, then the dean of women, for her absolute care in keeping confidences. Dr. Harvey McMillan chuckled and chuckled as he told us that on one occasion he knew certain things about a problem situation, and Miss Shipley did not know that he knew; he played a devious game for a time, he said, in talking with her and seeing how she would parry and change the topic whenever he pushed near to the confidential items. Thank God for the Mabel Shipleys!

A jingle we learned when I was about in fourth grade still has its relevance:

> While in this course of human life
> Five things observe with care:
> Of whom you speak, to whom you speak,
> And how, and when, and where.

● Remember often that your friends include more than the currently-present circle of friends.

The thousand interlinking decisions are always present, and you can't write, tonight, to everyone you'd like to keep in touch with. You can't telephone everyone every week, nor every month. But some contacts with California and Maine can keep friendship warm and joyous in Florida or Texas — or anywhere else.

Maybe the single person should deliberately permit himself a generous budget for long distance telephone calls, since friendship can be so important a part of life for any single. And he may cheerfully spend a lot more more on letter paper and postage than some of his associates ever do. Otherwise he (and you, and I, and we) can get so engrossed in activities with people who live within a few miles that he will neglect great opportunities, mind-stretching, heart-stretching opportunities, for continuing friendships with people half a continent away.

Conversation with a writer in West Virginia brightened all of my most recent weekend, after I talked with him on Saturday morning. After we talked about his writing, and about his wife's writing; after his assurance that they will be praying about this, my current writing. Yesterday the long distance wires brought a friend into my home from a town up by the Canadian border. In the mail this morning, a description-filled letter from the Great Lakes, and mind-stirring words from over toward the Atlantic coast.

C. S. Lewis comes to mind again as a great model. One simply cannot comprehend how he found the time to write all those *Letters to an American Lady* as well as the many other letters which have been collected. Clearly the persons who were with him in a British inn or in a Common Room at Oxford were not the only ones who were present to his consciousness!

● Be flexible. Don't push your friends to do your will, against their will.

There's give and take in any planning, of course. If it's an auto-
mobile trip together, then someone will have to decide about the
motels and the meal stops, and it is pleasant when each can defer to
each without being so overcourteous that all efficiency is lost. But if
Nan likes her likings too vociferously and grudges Mary's choices
too reluctantly, their friendship will fray.

I remember. I remember the bruising of a friendship. London,
1963. A transatlantic telephone call had brought the news of my
father's death. On the day of his funeral, I had gone off quietly to a
daily service at Westminster Abbey, and above all things I wanted a
meditative evening in my own room. But one of my acquaintances in
the residence hall wanted urgently to see a current comedy, and she
wanted not to go alone. She wanted insistently, demandingly, for me
to go to the play with her. She begged and wheedled, and was unwilling to accept either "No, thank you" or "No; please, no." Finally,
liking myself the less for it, I went along in order to sustain the peace.
A friend, I still think, should not have done that to a friend.

- Don't expect your friendships to stay static.

Life changes, and circumstances change, and friendships change.
It's the way of all life. Season gives way to season. (Outside my study
now, the lush full green foliage of summer, not the icicles and snowdrifts of the Epiphany season, not wild violets and blossoming
quince.)

It is good for sturdy long-growing friendships to be valued when
they, like the maples, are still sending out new leafage. But nothing
on this earth is changeless and inalterable, and undue pangs should
not accompany the updating of the address book.

The wonder, especially among Christians (and more especially
among Christians who have come to know each other in depth on
Christian college campuses), is that long-interrupted friendships can
be so often and so splendidly picked up again without strain, when
circumstances bring long-separated persons together again. During
my sabbatical year as Poet-in-Residence at Westmont College in
Santa Barbara, for example, I had opportunities for very happy
times with Anabel Schlosser Miller, who had greeted me at the little
Pennsylvania Railroad depot (then still a depot) when I arrived at
Greenville College as a student. Years and continents of distance had
intervened, but a deep and close friendship continued, and continues.

But the exceptions point back to the basic premise: changes
change. We thank God for what was, and we thank God for what is,
and where there are discrepancies that might embitter, we trust them
to him.

John, for example. John could talk to me for hours on end when

we were in the same city. We hiked together to look up historic landmarks and exclaimed together over architecture. He gave me complicated verbal reviews of his reading, of theology, of politics. Now I
may get a note from him at Christmas time, or I may not. He is still
a fine person, and we still value each other (I truly believe) but the
texture of this friendship has changed. So be it.

Kathleen, for instance. Christine, for instance. Look in your own
address books.

Especially, of course, one should expect a difference in the patterns of the tapestry that friendship weaves if two persons have been
really close friends and one of them marries. Howard may have
known Wilma's thoughts and preferences on a thousand topics, but
after Wilma marries she changes greatly, and changes toward Howard. Some brides certainly lose more than they need to lose of the
intellectual-social friendships they have had, and so do some bride-
grooms. But each must make the decisions that seem right and good,
inevitable and best.

Sometimes a former friend marries, and you gain a more durable
friending. Or you might lose the old and keep the new, as happened
with Ted. I had known Ted for several years before he married
Katherine. When she became Mrs. Ted, Katherine reached out in
warm and gracious ways to know Ted's former friends. A skilled
secretary, she once took down Ted's thoughts in a shorthand notebook while they were driving across Arizona, and she seemed to
have real fun in sending me their joint production. Well, eventually
the marriage came apart, and I wrote to them both for a Christmas or
two. Then Ted stopped writing, but I continue (glady, gratefully) to
hear from valiant Katherine.

● Value and cultivate wholesome opposite-sex friendships. (And
not just the friendships that might, might, might lead to a dating relationship.) Single women live more joyously, more creatively, if they
have close friends among both men and women. Single men live more
joyously, more creatively, if they have close friends among both men
and women.

For this whole topic, "wholesome" is a key word, of course, and
one's common sense needs on occasion to become uncommon sense.

Some of your associates may be shy, and some may be preoccupied, and some may be so very inexperienced in wholesome opposite-
sex friendships that you will have to go the second mile, and the third,
in extending "the right hand of fellowship." While I say that, I hear
myself in conversation again with a delightfully vivacious young
woman two or three years ago; she was hesitating about a social
contact she really wanted to make. "Go ahead," I urged her. "You

know how to be comradely without being predatory. Go ahead!"
And she did, and her shy associate was pleased, more than a little.

I think of Alice and Melissa, two single women who lived in the
same city, went to the same church, worked for the same company.
In the time that I knew them, I'm not sure either of them ever had a
"date." So far as my acquaintance indicated, Alice was far more
frustrated and angered by her singleness than Melissa was. Alice
tended to be brittle and harsh and stinging; Melissa tended to be
enthusiastic, appreciative, and creative. Many things must have
shaped them to be what they were, but one crucial difference seemed
evident: Melissa was the close and appreciative and loyal friend of
several men; Alice was not. Alice was brisk and efficient in working
with masculine colleagues, and she briskly kept them at a distance.
Melissa would have a group in to celebrate Sam's latest promotion,
or help Vincent and his wife to wallpaper their dining room, or listen
all through a coffee break to Ross's tribulations with his income tax;
Alice would not. Melissa was not a saboteur of her friends' other
loyalties; far from it. She seemed to be such a whole person herself
that she made other people around her more whole: the women she
knew, the single men she knew, the married men she knew. Alice
did not.

● Learn to joy in the joyings of your friends. Learn to grieve in
their grievings.

You're read it a thousand times, in Romans 12:15. Yes, but today
is a new day, and there are new opportunities. And the human heart
is a very strange instrument. If it stretches and stretches to put other
people's joy inside, their joy can warm you and gladden you, like a
hearth-fire in a winter room. If their joy stays outside that unstretched
heart, it can sear and burn until you suffer with dreadful jealousies,
until envy leaves horrid scars.

(And I'm not just theorizing. Yesterday gave me some new opportunities, complex and multiple, for vicarious experiences, and I was
not up to them. I just wasn't. Some self-pity welled up last evening,
and some tears dripped down. Along about midnight I awakened,
sore in spirit, and reached for my scribble notebook to jot down a
scribbled intensity of prayer, to fling the whole circumstances into
the Lord's capacious hands. And today is wonderfully different from
last evening.)

Have you lived long enough yet for a great and desperate grief to
come to you? If it comes, when it comes, grief can petrify this
strange thing called a human heart, or grief can stretch it and
stretch it, until your heart can shelter many other persons, time by

time. After Horatio had friended Prince Hamlet through his disasters, surely Horatio must have become the stabilizer of all Elsinore!

● Can you come to new friendships with a basic attitude of trust and good will? No, it won't always be reciprocated. But if love flows out from you, and flows out, and flows out (your love, and God's love through you), it will help meet the needs of earth.

● Do you often think about the friends our Lord would use you to bring toward himself? Do you listen to what he tells you about them?

If he uses you sometime as a lariat to catch some yearling that is skittering away from his herds, what greater privilege could you know?

Many Christians are much too slow and hesitant in forming friendships with the pagans around them — yet for the pagan to see Christianity happening in a friend is surely an argument beyond all the books of apologetics and doctrine. (Have you read what Sheldon Vanauken wrote in *A Severe Mercy,* about how Christian friends influenced him and his wife, Davy, at Oxford?[5]

Our Lord himself was a friend of everyone — of the ones the respectable people called scum and riffraff. Let us remember to remember it.

● Do you acknowledge the Holy Spirit as the other who is present, the chaperon in any association, in any friendship? Whatever the kind of love, from family affection to Eros to *agapé,* do you recognize him in all your loves?

In that vein, might I share with you some thoughts on friending, from one of the notebooks of my unpublished poems?

TRIANGLES

i.

You, Lord God, are three
and You are one,

and in the lives of Your making
love needs a threeness always
to be mortised or pinioned or chorded
into a one.

ii.

If we a two are only two
we will be dissonance
or blobby sentiment
like melting Jell-O;
we will be splintering bridges;
we will be bombs just ready to detonate;

if we a two are only two
if ever, if ever.

iii.

Put Your scarred hand, Lord Christ,
upon my hand
when it touches any other hand
whenever, ever.

Let Your spear-sundered heart
encompass and give compass
for each two tremulous, blundering hearts
when one of them is mine,
is mine.

iv.

Love needs a threeness always
to be truly
truly
one.

Notes to Chapter 21

1. C. S. Lewis, *The Four Loves* New York: (Harcourt Brace Jovanovich, Inc., 1960), p. 89.
2. Lewis, *The Four Loves,* p. 111.
3. *The Complete Poems of Emily Dickinson,* ed. Thomas H. Johnson (Boston: Little Brown, and Company, 1960), p. 143.
4. Lewis, *The Four Loves,* pp. 98-99.
5. Sheldon Vanauken, *A Severe Mercy* (New York: Harper and Row, 1977), pp. 77-78, 85-86.

"Male and Female Created He Them" 22

Last night I left the radio on softly, tuned to KWMU so that classical music could lull me to sleep. When dawn started bringing me up from deep slumber, the radio was singing, singing; my half-awake wondering mind caught bits of antheming, and more bits, until an announcing voice finally told me that we had been hearing *Pilgrim's Progress,* with music composed by Ralph Vaughan Williams from John Bunyan's great Christian classic. (The London Philharmonic, with Sir Adrian Boult conducting.)

A good background, I told myself, for the seminar we now approach.

A devotional book I have been using took me to Psalm 143. David's personal pronouns always fit many of the exigencies of human experience. Just now, they would speak pointedly to the Christian who is questing for right comprehendings and right use of his sexuality:

> Cause me to hear thy lovingkindness in the morning; for in thee do I trust: cause me to know the way wherein I should walk; for I lift up my soul unto thee.
> Teach me to do thy will; for thou are my God: thy spirit is good; lead me into the land of uprightness.

At some previous reading, my pen circled the pronoun "I" in one phrase: "the way wherein *I* should walk." That emphasis is an appropriate preface for any thoughts about sex in 20th-century America. We live among pagan mores, among pagan assumptions promoted by cinema screen and television comedy, among strange and contradictory assertions from voices of authority, until we need very greatly to ask and obey God's guidance: "the way wherein I should walk." Like the lady in John Milton's dramatic masque

Comus, we are beset by reveling monsters. Like another ancient Psalmist, we live within a Babylon. (Even as I write "Babylon," I hear moments of news interrupting the music on KWMU, and a financial reporter's voice mentions *Playboy* in the stock market review. Another voice, giving headlines, alludes to some city's newest legislation on homosexuality, and there is a paragraph of reporting about rapes and homosexual assaults in some public facility; I wasn't listening attentively enough to catch the details.)

Yet in any Babylon, among any followers of Comus or of Baal, God's Spirit is good, and is indeed ready to lead us "into the land of uprightness."

If your questions were all written down on slips of paper and placed here beside me, what would I read in your scribblings? In imagination, I stir bits of scented stationery and typed anonymous notes and torn pieces of theme paper around in a big wooden salad bowl. Stir, toss. I lift one out, and another, and another.

Why did God give me all this sexual machinery in my body anyway, reads one slip written in vigorous looping penmanship, *if I'm never to use it? I'm 46, female, never married, no prospects.*

Well, first of all, let's note that it is right and good to ask a good many "why" questions all through life, but it is good also, many times, to come to a point of confidence that what God did and does is good, whether we can understand his *whys* or not. Remember Job? He wept and pled and beat his fists against the shards of pottery and wanted to know why. Eventually he received a tremendous revelation of God which left him awed and humble and contented, but not through specific answers to his inquirings; the presence of God and the voice of God just dispelled his perplexity.

Beyond that, though, human beings do catch a good many glimmerings of why God said of man, made male and female, that his making was "very good." Of geology and botany and zoology, he had said "good." With man added ("male and female"), he said "very good."

And he could have arranged for reproduction in other ways. If any science fiction writer can think up innumerable possibilities for racial continuity, the divine Maker was not limited to spermatozoon and fetus. He could have let new beings rise from the ashes of the old, like the legendary phoenix; he could have let men plant dragon's teeth and grow new men, as another legend imagined; he could have devised clonings; he could have let nail parings grow into tall new mortals. But he gave us sexuality, and he said that it was very good.

Good within matrimony, someone mutters. Well, yes, certainly that — when it is indeed good. Sin marred Eden, and sin still mars our earth, and anyone would know that sin mars many a marriage, sometimes irreparably. But as the Song of Solomon so joyously affirms within Holy Writ, and as much as our literature keeps affirming beyond Holy Writ, human sexuality within matrimony is very good.

But to your question more directly.

You are not married, and may never be married. But the rest of your question does not logically follow. You are female, as God made you, during every moment of your life. One is not "female" only when she is in bed with a man. You are female while you eat your cereal, sign your name on contracts, walk to the post office, buy a dress or buy a car, talk with a neighbor or supervise a music student. To be radiantly, splendidly, joyously female is your gift and your glory. Add another modifier: sacredly. Without it, the glory can quickly tarnish into what *Webster's Collegiate Dictionary,* here beside me, calls "common and venal lewdness," into a prostitution.

"No prospects," you said. But you do have prospects, while you are mortal. The machinery within you enables you to be psychologically female: caring, giving, solicitous, thoughtful, irenic, unendingly kind. Adapting to others. Gracious. Gentle. Resilient.

"I adore ladyhood," said one eminent mortal when he was asked about his thoughts on Women's Liberation. A good term, "ladyhood," and your full privilege.

Hands seem to be starting up all over the room, but for now let's reach for another question from the Hawaiian salad bowl.

My boy friend wants to move in with me this weekend, and I think I'm going to say okay. Or should I? He really loves me, and we're planning to be married this fall.

No.

Unalterably, no.

The biblical imperatives coalesce firmly, in eight powerful words that I once heard spoken in a Wheaton College chapel address: "Before marriage, absolute chastity. After marriage, absolute fidelity." The words came with a quiet certitude that gave them a resonance like another set of stone tablets straight from Mt. Sinai. After these several years, I am not quite sure who was speaking; I think it was Paul Fromer, former editor of *His* magazine. (Or maybe Joe Bayly?) But I remember very well the sobered silence of the students as they went from the chapel. They clearly knew they had heard a voice of authority and validity.

Everyone's doing it, someone says. No. Everyone is not doing it. Old Elijah thought that he had been the only one who was keeping the divine commandments, when he sat whimpering under his juniper tree, until Jehovah revealed a very different reckoning: seven thousand in Israel had not bowed the knee to Baal.

And if everyone were doing it, that would not make it right or wise for you. The identity of sin is God's decision, and not ours.

Nor, in sober reality, is cohabitation as clever and desirable and liberated as your boyfriend wishes you to believe. You might like to look up the November 1977 issue of *Seventeen,* with its report of research by sociologist Nancy Moore Clatworthy, or to study the resumé of her findings reported in *Campus Life* for May of 1978. After 10 years of sociological research on "living together," Dr. Clatworthy thoughtfully opposes it "in any form." Only a fully committed marriage relationship, she finds, "is really suited to working out the best possible relationship."[1]

You might like also to look up Tim Stafford's book, *A Love Story: Questions and Answers on Sex.* Compiled from his regular column in *Campus Life,* Stafford's book is slanted toward teenagers but offers practical and careful and rigorously Christian comments that can be useful to singles of other ages also. Premarital sex, he is quite sure, damages and stultifies and wastes. It is not a good road to good living.

I hope you will choose the better choice, for this weekend, and always.

Next slip of paper. Typewritten. *I wish the people at my church were not so snide and judgmental; I'd like to go to church events sometimes, but people act as though I am a moral leper. Sure, my girl is living with me. But didn't Jesus himself say he didn't condemn the woman taken in adultery? How come his so-called followers are so everlastingly condemning?*

Well, maybe, dear sir, because you are dealing with things of "everlasting" consequence?

Pick up your New Testament again, and dust it off. The story you're wanting to hide behind is in John 8:1-11. Notice first that the condemnation which the Pharisees were asking for was not a mere reproof nor the raised eyebrow; it was capital punishment. Of more importance to our day, and to all the uses of this story, notice that the second of his assertions, curiously neglected by many people who use this story, was climactic and imperative: the woman was to "go, and sin no more." He was liberating her from her past, and she knew, and he knew, and we should know, that it was a great sin from which she was being liberated.

You want, apparently, to find a church which is so "loving" and "tolerant" and "accepting" that it has lost the word "sin" from its vocabulary. But if you find it, that will not be the church of Jesus Christ. He says to us, too, "Go, and sin no more."

He did not send the woman back to her paramour. He will not send you back to your girl's bedroom.

Yet if you go there, his love and his caring for your eventual

liberation will go with you. Be sure of that. And if your church is
indeed his church, the love of the church will be with you, also and
always. Sometimes love has a stern face, and sometimes it has a sad
face; the face that smilingly ignores your sin is not the face of love.

*How far can I go and still be a Christian? My roommate says
heavy petting is as bad as going all the way. But when I've been out
with a guy and had a nice time, he makes me feel so obligated.*

"As bad as" is usually a slippery phrase, isn't it?

Rather, try this: is heavy petting good, or is it not good?

Dr. Dwight H. Small, a Christian sociologist with very great
wisdom and broad counseling experience, has suggested that the girl
who considers petting to be "the price of an evening's entertainment" is accepting "the essence of harlotry."[2] And Dr. Small is
firm in his opinion: "Petting outside of marriage is sexual immorality."[3] A man's caresses prepare a woman's body, and her psyche,
for the ultimate expression of his affection; God and your own good
sense can help you to know when the caresses that are right in
friendship give way to the ones that are right only in courtship, and
then to the ones that are right only in marriage.

Two narratives flash to my mind; they are relevant to your query.

Several years ago I was asked to talk with a group of college girls
on the approximate topic of "Christian commitment means the commitment of your love life, too." Afterward, a pretty, vivacious girl
came to my apartment, sobered and stirred, for a desperate prayer
time. "I've called myself a Christian," was the essence of Beth
Ann's troubled statement, "and I've always insisted that I would be
a virgin when I was married. But in holding to that, Jed and I got
into the worst of sexual practices. And I do mean the worst." Beth
Ann's voice quivered, and her body quivered. "I've never thought
of praying about my love life," she said. "I really haven't." But she
wanted to pray then, without further delay, and she wanted to kneel
by my davenport for the praying. Later she came back to tell me
how jubilantly happy she was, now that Jed was out of her life. And
later words have come to tell of the newer happiness she has now
found in married love.

Veeda delayed the praying, real praying, longer — and too long.
She thought she was being clever and careful, because she and Jerry
were not actually having intercourse. But semen contains sperm
cells, and semen touching a girl's vagina may sometimes enter and
begin a new human life. Veeda's pregnancy was humiliating and
scarring, to herself and to Jerry and to their families; sometimes,
still, she probably thinks about that first baby of hers, and wonders.
And wonders.

Next slip of paper. Green, carefully ruled. Green ink. Fastidious
little circles to dot the *i*'s.

When I visit my roommate's family, they make me very uncom-
fortable with all of their kissings and huggings. I don't like being
touched and mauled and handled so much. I really don't. Am I
being squeamish?

Possibly.

Possibly not.

Not being there with you, we'd have to guess. Even being there,
we would have to guess.

Within a family or among friends, body language can become too
overt and too explicit; the "holy kiss" of New Testament Christians
can become the Hollywood kiss. But in general we need more and
not less of sincere concern and affection to be expressed by touching. Encouragement, trust, esteem, sympathy, concern: often the
touch of a hand can speak the deep emotions as mere voice cannot.
In one of his poignant lyrics, Matthew Arnold spoke of the great
loneliness of human beings:

> Yes! in the sea of life enisled,
> With echoing straits between us thrown,
> Dotting the shoreless watery wild,
> We mortal millions live *alone.*

A warm, warm handclasp or a literal pat on the back can reach
across the "echoing straits."

The touchings of affection and friendship, as distinct from the
touchings of Eros, are, in fact, a part of the total sexuality which is
your heritage and your gift. (Let me commend C. S. Lewis's splendid little book, *The Four Loves,* as an exposition of the rich and
wonderful roles of affection and friendship in lives that open to
them.)

Temperaments differ, and your family has apparently not made
you ready to be as expressive, yet, as your roommate's family is.
You will always need to use the responses that are right for you and
for the people you are with at any given time. Maybe thus far you
have held yourself back from caring deeply about most persons, or
about anyone. Maybe your roommate's expressive family needs your
affection more than you have realized that they do.

The sexuality in your singleness and the singleness in your sexuality can free you, if you let them, for rich and radiant dimensions
in *storgé* and *philia* and *agapé,* as C. S. Lewis lists them: Affection,
and Friendship, and Charity.

Next query.

Handsome gray note paper with an elegant crest.

People say I'm "sexy." Among the couples I know, the women
tend to ignore me, or to be jealous of me. The men tend to ignore
me too ostentatiously, or to flirt like mad. If God doesn't send me

a husband soon, I wish I could be neutered, like a cat! Any sugges-
tions?

Yes.

Don't wish your sexuality away, and don't try to smother it nor to evade it. It's you. With every breath that she breathes, a woman is a woman. With every breath that he breathes, a man is a man.

Ask God to guide you in the directing and fulfilling of your sexuality. It should, and can, make you a good cheering section for the happiness of the families you know, and not a competitor. As another woman, you can give wives your interest, your sympathetic insight, your warmth and tact and genuine kindness. And any woman needs sisterly strengthenings. As a woman, you can give a man a sharpened awareness that he is the head of his own home. While you obey the Holy Spirit in the details of your associations, your masculine asquaintances can become more genuine, and more holy, in their masculinity.

Give some thought to the degree of flirtation that you yourself exude. In a community of friends, Eros can try to drive out Affection, to the great loss of everyone. Real womanliness is a benediction and solicitude, not a seduction. Let your demeanor make it clear to everyone that you are not a Lilith-witch!

Next slip.

After all we have heard from the advocates of the E. R. A., do you really think that "male" and "female" are important demarcations? Now, do you? Are men all that different from women?

"Apart from the plumbing," you mean — as one of my friends who is brilliant at handling language would immediately remark.

Well, yes, I think the demarcations are tremendously important. Unisex was never God's idea for human beings. Many things men and women share, wonderfully and gladly. In many ways women have been denied opportunities, in America and in other nations, in our culture and in more ancient cultures, which should not have been denied them. But men are men and women are women.

Look out the window, at the different coloration of male and female cardinals. Watch almost any "Wild Kingdom" film. Caribou, moose, lion, coyote, bear. The male knows his roles, and the female knows her roles. A stallion is not a mare, nor is it a gelding. A bull is not a cow, nor is it a steer.

Maybe growing up on a farm helped me to have a little common sense which has defended me against the more shrill lunacies of "Women's Lib." And there have been the lunacies. Conventions which repudiate maleness to the extent of praising and advocating lesbianism have been a lunacy. What one reads about anti-male enthusiasm for satisfying one's own body through special gadgets used in orgies of masturbation is a lunacy.

No.

Male and female created he them.

Any list of special traits would have to be flexible and conditional, I'd think, for many qualities would vary from person to person, situation to situation, culture to culture. But the identity of "femininity" and "masculinity" are worth thinking about, and worth our respective aspirings.

A tiny episode several years ago gave me a glimpse — which both startled and interested me — of the deep depths of my own femininity. I had employed a young boy, maybe 10 years old, to help me with some yard work. At one point he asked where he should put certain clippings and trimmings. "Over here, under this bush?" he asked. And while I assented to that very small man's judgment on that very small topic, and assured him that the bush would be a fine destination, I knew myself curiously akin to any woman who ever assented to the decisions of a cave man or a medieval knight or an Indian chief.

Someone has suggested that for 20 thousand years (or however many there have been), men have stalked after some animals and grappled against others. If the frailer woman and the new children had run with the men in hunting, says the theorist, humanity would have become extinct aeons ago. It may be.

Have you read *Let Me Be a Woman*, by Elisabeth Elliot?[4] It was written as meditations for her about-to-be-married daughter and keeps rather close to that immediate situation, but it is full of useful ideas.

Let me be clear, though: women's ideas should be used, and women's skills should be used. I'm very glad my brain has had a chance to be disciplined in several universities and countries. I'd admit to a degree of pleasure when I, on some committee with a whole roomful of men, have suggested a plan of action and had it quickly accepted by the group. On some of those occasions, I don't know that I was offering man-ideas or women-ideas; just idea-ideas. I remember being almost angry one time when I showed a new poem of mine to a friend and his immediate comment was, "Well, it's certainly very feminine." I thought, and still think, that it was a poem, not a woman-poem nor a man-poem. A good many other things I've written have indeed been woman-poems.

Yes, we are different. We do not know exactly how. But it is exhilarating to explore both the common ground and the distinctives — and in the distinctives lie some of our gladness, some of our glory. We are sexual beings.

Next slip.

A tightly folded and creased little paper. Three words, printed in pencil.

What about masturbation?

Well, we would have to note first of all that counselors are not agreed on this topic — that careful and thoughtful Christian counselors are not agreed.

Two discussions you might find especially useful are Chapter 3 in Tim Stafford's book, *A Love Story: Questions and Answers on Sex*,[5] which I have already mentioned, and *My Beautiful Feeling* by Walter and Ingrid Trobisch. The latter is a series of factual letters written by the Trobisches to a German girl they were counseling, together with her letters to them.[6]

The Trobisches believe that "no other sexual behavior is so closely connected with a person's religion and relationship with God,"[7] and do not believe that the guilt feelings which linger after self-induced erotic thrills are simply a result of conditioning from society or family. Yet they are careful to say that their experience includes a variety of responses: some Christians find masturbation "an emergency measure" to achieve sexual release and count it a liberty which God gives to them; others feel that "their relationship to God is destroyed" when they indulge.[8] Some persons, the Trobisches continue, "became free completely through the experience of confession and absolution and through a new surrender to Christ." There were others whom "God guided patiently through a longer way of gradual overcoming."[9]

We do not have any explicit biblical instruction on the topic. Tim Stafford has commented with wit and vigor, "One thing I'm sure of: masturbation is no big deal. If it's a sin, it's one the Bible deals with less than gossip, overeating, and kicking the cat. Why can't we take up God's priorities?"[10]

Masturbation is a natural way for young people to get acquainted with their own bodies, say other counselors. It may be considered at at least an occasional necessity, they would add, for some formerly married persons. They would view it as one potential part of God's good gift of sexuality.

Then why, asks someone, do I feel so guilty? Why?

Maybe, suggests Walter Trobisch, because sexuality "is language, it is communication, it is relationship; it reaches out its hands, it seeks to touch others' lives, it is ready to give. That is its meaning and that is what makes sexuality human.

"The single person may also learn its language, although he or she will choose another vocabulary to express this language than the married person. Through masturbation, however, sexuality misses its target. Basically that is why masturbation is an unworthy or inhuman expression of sexuality, and precisely not 'at least something.' It divides a person in two, for he must play two incompatible roles simultaneously — that of the stimulus giver and stimulus receiver.

"Masturbation is not language, it is silence — mute isolation."[11]

Maybe the guilt feelings come because self-will and self-pleasing are so totally at the rooting of auto-eroticism, and just there is the essential seedbed of all human sin since Eden.

Another fact to be noted, an important one. The urge toward masturbation is often an indicator of some other problem, and that other problem should be receiving the attention. The Trobisches have found, for example, that girls who do not have a warm and loving relationship with their mothers experience more frequent temptations toward masturbation. If you are feeling heavy school pressure, job frustration, or a desperate lack of friendship, you may want to manipulate your own body into giving you some moments of suffused and glowing pleasure rather than doing the harder thing of achieving in new ways.

In such a case, some discussion with a counselor may be especially helpful. For most people, masturbation is not easy to talk about; it may be harder to discuss, actually, than less furtive sexual practices which the Bible explicitly condemns.

To the person who wrote this tightly folded little paper: do talk with God about your question. He knows anyway; you won't surprise him. (We human beings are so odd; we want to think God hears our silent prayers when we consciously pray them, but we want to assume that he is ignoring our most muddled perplexities!) So far as I can comprehend, there is only one thing to do with guilt, whether it is real guilt or imagined guilt: put it straight into God's loving hands. He knows precisely why your fingers stroke and caress; even if you haven't begun to untangle the whys, he knows. He knows what is or is not sin for you in his sight — and his view may be rather different from the views of your parents, your pastor, your high school counselor. (And their views may all differ from each other's, anyway.) As you obey God, he will lead you into new peace and new victory, and keep on leading you.

Now a raggedy piece of notebook paper, with block letters in purple ink. *Everybody talks about sublimation,* it says, *but if you ask me, sublimation is for the birds. Sure, I'm a Christian, but my body wants a man. Now. Often. And I don't even have a boyfriend. I had sex pretty often in high school, before I became a Christian, and I'm just about to go bonkers. Maybe a homo friendship would help?*

No. No, that's not the solution.

You would be inviting bigger and uglier demons to camp on your doorstep.

Look, pick up your New Testament. Turn to 1 Corinthians

10:13. Read it aloud about 15 times, and then memorize it, and carve it into the inner surfaces of your soul: "There hath no temptation taken you but such as is common to man: but God is faithful, who will not suffer you to be tempted above that ye are able; but will with the temptation also make a way to escape, that ye may be able to bear it." Note that St. Paul was writing to the new Christians in the old seaport city of Corinth, a city that was notorious for its immorality. Earlier (5:1) he had specified: "It is commonly reported that there is fornication among you, and such fornication as is not so much as named among the Gentiles." In 6:9-20, he specifies candidly the kinds of temptation the Corinthians were experiencing, as he tells us who will not "inherit the kingdom of God" — not fornicators, not adulterers, not homosexuals. But triumph over the Corinthian temptations is available, he goes on jubilantly: "And such were some of you: but ye are washed, but ye are sanctified, but ye are justified in the name of the Lord Jesus, and by the Spirit of our God."

There, my dear, is your "way of escape," too: in the name of the Lord Jesus, and by the Spirit of our God.

The forgiving of old sins is a miracle, and the avoiding of new sin is a miracle. And God does continue to work miracles.

Often the "way of escape" includes practical common sense on your part, of course. It may mean switching the dials when a TV movie starts getting heavily erotic. It may mean reading a sturdier and less lurid book that a current best seller which the reviewers say has "redeeming social values" — but you well know it would light intense little fires inside you. It may mean turning down a date with an office acquaintance whom you recognize to be a very citizen of old Corinth.

And, yes, it may mean some "sublimation." What are you doing to keep your whole body disciplined and controlled? Does it hike, roller skate, fling basketballs, play tennis? Does it diet sensibly?

How deeply are you engrossed in doing things for other people, in general sociabilities, in the projects of your church? Someone has spoken wisely of the expulsive power of a new affection; if you start caring more and more deeply for people in your community whom you can help, really help, will your clamoring body get more busy signals when it sends messages to your brain?

Do you briskly, deliberately, curb the daydreamings which would take you back into your now-forgiven chapters?

Can you send up more frequent emergency prayers?

Listen for, and follow, the obediences that God will tell you about. He is faithful. Quote it a thousand times a day: God is faithful. And the recognized presence of our Lord Christ will teach you, more than anyone else possibly can, of how to avoid the thoughts and the deeds that would hinder your new relationship with him.

When the sexual hungerings are hardest, grip hold of Hebrews 4:14-16, too. Jesus, the Son of God, is your high priest. He is "touched with the feeling of our infirmities." (Try translating that into the colloquial language of your community, and feel the power of it!) He knows, because during his mortal sojourn he himself "was in all points tempted like as we are, yet without sin." Has it occurred to you, ever, that our Lord was on earth as a bachelor, a single man with muscles and blood and sexual capacity? The writer to the Hebrews did not speak carelessly, you may be sure, in saying that he was "in all points tempted"; his full divinity was also full humanity.

And he is the one you will get to know better and better as you handle, through him, the successive temptations.

Yet another slip of paper from the big wooden bowl.

Male and female, huh? What about the homosexuals, who walk somewhere between?

Far too much is being written these days by people much more trained in theology and in psychology than I for me to spend very long on your query, I'd think. A few comments, though.

The very existence of homosexuality in our world surely affirms the Fall, that all is not now as it was when God looked upon male and female and pronounced his creation "very good."

A good many of the recent discussions would seem to point up the fact that there is a difference between a homosexual proclivity, which may have come about through early childhood circumstances or other factors beyond one's own volition, and homosexual practices. In the light of the various apposite Scripture texts, I would concur with C. S. Lewis: "I take it for certain that the physical satisfaction of homosexual desires is sin."[12]

Some grateful Christians affirm that they were formerly homosexuals, and that (like the ancient Corinthians), they have been "washed," "sanctified," "justified in the name of the Lord Jesus," (1 Corinthians 6:11, again), that they are now heterosexual and well married.

In some recent writings, strong pleas have been made for the acceptance, among Christians, of homosexual "marriages," of professedly loving and permanent commitments between two homosexuals. The argument goes that the person with a homosexual proclivity which he has not chosen is incapable of a traditional marriage and that he should be permitted by a loving Christian community to find whatever happiness he can find in a homosexual partnership. Otherwise he must remain single.

This kind of argument seems, candidly, to be a pitiful sort of nonsense. That he may be homosexual in condition and also be a new Christian is a premise I can accept. (I must; I remember very vividly the glad, glad face of a student who talked, sincerely and often, in class and out of class, about how wonderful it was to be a new Christian. I could not doubt his testimony. But I remember also the jolting knowledge that came: Tom had given way again to homosexual practices he had known before he accepted Christ, and he was being dismissed from college. I remember how he wrung my hand when he came to my office to say goodbye, to ask me to pray for him. I am confident that his new sins had been newly forgiven, but Tom's homosexual proclivity had not been expunged.)

Back to the argument. If one Christian must remain single because he is still a homosexual, is he so different, really, from the thousands of heterosexual Christians who remain single because God has led them, for now or for always, into their single state?

Homosexuals, too, should be free to be single.

The real love of the church, someone has suggested, should not go into condoning any homosexual unions, but into building a climate of thought which freely recognizes that to be single can be satisfying, fulfilling, and good.

We hear often about "gay rights." It's a rather ridiculous phrase, really, since the homosexual state is so troubled psychologically, rather than merry or glad, in the basic and valid sense of gaiety. The real right of the homosexual, surely, is in his access, with everyone else, to the Cross; to the atonement; to God's forgiving love, as he, with all the rest of us sinners, confesses his sin.

I put down my hypothetical bowl and look out the window. A glint of scarlet moves through the maple tree. A male cardinal. He has no problem of finding his sexual identity, and he is splendid in his maleness.

The morning mail has brought a wedding invitation. On the front of it, an embossed design contains two butterflies: two symbols of immortality. I think again of C. S. Lewis's powerful concluding paragraphs in *The Great Divorce,* of his conviction (and any Christian's conviction) that what we do now shapes the dimensions and textures of our Forever. I glance inside the invitation. "In celebra-

tion of our Saviour's love," it says, Edward Mark and Ruth Eileen request the honor of my presence. Male and female created he them: Edward Mark and Ruth Eileen.

His, the creating of our sexuality. Ours, the using of our sexuality: in celebration of our Saviour's love.

Not many people in our contemporary blatant and hedonistic

America may understand it so. Not many weeks ago I heard a university professor, lecturing on TV, say casually that any man who asks a woman for a date can be assumed to be ready to go to bed with her. A sociologist, gathering facts as sociologists do, has reported that only five to 15 per cent of his respective samples felt that "one had to be in love or care for the other person deeply before having sex."[13] The Christian blinks and shudders at reading such a comment — but then the Christian reminds himself of our Lord's own words: "Wide is the gate, and broad is the way, that leadeth to destruction, and many there be which go in thereat." To be in a minority is not new to Christians. And in the splendid phrase of Dean Francis B. Sayre, one can "dare to be eternity's man and not the prisoner of Earth's lovely blandishments."[14] Dean Sayre, I recall, was writing of the resolution that Jesus must have shaped during his temptation in the wilderness." In all points like as we are, yet without sin."

Now the cardinal has disappeared from the neighboring maple tree, but his strong and splendid trilling voice is filling the whole neighborhood with sound. Male cardinal sound. God-tuned and lovely sound. And very good.

Notes to Chapter 22

1. Tim Stafford, "Love, Sex, and the Whole Person," *Campus Life,* May, 1978, p. 82.
2. Dwight Hervey Small, *Design for Christian Marriage* (Westwood, N. J.: Fleming H. Revell, 1959), p. 56.
3. Small, p. 173.
4. Elisabeth Elliot, *Let Me Be a Woman* (Wheaton, Illinois: Tyndale House Publishers, Inc., 1976).
5. Tim Stafford, *A Love Story: Questions and Answers on Sex* (Grand Rapids, Michigan: Zondervan Publishing House, 1977).
6. Walter and Ingrid Trobisch, *My Beautiful Feeling: Correspondence with Ilona* (Downers Grove, Illinois: InterVarsity Press, 1976).
7. Trobisch, p. 57.
8. Trobisch, p. 84.
9. Trobisch, pp. 80-81.
10. Stafford, *A Love Story,* pp. 83.
11. Trobisch, pp. 64-65.
12. Cited from a letter of C. S. Lewis in Sheldon Vanauken, *A Severe Mercy* (New York: Harper and Row, 1977), p. 147.
13. Peter Stein, *Single* (Englewood Cliffs, New Jersey: Prentice-Hall, 1976), pp. 58-59.
14. Francis B. Sayre Jr., *To Stand in the Cross: A Book of Meditations* (New York: The Seabury Press, 1978), p. 54.

"Of Shoes and Ships and Sealing Wax" **23**

We live among high dreams and noble aspirations; we sing lofty hymns and pray words of all-encompassing devotion. But we also live among daily practicalities, "where the rubber hits the road," as one of my colleagues often phrases it. Do we bring the niggling, vexing details of life to our Lord as often as we might? Do we ask his guidance, and use all the good sense he gave us as we try to work out his will?

How about a miscellany of thoughts on some of the practicalities of being single? Especially some of the practicalities of the single who lives alone? As I toss some ideas into a mixture, like shreds of lettuce and bits of radish into a salad bowl, maybe you will be reaching for other ingredients.

On that culinary metaphor, let's think a little about your meal-times. Have you swallowed a vitamin pill yet today? Any person who lives by himself, a medical doctor once told me firmly, should be sure to take a regular food supplement. We tend to be impulse-prone in our eating.

Following some impulses can be a part of the fun of life, though. Do you sometimes devise odd new recipes for yourself? Do you prepare standard recipes with different ingredients? One of my newest experiments, hours ago, was to mince some orange peel into a bowl of breakfast cereal. Zestful. I've sometimes said I don't know which is more fun: to buy the food, or to cook it, or to eat it.

Sometimes, and often, your meals will be very brisk; you may munch an apple and a peanut butter sandwich while you are doing other things, and not even sit down. Fine. But do you sometimes honor yourself with meals of pleasant elegance, too? I often like to make Sunday more special, a more set-apart day, by bringing out bone china, blue jasper Wedgwood pieces, sterling silver flatware, crisp linens. Maybe flowers in a bowl. And candles; quite certainly candles.

Eating out. When circumstances permit or require restaurant meals, do you enjoy them to the full? I read a pathetic little article recently in which the author was describing, almost caricaturing, the woe of her loneliness. She usually eats in quick-serve "greasy spoon" places, she confessed, because the waitresses of the nice restaurants intimidate her. They seem scornful of the table-for-one customer. "Good grief!" I cried to myself as I read, and my exclamation had even more intensity in it than Charlie Brown usually musters. "Good grief! What nonsense!"

There are exceptions; I've had the occasional dismal experience. But in several states and in several foreign countries, I have had sustained (and sustaining) glee in exploring the local restaurants alone, when I happened to be traveling alone. Seafood places on Prince Edward Island. Seafood, Mexican food, Danish food, other specialties in the Santa Barbara area of California. Quaint little restaurants all over Switzerland, during the summer I studied there. (I close my eyes for a moment and am back in Grindelwald, at a little outdoor cafe with a superlative panorama of snow-topped Alps. What a glory!) Teashops and old hotels in Britain.

And I don't wait for the foreign excursion. If I don't have other commitments, I rather often take myself out for meals on special days, or on ordinary days that become special when I drive to an old inn in Hillsboro, 20 miles away, or to the Holiday Inn in Vandalia; when I hike through the bird choruses of a summer dawning to Hickey's, two miles away, out at the highway junction.

Such meals are more fun for me. I'd quickly add, because I regularly take a scribble book along. I may see part of a short story happening as people come and go, and jot down a potential plot. I may catch an idea for a new poem. I may write some paragraphs of description to put into a letter. Friendships may deepen as I invite Beth or Bill or Meg or Marian to join me at my table. Sometimes I go to a restaurant straight from Sunday church, and a little leatherbound hymnal or a magazine from the literature rack at church may help me to absorb much more than calories, and more than my small adventure of the day.

Books and magazines and newspapers can accompany the at-home meal, too, of course. Do you experiment, and change your mealtime companions from time to time? For a while I took the daily St. Louis Post-Dispatch, and regularly conversed with the columnists while I ate dinner. *Time* might talk with me, or the *Saturday Review*. In the present chapter of my life, some selective TV watching has its supperly sociability.

Back to the restaurants for a moment. Another "Good grief!" crossed my startled mind a few days ago when I met a comment by a professional woman who has a good deal of common sense and *savoir faire*. Many single women entertain couples at home, she thinks, because it is such an embarrassment to have the waiter insist on leaving the check with the man in a party of three. Good grief! If she likes to cook and wants to entertain at home, that's fine; but to let waiters intimidate her that much — well, I reiterate, good grief! If Sue and Maurice Brown are people she likes enough to take them out, surely she can grin at Maurice and reach over for the check without any huge fuss! Or she can smile a little more, hand Maurice her billfold, and let him do the honors at the cash register. Why not? One elegant woman I know likes to patronize a trusted restaurant which she knows will accept her personal checks. Meal ended, she puts a signed blank check into Maurice's hand and asks him to take it to the cashier for her; he needn't even glance at the size of the bill, and he can feel chivalrously efficient.

Let's move on from the food.

"My hope chest." Have you heard the term recently? Some women who would not use the phrase still have a hope chest mentality, and so have their families. Grandma's linens, which Susan will get when she marries, and not before. The Spode tea set Lucy received three Christmases ago; it's still in the carton, back in the bedroom closet. The crystal that Lynette thinks vaguely about buying some day, when she gets engaged. If she marries, chances are that Lynette's husband, liking her, will also like her taste in crystal. If he doesn't, she can have a garage sale. Or she could make it a magnificent gift to some other single girls who are using chipped plastic mugs!

Pets.

Is it a good idea to have a pet? For you, maybe. How much do you enjoy purrings, barkings, and tail-waggings? How are your facilities? Would a pet be a super-nuisance for you to look after?

For many singles, as for many families, a pet is companion, comrade, amusement, emotional safety valve. But sometimes affection that could well be going to neighborhood children or to a church family goes toward pets in unwholesome and ridiculous quantities. If Itsy Bitsy Woofums is overfed, overpampered, and clothed with itsy bitsy sweaters that cost enough to feed a whole mission compound in Bangladesh, then surely Itsy Bitsy's owner needs to do some hard thinking about Christian (and human) priorities.

Exercise.

Mens sana in corpore sano, the ancient Latins said. A sound mind in a sound body. The body is the temple of the Holy Spirit, added St. Paul; you are to "glorify God in your body." (1 Corinthians 6:20.) Tennis? Cycling? Hiking? Swimming? Jogging? Calisthenics on your living room floor? The popular magazines and TV keep us informed, these days, about the importance of diet and exercise, but sustained effort still requires will power and rigorous maneuvering of schedules. Ask any businessman who jogs during his lunch hour or spends evenings on a handball court.

Or ask me. Just ask me! Several years ago a doctor said firm words to me about brisk walking, and I nearly laughed aloud at being commanded to do what I already wanted to do; I have always enjoyed hiking along country roads, or over mountain trails, or through the plazas in new-to-me foreign cities. But usual impulse suddenly became a disciplined regimen, that day in that office. Later, a young colleague asked whether I had thought of an exercise bike as an alternative; he and his wife were enjoying theirs a lot, he said. Fine, said my doctor; fine. So I placed an order, and the young colleague kindly brought his tools to assemble the hardware. And — time out for a moment, while I go to look at the odometer — 7317.0 miles is the current reading. I often thank the Lord for our educational channel on TV, and I scan the guide for other worthy programs; about half an hour of news or music or drama can mean seven or eight miles of my pedalling.

In "Rabbi ben Ezra," Robert Browning asked for a unity between body and soul:

> "As the bird wings and sings,
>   Let us cry, 'All good things
>   Are ours, nor soul helps flesh more, now,
>   than flesh helps soul.' "

St. Paul would have agreed, wouldn't he? In disciplined Christian living, right use of body can indeed help toward right use of soul, and vice versa.

Clothes.

Is there anything concerning clothes which a single should think about, that any human being isn't already thinking about?

Well, maybe. Do some singles tend to get me-centered and become almost pathologically interested in their wardrobes? Insecure emotionally, do they try too hard for security through shoes and boots, sequins and silks, new and newer suits? Is shopping for clothing an over-engrossing hobby? It may be.

Do some singles, at another extreme, dislike themselves and unwholesomely deny their sexuality by wearing too often the dowdy and the drab? Single women especially? Surely no single woman of any age should repudiate her "ladyhood" by what she wears. Some while ago, I was in a restaurant when two women came in who made me almost want to leave my dessert and run out to buy each a flamboyant scarf, or a something. Drab faces. Drab hair. Drab clothing, in dull browns and tired grays and practical blacks. No sheen nor shine about them. (And no ring on the left hand of either.) Perhaps they exemplified a commendably self-forgetful thrift — but surely no woman should often be so lacking in the exquisite and the winsome as those two seemed to be on that evening!

Entertainment.

Along with the restrictive myths that circulate about singles in restaurants, some singles are much too self-pitying about what they simply cannot do alone. Some things are more fun in twos or in fives, granted, and some cities are safer than other cities for the woman who comes and goes alone. But I certainly would not wish to delete from my memory all the concert-going and play-going and banquet-going that I have done on my own. London was inexhaustible, during a sabbatical year. New York has been splendid, when I have been there after a convention or en route to Europe. Other sites of professors' conventions have offered their operas, their art museums. If I found someone else to do with me what I wanted to do, fine; if not, here was this head of mine, ready to be filled with great music or great art.

One chooses a hotel with care, naturally. One uses sense about deciding between a matinee and a late evening performance. One keeps the sixth sense (or seventh) turned on. One schedules events in Bern or Lucerne, let's say, that one would not schedule in Venice or in Naples.

But one goes, and does, and is gladdened.

A while back, a delightful dinner-concert was announced in our town. Most people were going as couples, and many girls in the campus community stayed in their rooms and mourned rather than going unescorted. One braver woman took a neighborhood couple and her housemate as her guests. One zestful married woman went alone; her husband thought he wouldn't care for the music, and she wanted not to miss it. I asked a recent graduate if she would like to go, and we caught up pleasantly on her post-college experiences.

And each who went was glad she hadn't let the absence of a dately escort keep her with the TV screen or with usual tasks through all that memorable evening.

For travel ventures, let's not forget the package tour. If it's a good one, a tour can be wonderfully efficient, and you can let someone else worry about getting you home from "Faust" at the Paris Opera House or "Aïda" in the Roman Baths of Caracalla.

Time.

If you don't spend most of your off-work hours at the shopping centers finding newer togs — and let's hope that you don't — how do you spend them?

Every human being, every Christian, faces the matter of the stewardship of time. But the single faces it with a difference; outside his working hours, he has a flexibility and a freedom which family persons simply do not have. (Inside working hours, too; some singles pull much more than their own weight in job situations because they're more available and more flexible.) And the freedoms stand behind an old proverb:

"Whether down to the pit or up to the throne,
He travels fastest who travels alone."

Like most proverbs, it could be debated, but do you know some singles who are traveling downward? Do they go through their evenings and their weekends with no plan, no evident purpose, pulled only by impulse after impulse? For such persons, Nicholas B. Christoff, the popular Lutheran minister to singles, puts laziness at the top of his list among his "seven deadly sins" of singles.[1]

Other singles, compulsively busy, seem to be so ruthless with themselves and so desperately tense in their schedule-making that joy drains away from them and from their associates. They are like what we read of young John Wesley, before his heart was "strangely warmed." After his life-changing evening in Aldersgate Street, Wesley became a person of great method in his daily living, but also a tool of joy and of redemption.

As I think, now, of Lucy, one of the most admirably disciplined singles I know, I think of the time she must spend writing her cheery letters. She doesn't go about vaunting her dedication to the task, but every now and again I learn of her correspondence with some missionary, with some person who has moved away from her church, with someone who needs a brightness. Lucy gives herself unstintingly to people who need her in her local community, but she keeps the neighbor half a state away or half a world away in her love, as well as the one only half a block distant. And she keeps a firm hand on the daily apportioning of her time.

Devotions.
One of the things that does not happen when you live alone is family worship. If you have a housemate, is shared worship important to you? If you're alone, do you keep alert to the other soul-tunings? "I prayed that God would give me someone to pray with, and he did," Marie told me when she was describing her move to a new university town, a new university job. Her voice quivered with intensity.

Sometimes a small group from church becomes a "family worship" unit. Sometimes you may invite a friend over for a time of special prayer that you both need. Sometimes telephones help. Every now and again, my friend Celesta may come to my home for a prayer time via long distance wires. After we have talked about this topic, and this, and this, it sometimes seems quite natural to Celesta for one of us to voice a prayer.

Sometimes I have found it useful to my spirit to flick on the tape recorder while I read aloud from devotional books, while I tell God aloud about my current aspirations or desperations. Then I can think those concentrated devotional thoughts with new reiterations as the tape plays again while I do a bit of sewing, or while I am midnight-wakeful.

As I think of the tape recorder, I think of other electronic devices, and I am grateful.

Soon after my first living-alone chapter began in a Seattle cottage, I mystified my family by writing to them that I had acquired a new roommate whom I was calling Gwendolyn Gabble. Soon I let them know that Gwendolyn was my new clock-radio. She was a pleasant and useful associate. In the present chapter of my life, I am most grateful for two FM stations in St. Louis, KFUO and KWMU. Their classical records can help to make my life a celebration, day or night. Sometimes I tune my living room set and my bedroom radio to the same station, and let great orchestras just fill the house with double-stereo sound.

If you like, you can even leave a radio on while you are out doing errands, so that you can come home to the welcoming sounds of music. If the triumphal march from Verdi's "Aïda" should happen to greet your return, it could celebrate any number of completed errands!

You do leave lights on when you will be returning in the dusk or later, don't you? Even a long-loved house can seem harsh and strange while it is not sending out any electric light to symbolize all of the other light, and the Light, within it.

If you thought I was going to talk about insurance and income tax and retirement plans when I said "practicalities" a while ago, I'm sorry. I'm not the one to offer ideas on those topics. When a circle of students filled my living room a few weeks ago to talk about some ideas on singleness (at a student committee's request), I mentioned to them that they might think seriously about signing up for a course in "Consumer Economics," if they are really thinking about how to prepare well for creative singlehood. I realize that my check books, and all related items, leave me feeling more queasy than they should. I don't try to do it all alone; year by year I ask an experienced consultant to compute my debts to our sovereign Uncle, and from time to time I address specific inqueries to my friends who have numerical computers built within their very skulls.

And I add to my various doxologies a gratitude that I am not a corporation president, nor the heir to any oil company.

Oh. Did you notice that my typewriter says "heir" and not "heiress"? Mildly interesting to me, this typewriter's preference. The generic masculine pronouns do not irritate me; I've studied too many languages, and have too deeply rooted a sense of the grammatically smooth correctness of "Each one must choose his own path, in his own way." But those -ess nouns often seem to have a condescending and patronizing quality. *Poetess* or *authoress* I cordially dislike. Once I protested to an editor that in my other roles I am not hikeress nor lectureress nor professoress, and I really did not see why he must list me in his journal as *poetess*.

Other locutions? If you want to know, I find that as time goes by, "*Ms.*" still annoys me a little, with its echoes of the more strident shrillnesses of Women's Lib. It seems not a full courtesy to the "ladyhood" which I value. It's too much like the American propensity, of another sort, for using first names on first encounters. Spoken with dignity and grace, "Miss" is a term of full courtesy. In practice, I myself hear my professional titles and nicknames so much that the other prefixes almost seem needless. Soon after I started teaching at Greenville College, the students affectionately dubbed me "Doctor Mac" and sometimes it's all I hear throughout a working day. Which is fine. Last fall a dear little freshman girl who had transferred to our campus from a parochial preparatory school started to ask me a question. "Professor . . . ," she began. "Professor. . . ." Then she twinkled. "I want to call you 'Sister,' " she said. "Call me 'Sister,' " I urged her. The term has an honorable lineage, back to the New Testament. "I commend unto you Phoebe our sister," wrote Paul to the Romans. (And I wonder what sort of corporate or personal business Phoebe was carrying through in metropolitan Rome — but that curiosity would take us rather far afield even for this discursive essay.)

Joking.

It's great. I'm in favor if it. Singles need a sense of humor, and one can find fun in nearly everything on this earth.

But some of the singles might give a little more thought to Ephesians 5:4, and the "foolish talking" and "jesting," which, Paul thought, "are not convenient."

Some single persons are unduly preoccupied by their singleness. It is our state of being — but we need not make a career of it! You might like to be introduced as Joellen, who makes a great tamale pie, or Joellen, who has the Bach collection, or Joellen, who is an ecology nut, or Joellen, who writes all those crazy limericks, but you might not like to be introduced as "Joellen, the single girl in our office." Well, if you make too big a deal about your being single, that's the way you will get introduced — in the overtones, if not in the spoken words.

A man or a woman who is comfortable with singleness can afford to laugh about singleness, or about anything else. But there *are* 10 thousand other topics for humor! If you jest too constantly about your mate-hunting and your availability, you may be sabotaging your own morale needlessly, and making it harder for other people to think of you as a whole person rather than as an awkward single.

Sometimes the jesting truly is not convenient. The president of a Christian corporation talked with me, a while back (and blushed like a schoolboy as he did so) about a very risqué quip that one of his single staff women had made about her single self; she was either much more naïve or much harder in her sophistication than was good within his offices. When we talked, he had not decided to make an issue of it, and he may not, but her kind of quip — like other uses of the tongue that St. James talked about — "ought not so to be"!

Like Lewis Carroll's Walrus and the Carpenter, we have talked today of many things. And many more are on your mind. Life, someone quips, is so daily. And it is. In all that you decide and think about and work through and live out day by day, day by day, in your various versions of topics like "shoes and ships and sealing wax," may our Lord be with you. As I know that he is; he truly is.

Note to Chapter 23

1. Nicholas B. Christoff, *Saturday Night, Sunday Morning: Singles and the Church* (New York: Harper and Row, 1978), pp. 70-73, in Chapter 6, "What Ails Singles: Seven Deadly Sins."

With Christ
Himself as
My Escort 24

My breakfast tray this morning, as I watched a few minutes of news in my living room, was brightened by a corsage of yellow roses. The same roses are here beside me in the study now, an exquisite still life of yellow petals and greenery on a white milk glass plate. I always enjoy getting full benefit from flowers, and often move a bouquet from room to room in my home as my activity center changes. And these flowers have a particular speaking, to which I especially want to listen.

Shall I explain?

To me, one of the most powerful verses in Scripture has always been Matthew 28:20. For years I have realized that the promise, "Lo, I am with you alway" has a really total implication for the Christian. It is all-inclusive. It doesn't just mean during quiet Bible study times at church, nor during sermons, nor during consciously pious efforts at evangelism. It means *always*. Once I wrote a meditation for my sister, assuring her that *always*, for that time in her life, meant that he was with her in the midst of diapers, bottles, laundry, pabulum, toddler mischief. Very recently, the implication of that tremendous promise for me was stirring at deep levels in my consciousness: for me, and for any single. "Lo, I am with you alway."

He really is.

We need to remind ourselves of it, to live by it, much more often and much more totally than we do. Or, let me speak for myself; much more totally than *I* do.

Well, while I was thinking in such veins as that, some 10 days ago, a banquet occasion came along. Just about all the people there, I could assume, would be my friends, but no one was sched-

uled to be an escorting friend. As I looked forward to the event
and settled with myself on what I'd be wearing, an impulse started
welling up and finally took on the urgency of command. It was as
though Christ were reminding me (if I can approximately verbalize the depth of the conviction), "My child, my child, I am with you
always. I am your Escort, in any crowd or in any solitude. You are
not alone, ever. And things would go better for you if you realized it
more totally than you do. Now, for this banquet, to which you will
be going 'alone,' I want you to use a definite symbol that I am with
you. To the greenhouse, my child; briskly, now."

So I placed the order, and the corsage was duly delivered.
"Lovely flowers," commented various friends, and I smiled quietly
each time. It was not yet a time, then, to speak of the symbolism,
but now I touch a finger to a delicate yellow petal and thank him.
He who made all petals made me also, and he is with me.

(Oh. Lest you wonder a litle about my veracity, let me mention
that my refrigerator has an excellent crisping tray for fresh vegetables, and I have more than once enjoyed a florist's craftsmanship
for two or three weeks of successive uses.)

Looking back through the panoramas of my thus-far life, I would
have to know that much of the peace and joy and zest I have
known has been linked with what these yellow roses symbolically
affirm. As a child, I decided to follow Christ utterly, and to follow
means also to walk with: to be escorted by him. I would have to
know that much of the stumbling and pain and dismay, when they
have come, have been linked with the tendencies to take his presence for granted, to ignore him in the daily actualities.

I am not wise nor clever in the practical decisions that tumble in
upon one constantly. How often would I decide more serenely and
more efficiently if I were more ready to look to my Escort for his
counsel?

At this moment, I touch the yellow petals again, thankfully, and
go to my bookshelves to find a slim volume which I value: *The
Practice of the Presence of God*. It contains the conversations and
letters of Brother Lawrence, a sweet-spirited French monk of the
17th century. In the presence of God, Brother Lawrence purchased
provisions for his order. In the presence of God, he worked among
the pots and pans of the monastery kitchen, a kind of work for
which, he said, he had naturally a great aversion. Going straight to
God about everything, and doing everything for God: that was the
way of life for Brother Lawrence.

The single person in 20th-century America often has rare and
splendid opportunities for "the practice of the presence of God."
Comings and goings of many sorts can be "alone," but with him.

If one lives alone, there are mealtime solitudes when his presence can be joyfully recognized. One can talk with him in little exclamations of joy and gratitude during dishwashing or laundry. While one cooks a meal or makes a bed, one can talk with him about duties, pressures, friends, opportunities, decisions. Surely our communities, our nation, and our world would be different if Christian singles more truly practiced the presence inside their own apartments!

And whenever we go out from the home, he goes with us.

I think back, joyfully, to many episodes of his grace and his guiding. In retrospect, I am in London again, on sabbatical, coming back to my residence hall alone after lectures or plays or concerts. (Alone, but not alone.) I am catching trains alone here and there all over Britain, looking up literary landmarks. (Alone, but not alone.) I am driving alone from Santa Barbara, California, up to Santa Cruz, to speak at a women's retreat. (Alone, but not alone. Oh, indeed not!) How that day lingers in my recollection! Huge prayer topics were in my mind, as well as the responsibility for the retreat, and I talked with him consciously, earnestly, often and often through the miles. I talked with him, too, about practical matters as evening came nearer and I wondered where to stop en route; after I had settled my suitcases in a graciously rustic and pleasantly thrifty cabin at Carmel, I thanked him very joyously for guiding me to that precise spot.

I am out on Swiss mountain trails, during the summer of my study at St. Gallen, rejoicing in his mountains and his alpine roses and his edelweiss or blue gentians (Alone, but not alone.)

Sometimes one is companioned by another person, or by many persons, and is still conscious of, very grateful for, his companioning presence. Retrospect again. Now I'm in the midst of thousands, at a national conference for which I was a speaker. Great emotional pressure was there, that week, and loneliness was not absent among the thousands. But he was my escort.

Another sort of remembering.

When I was finishing my doctoral program, I was under fierce time pressures, but I also knew I had to take some time off from writing a dissertation to do some shopping for things to wear during the next year. I had been living on a very narrow shoestring during the graduate grind, and I knew that what I had worn while I wrote examinations and research papers would not be at all adequate for faculty roles. Well, the post-Christmas sales came along, and I took one day away from my piles of books and note cards. I talked with Christ before I caught a city bus, believe me. And when I returned, I had (to the amazement of the other women in the

residence hall) found four classroom dresses, an evening gown, and
a suit that was rather beyond my dreamings — all with fewer shopping hours and fewer dollars expended than one could ever have
credibly hoped for. I had to believe, and I still do, that Christ had
been my Escort.

He does not make us into automatons. Certainly I was no pup-
pet during that brisk day of shopping in Champaign and Urbana,
nor in other practical episodes ever since. He has left me free to
make wrong judgments and to blunder. But he has not left me
alone.

Sometimes we sing with our lips and with our hearty voices the
gospel songs that talk about God's presence. Sometimes the songs
are a mere sentimentality to us, and not a reality. But it is a truth
we sing about, and a truth we affirm when we read Matthew 28:20
again.

In context, we should note that he was promising to be with his
disciples (his then-disciples, his now-disciples) to the end of time
within their mission of discipling others. It was not a promise of his
presence just to make us feel stroked and pleased, like well-fed
petted kittens. His presence is to be with us as we do his enterprises. If we were more totally concerned about the teaching of all
nations, we would certainly be more continuingly aware of his constant presence.

Singles who are ardently concerned about the Great Commission, in Africa or Taiwan or in their own apartment complex, are
just the singles who are most aware that he is their continuing
Escort. Singles who ignore his world-reaching commands also keep
ignoring his presence. But if we acknowledge him, if we listen, he
is giving us special opportunities, and he is with us. For a banquet
a few days ago, yellow roses were for me a new and memorable
symbol that he is.

For your today, whatever it is, I hope that there will be some symbol. Some yellow-rose equivalent. He is your Escort also. Acknowledge him, and thank him that he is!

part three

WITHIN THE COMMUNION OF SAINTS

Within the Communion of Saints 25

Whenever we recite the Apostles' Creed, we affirm a great affirming: "I believe in the communion of saints."

It is a declaration of greater magnitude than any mortal can comprehend. First-century martyrs kneeling in a Roman arena kneel within that phrase, and present-day missionary translators in remote South American villages, and Irish monks evangelizing seventh century Switzerland, and the believers with whom we sing hymns Sunday by Sunday. The communion of saints.

Once on a Christmas Eve I went to a midnight communion service at the Priory Church of St. Bartholomew the Great in London, and my imagination fairly reeled as I realized that I was worshiping under stone arches where other Christians had been worshiping ever since A.D. 1143. For more than 800 circling years, Christians had come to kneel among those very same stone pillars, had gone out again after receiving there the sacramental bread and wine. I have joined with other believers at little meeting halls in Edinburgh, in Paris, in Switzerland. I have joined with other believers at great cathedrals in London, St. Louis, Washington, Venice, Florence. I have joined with other believers in a huge stadium, when busloads of God's children were thronging up the concrete ramps toward an evangelistic rally. The communion of saints.

One of my research projects in graduate school gave me a chance to look closely into the history of the great Methodist Revival, and I stood in imagination with John Wesley, hearing thousands of voices singing Methodist hymns in Cornwall before the men went down into the tin mines for their working day. Through my doctoral dissertation, I came to know the Anglican Revival of 19th-century England, and in imagination I knelt often among the soaring earnestnesses of

John Keble, John Henry Newman, E. B. Pusey, Christina Rossetti, Gerard Manley Hopkins, and scores of other valiant spirits who were leaders or inheritors of the Revival. The communion of saints.

All of this leads me to say what in fact we ought often to be shouting: the Christian single is never, never solitary. We are within a communion. Thank God, thank God for the communion! A stance of gratitude for his work among his people is an enablement, continuingly, for our now.

In the familiar language of the New Testament, the individual single is a part of the Body of Christ. And the joyous, fulfilled Christian single is, it seems to me, the one who has found, and keeps on finding, his own role-identity within the Body of Christ. No Christian is meant to "go it alone"; certainly the Christian single is not meant to go it alone. Affirming that fact, my mind skips back to a lively argument in a general psychology class when I was in junior college, out at Garden City, Kansas. "Nobody has to go to church to be a good person," someone was asserting truculently. "Well, sure," acknowledged a benign voice. I don't recall now whether it was a student voice or Professor Farquharson's. Probably his. "Well, sure. You might be able to cross the Atlantic in a rowboat, but you'd have a much better voyage of it on a big ocean liner, with the others."

To find one's role within the Body. To keep on finding. Thought dips and leaps through Christian history. The missionary Mary Slessor. The missionary Amy Carmichael. Joan of Arc. Mary of Bethany. Stephen, flung into glory by the flinging stones. (Was he a single? So far as we know, he was.) St. Paul, who frankly affirmed his singleness. Names I named a moment ago, the poets Christina Rossetti and Gerard Manley Hopkins. C. S. Lewis, a single through most of his lifetime, through most of his role-finding. Corrie ten Boom. A library administrator I know, a single who is valiantly Christly within his diocese. Mother Teresa of Calcutta, with her ministry to the "poorest of the poor." The girl who plays the organ at a church I often hike past. Sunday school teachers. Wycliffe translators out in New Guinea. The quiet widow who leads no public act of worship, ever, but who lights altar candles in us all by the depth of her devotion. The Jesuit priest who has assured me that my tasks are within the scope of his prayers. My former student who is a secretary with the Billy Graham Association.

Now to think about some of the practicalities, if we may, of our role-finding. I recall the great panels of mosaic-pictured saints and martyrs in the basilica of Sant' Apollinare Nuovo, in Ravenna, Italy: white robes, palm fronds, crowns in their hands. What daily little decisions in mundane events led mortals to become that golden host within the communion of saints? Of greater importance to us: what little decisions can help us to right roles within the present assemblies of persons who are becoming saints?

Bluntly and directly: what about you and your local church?

From my contacts with all the churches I've ever attended, spoken in, and visited, both in America and abroad, and from all the people-watching I have done among Christian singles, may I offer a few thoughts, a few urgings?

● Take your church membership seriously.

It isn't Rotary or a photography club or a bowling team. Not A.A.U.W., and not the Young Republicans. It is one part of Christ's Body. It is the communion of saints. Maybe we should each review more often the vows we affirmed in baptism, or in confirmation, or in our first joining of a local denominational unit. Do you say to yourself now and then, "I am Christ's; these other believers are his; they are my brothers and sisters in him; for now, are we working together to do his will in this place"?

● Keep involved.

Keep involved beyond attending the Sunday morning worship service. Just *how* you are involved will depend, of course, upon your skills, your energy levels, your other commitments. But do you think seriously, and often, about those other commitments and their relative priorities? Sometimes zeal outruns wisdom, and one loyal single may try to carry far too many concurrent responsibilities, but more often sloth is a deadly sin very active among us. (Isn't he?) Your local church proably has more continuing staff needs than you would dream: youth sponsors; choir voices; hands to paint walls, to weed and water the grounds; officers; committee persons; crib-room staff; ushers; secretarial helpers.

If none of those is right for now, or along with them, what about letting some of Christ's love show through you as you greet other persons before and after the services? "They will know we are Christians by our love, by our love," we sing. Do they know?

● Be creative enough, and caring enough, to step over the barriers to fellowship that you may find.

In some churches, it seems to be assumed that young people will associate only with other young people; that young couples will associate only with other young couples; that only senior citizens are to spend time with other senior citizens. But you do not need to like those invisible walls, any more than Robert Frost liked the walls between pine woods and apple orchard, in his "Mending Wall" poem. Take some initiatives! Experiment!

● Look for ways to develop contact with families. How? I don't
know what would be right for you. Have a family over for a Sunday
supper? Write some notes of congratulations? Keep aware of griefs
and joys, and do something about them? Let parents know you are
caring and praying when their children go through childhood illness
or adolescent rebellion? The church will be stronger and the families
will be stronger if you will keep investing some auntly or avuncular
concern.

And the fringe benefits can be delightful: the tiny blonde cherub
who runs over to fling her arms around you when she sees you in the
parking area; the young adult, home from a dazzling new job, who
says warmly, "You were one of the few who wrote to me about the
promotion. Thanks so much!"

● Consider, from time to time, the length and depth of the ruts
you are in. This, if you have attended the same church for much
more than six months, I'd say!

Do you sit in the same pew, greet the same people, participate
with a dull sameness?

Have you tried a front seat lately? Have you come early, for silent
prayer? Have you sharpened your listening by outlining some sermons? Whom did you last invite to come along with you? If a novelist were putting you into his next book, how would he describe the
church-going you? What adjectives?

For too many of us, church attending is tired and empty and in-
hibited and bland — a mere habit. We need new chapters for the
book of Acts. To use Malcolm Muggeridge's phrase, we need "a
third testament" being written among us!

● If your church has singles' groups, then by all means feel free
to enjoy the singles' groups — but don't let them be your whole preoccupation.

Time is limited, within any mortal life. Emotions are limited. And
it will be your loss if lunching with the singles, ski trips with the
singles, Bible study with the singles, and concert-going with the singles fill your whole life. Here is a corollary to my urging, a minute
ago, that you look for ways to associate with the families of your
church.

If you're a woman and your singles' group is predominantly feminine, the wholesomeness for you of reaching out becomes all the
stronger. If you share a dwelling with another woman or two, and if
you work mostly with women, the valuing of families becomes yet
more emphatic. Women can give themselves the narrowing and stul-
tifying that might threaten a convent-enclosed nun, without the

counterbalancing ecstacy and glory that a nun could know in her chosen life!

● Recognize that the children of your church are also *your* children.

With a difference, of course.

You won't pay for Judy's dental braces, probably, nor ration out daily vitamins for all the infants. If there are 20 sixth-grade girls and you are one you, you probably won't ever stitch up a new frock for each of them, one after another.

But you may lie awake praying after the Joneses telephone you that their Judy (your Judy, too) has hepatitis. You may lie awake even longer when their Jimmy, age 17, is arrested for drunken driving. (He's your Jimmy, too.) You may be gladder than anyone not in the communion could ever understand when their Jerry realizes he must be a preacher, and not a research chemist.

● Don't just stay away, miffed, from all "family" events.

Don't, and don't, and don't!

You are a wholeness. You are not an incomplete part of a unit. You may be a one-person family unit, but you definitely are a unit.

And it will be your own loss if you don't go.

At a holiday time, for example, the church I attend once announced a twilight communion time for families; people were to come and go as they wished, and to take communion in family units. I was under deep stress at that season, and I could have lingered at home whimpering all evening, or yelling at God for causing me to be single. But I went quietly, gladly, knowing my need for the Eucharist. My love touched the family groups who came and went. Alone, I was free to linger and to linger. And I remember with awe and great gratitude the recognized Presence of that evening.

Sometimes you may want to borrow a nuclear family to take with you, if it's a "family picnic" or "family potluck."

Sometimes your calendar will be full of other events and you will choose not to attend. Fine. You're free, in Christ and among his. Single and free.

● Be alert to God's new leadings, for yourself and for your church.

Sometimes a single person who is detached from some other involvements and "careth for the things that belong to the Lord," as

1 Corinthians 7 puts it, can be a sensitive discerner of new guidings from the Holy Spirit for a group of believers. Sometimes the single person has a freedom for intercessory prayer which can make a difference in board decisions, in community projects, in revival movements.

Some years ago when I was helping with the youth program of a summer camp, a single woman who had spent many years in China came to the campground as a missionary speaker. One of my co-workers said to me, with a deep yearning that still burns in my bones, "Oh, if we could just arrange the schedule so that Miss X could be here when we have our teen-agers' chapel every day! If she didn't say a word to them — if she were just present and praying, it would make such a difference!"

Surely the single person who is totally God's person, present and praying, can often make a difference, "such a difference," within the community of saints.

To find our roles within the community gives purpose, and strength.

To recognize that even now we are leagued with "a great multitude, which no man could number, of all nations, and kindreds, and people, and tongues" is to be touched with eternal glory, even in the midst of the most mundane realities. Perhaps we should read Revelation 7 much more often than we do, and play *Messiah* records much more often than we do, to affirm it: we are within the communion of saints.

To the (Married) People Who Run Our Churches 26

Thank you for inviting me in to talk with your church board. No, no coffee, thank you. The lectern, if you don't mind; I can keep all of your faces in focus better, around this big conference table, if I'm standing. Fine. That's fine. Thank you very much.

All right. Shall I pose some inquiries, and see where they take us?

1. Are singles attending your church, these days, in an appropriate ratio? Various books are telling us that approximately one-third of America's adult population is now single. That would include widowed and divorced persons, as well as the single-singles. So if your church is reaching its adequate share of the population, one-third of your adult attendance on any given Sunday morning would be single adults. If your program is more attractive to singles than most in your city, you might have more than that.

Now, two other questions would immediately follow. If the singles are staying away from your Tenth Avenue Church, precisely *why* are they staying away?

If they are coming, are their needs being met? Maybe we should send a recorder over to the chalkboard to write down some comments about *how* the needs are being met. Okay. Anything else?

Look, have you recently asked your singles themselves how *they* feel about their needs and the Tenth Avenue Church programs? One weakness in churches across the country seems to be that married people sit down to decide what singles want and need, and may guess wrong. If you haven't asked, you may just shrug and decide that the programs in your church always have been fine and always will be fine, world without end, Amen; there is the excellent youth program, and the excellent program for young marrieds, and the excellent. . . .

215

Yes, but what are your singles, and the potential-attender singles, saying about their needs?

2. Do you give your people the freedom to be single? At deep, subliminal levels of your attitudes, in your conversations and even in your jestings, do you truly encourage your young people to follow God's full leadings for themselves, or do you constantly push them toward a marriage expectation?

If a handsome Bill Business, age 27, starts attending your church, is he constantly bombarded with tactless queries and remarks and tormentings (otherwise called teasing) about his single state? When Elegant Ellen comes home from the university, is she quizzed slyly about her "prospects"? Do you tell your teenagers that you are praying about *whether* they will marry, rather than *whom* they will marry?

3. Are your pastors here? Dr. X, Mr. Y. Good. They may need a few earnest words; most preachers do! It is my observation that among Christians in general, preachers are often especial offenders in wanting to push everyone, everyone, into matrimony.

Maybe it should be mentioned to them quietly that in many Christian communities, total matrimony would mean either Christian girls marrying pagans, or bigamy and polygamy in the church homes.

If a preacher is himself happily married, I am ready to rejoice and thank God with him. But I am ready also to be both grieved and amused at his readiness to view marriage as the expected pattern for all Christians — as though he knew more that God about God's plans for us all. When young people admire their preachers (which they should) and hear the preacher's humor and exuberant extroversion proclaiming marriage as the only doorway into excellence, it can put young people under an emotional strain which they should not have to face, along with their other strains and pressures. And it can put a dash of bitter spice into the older single's morning coffee.

4. In many churches, there is a subtle attitude of smug superiority among the nuclear families. Sometimes it's a blatant attitude. "The church is for us," families seem to say or imply. "Singles are inferior; singles don't belong. They can look after themselves." How is it at the Tenth Avenue Church? Do you essentially ignore and ostracize the singles? Do you find their freedoms a little threatening, and wish they were not around?

5. Have you reviewed your Sunday school structure recently, to consider how fully it meets the needs of singles? This question is pretty important, since in many churches the general social life of the church is closely linked to Sunday school patterns. Do your singles feel welcomed, or excluded? Do they find themselves barely-tolerated fifth-wheel beings? Are they given such unattractive options that they just skip Sunday school?

Consider Mary. Mary attends a thriving Sunday school (it would say), with over four hundred persons usually present. But there is no class beyond the college department except "Young Married" and "Older Young Married" and "Older-Older Young Married." None. They are completely couple-oriented. Mary is not a couple. Nor is she a college student; she has been a professional chemist for 17 years.

Consider Marvin. He attends a church which has a pattern about like Mary's, with one addition: a class or two for "Business and Professional Women." Marvin is not brave enough nor foolish enough to invade such a class. He's 32 now, and really weary of the college department.

Marvin and Mary, and their friends, would welcome some topic-oriented classes which do not make matrimonial status the prerequisite for admission.

Marcia would welcome some new creative thought about Sunday school structures, too. Marcia goes to Marvin's church now, but she is looking around for another church home with less segregation. Wholesome women, she believes, need to interact wholesomely with both men and women in many circumstances, and she would like to find a coeducational Sunday school class rather than one with a built-in "women only" limitation.

6. Does your church have, or is it organizing, a variety of programs for single adults?

"Just for *them*?" mutters some one. "Well, why? There's the whole church. . . ."

Yes. But singles need a sense of identity, of worth, of status. They need a sense of being special, and of belonging. Persons in family units find those needs met in their homes. Increasingly across America singles are finding the same needs met in single adult fellowship groups. A notable example is Park Cities Baptist Church in Dallas, Texas, for which the Rev. Britton Wood became a full-time minister to single adults in 1970. By 1977, when he wrote *Single Adults Want to Be the Church, Too*,[1] Park Cities was serving some 800 singles. (His book is full of ideas that might be lifted out and examined in your discussions here at Tenth Avenue. For other ideas to examine and argue with, you will want to get your hands on *Saturday Night, Sunday Morning: Singles and the Church*, by Nicholas B. Christoff.[2] (He is an American Lutheran Church minister, a live-in pastor and counselor in Chicago's largest apartment complex.)

Any program needs to be what the single adults themselves need and want, but encouragement and leadership from the church staff will be important in developing a program. One church I visited showed its real vitality when it sponsored a much-valued informal Bible study in a home on Sunday evenings after church. The singles rotated in bringing refreshments; they joined eagerly in discussion, opened their lives to each other, and found themselves enriched. They were deeply grateful to the sponsoring church.

7. Looking around a big conference table, I cannot guess, so I'll ask outright: are singles well represented on your official boards? Nic Christoff thinks one-third of you should be single, in proportion to the American population. Are there at least a few singles here, to keep you aware of single awarenesses, and sensitive to their sensitivities?

By the way, Nic Christoff thinks, too, that any church with a second pastor should see to it that a single person is hired as that second pastor. Does he have a useful suggestion?

8. Some of your people are "single" through the trauma of death or divorce. Are you making particular efforts to help these toward healing and new strength?

9. Is every single in your church a stand-in aunt or uncle to some family? Singles need involvement, close involvement, with families. They need to be giving warmth and caring and strength and joy to a family. They need to be receiving the same qualities from a family. The well-balanced single needs contact with little children, with adults of his own age, with older adults.

I could wish I had a transcript of a conversation I endured several years ago which a pastor — call him Pastor Blank, for in one area of his thinking he was very blank. He told me, with sizzling earnestness, how very much he wanted to build a family-centered church. Strong families. Loyal families. Christian families. For him, singles hardly seemed to deserve even a shrug. I don't recall now just how that conversation got started, and I don't recall just how it ended; I do recall that Pastor Blank left me battered and blue-bruised in spirit. He almost made me feel that any singles would deserve his antagonism rather than his pastorly care. Looking back, I wonder how many singles Pastor Blank drove away from his church. And I wonder how many of his family priorities would have been met more quickly, more permanently, if all the surrogate aunts and uncles he was ignoring had been recruited to help his young parents in their parenting.

With that wondering, try this one.

What might happen in a year's time if your church became known all over town, through your advertising and through your innovative programs, as "Tenth Avenue Church, where singles are really special"?

As one of the innovations, might you try a special service or a social event, now and then, to which families are permitted to come *only* if they bring a borrowed aunt or uncle for the occasion?

10. Is the Christian fellowship so alive in your church that syn-

thetic "family groups" sometimes form and re-form across the usual boundaries of age and married-single dividings?

Pretty Rayanne came back to the Greenville College campus a few months ago, glowing about the church she has found near her metropolitan bank job. A special joy, she told me earnestly, is her Bible study group which meets on Monday nights. It includes Rayanne herself; several youngish couples; an older woman who leads the group; one or two other singles. "It's my family there!" she told me happily. "They even had a birthday party for me before I came on vacation!" And it was clear that other events in Rayanne's busy life have to be scheduled around the Monday commitment.

In the singles program at Park Cities Church, Britton Wood reports that some "family" groups of five to eight mutually supportive single persons have been formed, and have been useful. The "family" may lunch together, go bowling together, telephone each other with community news, or meet to share Christian concerns.

11. Do your planning committees keep singles in mind when they schedule social events? Do you care whether the singles feel genuinely welcomed?

Some singles would say they feel at home and joyful within the sanctuary, but that they strangle with loneliness in the narthex. Some new widows would say that church events are the events that hurt most of all. And persons who are already feeling a little alienated or ostracized may not listen in total joy to an announcement of an all-church family picnic, for which each family is to bring thus and thus and thus. What instruction, they would ask, for the one-person units?

If Suzy Single gathers her courage and goes to the picnic, will she be glad she went?

12. One of the singles' continuing needs is a need for status: recognition, identity, belonging.

Do singles take part often in your worship services? Sing in your choirs? Usher in your aisles?

If you have church newsletters, do singles get cited often in the personal news? Do you mention their trips and conventions and job changes as often as you might? Family news, such as the wedding anniversaries and the christenings, may be easier to track down, but singles' news is also news.

Do you find ways to recognize the single for his unique worth and merits? Says Tim Stafford, "I've never heard anyone compliment a person for having created a good single life style."[3] Is such praise often being given among you? And the other praises that singles might deserve?

13. Do your people care about the singles' carings? When visiting

singles come to visit your services, or when regulars come for the thousandth time in a row, are they greeted only with hollow "How-are-you?" phrases? Are they greeted at all? Does someone *care* about Terry's housing problem, Jim's graduate school exams, Joni's dreadful boss, Jerry's excitement over a splendid new book he has just been reading? And are they becoming *Terry* and *Jim* and *Joni* and *Jerry* to the whole church, and not just "those singles"? Is *agapé* love reaching out to them, one by one by one?

Some single people would say that married and formerly married persons have only an atrophied gift for vicarious experience. Would there be grains of truth in that assertion? Married Alicia, they would say, is quick to tell everyone about her children's latest school grades, her new draperies, or the extraction of her molars — but she could talk with Single Samuel for half an hour and never learn that he was elected chairman of a city commission last week. "You're single," she seems to imply. "Nothing in your life could interest me." Or Married Minnie hurries through the narthex to talk with Married Mildred about chicken pox and pinafores and Little League; both Minnie and Mildred assume that nothing in their child-bound lives could interest Sally Single. Actually, Sally would be glad to be inter-ested, if they would let her. (Well, within limits she would be inter-ested; she doesn't need to know about the centrimetric progress of little Jackie's every tooth.)

I chuckle. I am remembering one particular Minnie, once upon a day. I had just entered a restaurant with a fat envelope in my eager hands: a contract for a book, with a very exciting letter accom-panying it. Before I could even read the publisher's letter, Minnie saw me and hurried to my table to join me. I thought for a moment that the meal might become a jovial little announcement party, but Minnie talked so steadily about so many things from her immediate world that I, quaking a little with inner laughter, spoke nothing more dramatic than "Umm-m-m" and "Oh?" and "Yes, probably." Every paragraph engrossed Minnie spoke made it clear that she had no time and no emotional energy, that day, to care about any of my carings.

14. What about helping singles from your church get to area or national conferences for singles?

Exciting things are happening at many Christian renewal centers here and there across the nation. For representatives from your church to attend a conference might be like flinging an electric switch, for new power and new light to touch your whole congregation.

Are your denominational offices (or synod, or diocese, or region, or district — whatever you have) giving leadership in organizing and directing such conferences? Do your singles here at Tenth Avenue know what is going on regionally or nationally? Is your local church leadership helping good things happen, beyond the local events?

"Good things" might well include creative and invigorating things that Christian singles do with other singles in addition to talking about singleness and all of its implications, of course. Maybe some of the best singles' conferences talk relatively little about singleness and relatively much about the Psalms and the Gospels; about photography or the trees of the Adirondacks; about the writings of C. S. Lewis; about sainthood.

You might like to urge people from your church to inquire about the singles' retreats or conferences at one of these conference centers while they plan their coming vacations. Each has been commended to me for offering special events for singles — and Christian renewal, personal renewal, for your singles may be a part of God's plan for renewal in your church.

* * * *

America's Keswick
Keswick Grove
Whiting, NJ 08759

Mount Hermon Christian Conference Center
Mount Hermon, CA 95041

The Firs Bible and Missionary Conference
4605 Cable Street
Bellingham, WA 98225

Word of Life International
Schroon Lake, NY 12870

Forest Home
Forest Falls, CA 92339

Mission Springs
1050 Lockhart Gulch Road
Santa Cruz, CA 95066

Pine Cove
Route 8
Tyler, TX 75701

Hume Lake Christian Camps
P.O. Box 2267
Fresno, CA 93720

Monadnock Bible Conference
Dublin Road
Jaffrey Center, NH 03454

Campus Crusade for Christ
Arrowhead Springs
San Bernardino, CA 92414

Gull Lake Bible and Missionary Conference
Box 1
Hickory Corners, MI 49060

I take a deep breath and look around this long walnut conference table again.

In brief: is God leading you toward some new thoughts about your potential ministry to the single persons in your community? Is he directing you toward some new dialogue with them, to know their needs? Toward new evangelism among them? Toward new uses of their energies, their abilities? Does Isaiah 35 describe the new currents of spiritual power which await your church? From place to place, the winds of the Spirit seem to be blowing these days, where people are thinking creatively about the place of the singles in the church. For you, too, may waters break out in the wilderness, and "streams in the desert!" For you, too, an ancient promise:

"And the ransomed of the Lord shall return, and come to Zion
with songs and everlasting joy upon their heads: they shall
obtain joy and gladness, and sorrow and sighing shall flee away."
(Isaiah 35:10)

That kind of joy sounds like a fruition from another Isaiah verse — Isaiah 41:10: "They helped every one his neighbour; and every one said to his brother, Be of good courage." In our day, the "brother" may be the alienated brother who has been paying dues to a hedonistic singles club, or going week by week to a raucous singles bar. Someone needs to take words of courage and hope, of forgiveness and redemption, of Christian love and fellowship, to millions of American singles. To the singles around your church.

Oh, yes, Dr. X, I'd be happy to linger for some discussion. And a cup of coffee would be delightful now, thank you very much. Yes, cream and sugar please. You were saying. . . .

Notes to Chapter 26

1. Britton Wood, *Single Adults Want to Be the Church, Too* (Nashville, Tennessee: Broadman Press, 1977).
2. Nicholas B. Christoff, *Saturday Night, Sunday Morning: Singles and the Church* (New York: Harper and Row, 1978). Another book to consult is William Lyon's *A Pew for One, Please: The Church and the Single Person* (New York: The Seabury Press, 1977).
3. Tim Stafford, *A Love Story: Questions and Answers on Sex* (Grand Rapids, Michigan: Zondervan Publishing House, 1977), p. 93.

Single Again: Widowed 27

A while ago, while I was filling a breakfast bowl with granola (of my own making, from the recipe Ruth Joseph gave me), and heating the teakettle for a mug of instant Highpoint, I reached for a place-mat. I chose one from the Audubon set of butterfly paintings, and looked at it very thoughtfully. How incredibly much more it means than it would have meant three years ago this morning! Then, it would have been an attractive bit of art, a nice touch of stimulus toward enjoying outdoor nature. Now. Now my eyes trace the wild blue phlox in the sketch, and my mind is back in Danny's woods; I walked there, and picked wild blue phlox there, during the first springtime after Danny's ashes were scattered there. Now. Now I look at the lovely big butterfly in the design (wide black wings, gold-edged, a patterning of bright blue dots) and for about the ten thousandth time I am glad that the butterfly is an ancient Christian symbol of the resurrection.

Three years ago tonight Danny Cade drove over from Vandalia for a desperately earnest prayer time with me. Not yet three years since murder ended his mortal life.

A while ago a new beam of morning sunlight caught my little photo of Danny, in a moment's transfiguration, and new gladness edged by pain shook me again, and new pain edged by gladness.

* * * *

And in their homes this morning, O Lord my God?

If such emotion still whirls and glows inside me, since death ended a friendship with one of my students, what about them? The widowed ones.

The new-widowed, still stunned and reeling through first incredulities. The older women, 20 years alone, and more. The men who struggle to be both father and mother to their children. The five-years-long lonely, for whom five years seems more like five thousand. How is it with them?

Be with them in their now, whatever it is, O Lord my God! If I could talk with them each one, and ask gently how it is with their now, and listen for a little while to the ones who would like for me to listen. . . . If I could. . . .

*   *   *   *

In one way, much of what I am talking over with all of the singles touches you. You were "I," and then for a space of your life you were "we," and now, as day paces after day and day paces after day, you are again an "I." (Of course, if you have children at home it is "I/we," and that has a differing dimension.) What the other singles face in their ways, to some degree and with some differences you must face in your ways. And I hope that you will gain ideas and resources from my various conversations with them. But you are you.

Do you want to talk with me a little? Do you want to know what I think about as I catch step with you and walk a distance with you in your dark valley? Do you want to know what I am seeing in these forests, and hearing in these storm winds?

Well, first, to note that you are accompanied by a whole troop of rememberings. You never, never journey alone. And thank God for the rememberings! They can be too much sought after, until yesterdays try to become a substitute for the now and the new, but they can also be a good and joyful source for constant gratitudes. The books he liked, the tree he planted, the first corsage he sent, the trip to Mexico with him, the caress-inflection when he, awakening, spoke your name. Thank God for the flick of a special remembering, in the midst of the absence that is like another epidermis over your entire self. I think of my friend Fran, who told me once with a lilt and a chuckle that her daughter Betty had a very special place in her affection, because while she was dressing hurriedly to get to the hospital for Betty's arrival, her Jim had told her that she was *very* beautiful. She didn't know then how very soon he would be unable to give her other spoken admirations, but she put that shining one away in the treasuries, and it had obviously come out many, many times within her grateful fingers.

Some rememberings you won't ever share with any one on earth, naturally. Some you will tell to a few, as Fran told me about Jim's lovely word to her. Some you will linger over at one time, and some at another.

Before we go on, let me suggest a widening out of the tentative and "some of this, some of that" attitude I am suggesting. Each person on God's earth is a different person. Each bereavement is a new and separate bereavement. What helps you may not help another, and what helps another may not help you. If a friend tries to push you into using crutches that are not your size, maybe you need other crutches, or other friends. Maybe the crutches will be just the right fit for next month, or next year. Once, I remember, when an acquaintance talked to me with a fierce eagerness to be helpful and to make me see from her seeing, I could only dab away tears and say, and repeat, "I will have to grope my way." Afterward, I could tell God about her, and reach for his hand, and let him carry both me and the dreadful crutches she had tried so hard to offer. If one thing I say to you isn't helpful, will you go on to the next, and the next?

My first thought, then: thank God for the rememberings. Big ones, little ones. Maybe especially the tiny, tiny ones, that dart through your mind like humming birds through breeze-bright mornings.

My next thought is more vast than my hands know how to take hold of. I'll try it like this: for the Christian, the closer death comes to us, the nearer we come to Immortal Reality. Man is more than mortal, though we often forget it in the hurry of our daily now, of getting and spending, of job and schooling. When death touches a casual friend, the veil trembles. When a neighbor, a relative, a loyal friend is summoned, the veil is shaken and seems thinner. When the dearest of all goes from us, we may almost feel ourselves on Patmos with St. John, and looking over his shoulders. "I don't know, I don't know," we may tell others, or tell our own questionings, "but I know that God is, and I have trusted my dear one to him, and I am utterly confident that life is eternal and love is immortal, as the old rituals of the Christian church have told us." And there can be a radiant, durable joy in the knowing. To some it may come more slowly, to others more swiftly: the joy of our confidence in the immortal.

Because of it, what we have previously known of Christian faith and experience may now seem, in retrospect, to be very pale and immature. Like the chambered nautilus in Oliver Wendell Holmes' poem, the Christian soul can be building new and stately mansions as it works its way through grief.

Our consciousness of Forever and our turnings to the God of Forever can constantly link with the gratitudes, with deep praise to God for what one has had. In my measure, I know it can; on a Wednesday I shall never forget, surely, as long as I remember anything, several faculty and church friends stopped by to talk, to voice words of prayer in my living room. The news of Danny Cade's death had come on Tuesday night. "There is such radiance, though," I kept saying to this one and this one, "in having known him, in having worked with him." And through succeeding months, as new kinds of pain linked hands with other pain, the radiance came and came again, and I praised God. And I praise him, now, again, after a new sunbeam touched a little photo this morning.

Near the end of *A Grief Observed*, C. S. Lewis recorded his new perception (after the numbness, the shattering, the terrible gropings) of the role of praise: "Praise is the mode of love which always has some element of joy in it. Praise in due order; of Him as the giver, of her as the gift. Don't we in praise somehow enjoy what we praise, however far we are from it? I must do more of this. I have lost the fruition I once had of H. And I am far, far away in the valley of my unlikeness, from the fruition which, if His mercies are infinite, I may some time have of God. But by praising I can still, in some degree, enjoy her, and already, in some degree, enjoy Him."[1]

C. S. Lewis brings me directly to my next topic. All of us can thank God for rememberings; all of us can praise Him for the "intimations of immortality." For some, there is another kind of praise which I mention hesitantly, for different persons' experiences differ very, very greatly. If you, too, have been granted moments of knowing a continuing presence, you will want me to say: praise God, praise God for those moments.

Before the end of his grief notebooks, Lewis recorded that he sensed one night a moment, "incredibly unemotional," of "the impression of her *mind* momentarily facing my own." "Certainly the reverse of what is called 'soulful,' " he went on. "Not at all like a rapturous reunion of lovers. Much more like getting a telephone call or a wire from her about some practical arrangement. Not that there was any 'message' — just intelligence and attention. No sense of joy or sorrow. No love even, in our ordinary sense. No un-love. I had never in any mood imagined the dead as being so — well, so businesslike. Yet there was an extreme and cheerful intimacy. . . . Wherever it came from, it has made a sort of spring cleaning in my mind. The dead could be like that . . . I'm almost scared at the adjectives I'd have to use. Brisk? cheerful? keen? alert? intense? wide-awake? Above all, solid. Utterly reliable. Firm. There is no nonsense about the dead."[2]

Lewis was carefully not venturing on any undue generalizations about the afterlife on the basis of the moment of cognition he had experienced, and he had not sought it. (Earlier, he had thought that if he "got what seemed like an assurance" of her presence, he would not believe it.)[3] Yet he was clearly very grateful for the moment. A valid attitude, surely, for what has happened to some other bereaved persons: a strong sense of the continuing identity, presence, and cognition of the one who is now in Forever.

"I feel as though I could just take her hand and show her all these flowers that have come," Minta Tenney Secord told me, with an incandescence in her voice, while we were at the funeral home after the death of her sister, Dr. Mary A. Tenney.

"I feel as though" may be for others of us — as it was then for Mrs. Secord, as it was for his cognition-moment for C. S. Lewis — one of the aspects of the impinging of Forever against our now.

I myself thank God, often and often, that he has permitted me a good many times of "I feel as though." As though Danny himself were standing right beside me, consoling me for what I was facing in the first weeks after his going. As though he were turning this corner of this little street with me, while I hiked there. As though the glory of a sunset had an additional glory. I speak of a quiet joy, not of anything "spooky" or weird. Not at all.

I know that I am a moderately imaginative person, and I have not wanted to give undue credence to these touches of luminous joy; I have spoken of them only a very little, thus far, except in my poem notebooks, and some awed moments I shall perhaps never describe to anyone on this earth. This much I have wanted to say in order to say this: if you have, often or ever, a sense of a presence, why not thank God for it? If you have an impulse to tell her "Good Morning" as you walk past her desk, why not tell her "Good Morning"? If you feel like talking your day over with him as you drive home through the twilight, why not talk it over?

Sheldon Vanauken in his very memorable book, *A Severe Mercy,* tells, among his other carefully honest tellings about his wife, Jean (nicknamed "Davy"), of a particular day in Lincoln, when he sensed Jean's presence in an extraordinary way and for one final time, more than two years after her death. "In later times," he says, "I was to think of it as the last thing *we* did." This he describes for himself as "The Second Death," bringing with it "Davy's withdrawal toward the Mountains of Eternity."[4] For you also it may be as for Vanauken: a great sense of conversation-close presence for a while, and then a termination of that sense. If so, to praise God for what one has had — all that one has had — would certainly be a right praising. The familiar saying is true: What I had, I have.

Now, on to a variety of topics, if we might.

In spite of the dozens of books that have appeared and keep appearing on the good Christian marriage, not so much is being said — not yet — on good singleness, whether apart from matrimony, or after it. I hope that your friends are giving you helpful and timely thoughts, and your church.

If your loss is new, I could hope that you might find your way to the literature stand of an Episcopal church near you, or send an order note to Forward Movement Publications (412 Sycamore

Street, Cincinnati, Ohio 45202) for a little booklet, "For Those Who Mourn." I came upon a copy just a few days after Danny's funeral, and it spoke to me at deep levels. Never, ever, have I spent two or three dimes to better purpose, I'm sure!

When you are ready for them, accounts of other persons' journeys through their own dark valleys may be rod and staff to you. I have mentioned Vanauken's *A Severe Mercy* and C. S. Lewis's *A Grief Observed*. (In truth, I have always wished that Lewis had written another notebook full before he stopped his record; it might have gone on to show us more of the landscapes with rainbows and later verdure, as well as the night and the storm. But it is a deeply valuable book.) Catherine Marshall's *A Man Called Peter* and *To Live Again* have been a strength to many readers. The works of Elizabeth Kübler-Ross, a psychiatrist who has specialized in the study of death and dying, have many valuable thoughts and profound insights, although Dr. Kübler-Ross would leave many Christian readers unsatisfied at some points. A St. Louis journalist, Clarissa Start, wrote a very personal account in *When You're a Widow* (Concordia Publishing House, 1968) and was able to give her own story useful links with what many widows experience. Bea Decker's *After the Flowers Have Gone* (as told to Gladys Kooiman) not only tells of Mrs. Decker's bereavement, but also of her effort in organizing THEOS.

Her book is available through THEOS offices, 10521 Lindberg Avenue, Pittsburgh, Pennsylvania 15235, as well as from the Zondervan Publishing Company.

Have you heard about THEOS? The initials stand for "They Help Each Other Spiritually," as well as spelling the Greek word for God. After losing her own husband in 1962, Bea Decker felt inner commands to reach out to other persons with problems like her own and started building THEOS. It is a Christian self-help fellowship group, for young and middle-aged widows or widowers and their families. Chapters now exist in a good many communities across the United States and Canada; members meet to discuss the topics that widows and widowers would discuss: loneliness, legal matters, children, finances, other practical problems. A monthly newsletter goes out to all participants, and weekend conferences are held periodically. These events have been co-sponsored by the Pittsburgh Pastoral Institute and Guideposts Associates, Inc.

If you would like to have more information immediately, pick up your telephone and dial (412) 243-4299.

Sometimes, then, to *read* will be a therapy.

Sometimes, for some persons, to *write* is also a therapy. If you are new in grief, writing may be a particular therapy — though it can also help one find waymarks as a journey lengthens out into decade-long distances. For example, Sheldon Vanauken's Davy died in 1955, and his account of her going did not come to publication until 1977. If you are easily verbal, you may already have said in letters to close friends what you want to be saying. Maybe, though, a journal which is only between you and God would have its usefulness. In a kind of journal, the poet Tennyson recorded for some seventeen years his meditations after the death of his college friend Arthur Hallam, and shaped them into his great poem *In Memoriam.* (Another to add to the list of readings?)

You will be expecting me to say that I found writing a help after the death of my young friend Danny. Yes, I did. I am always jotting down all sorts of things. For ten years, I suppose I have seldom taken any trip by bus or plane or train without having a jotting journal handy. Who knows when the poem will come? For months before Danny's death, I had been jotting down prayer thoughts about him, and memoranda about conferences with him, and my joy at the progress of his brilliant mind. My unformed rough jottings continued and continued, after his death, and often they shaped themselves into poems. One day perhaps I will release to some publisher the accumulation of poems from the notebooks. Sometimes I didn't write at all; sometimes the brinks of tears were much too close, and I needed not to dissolve too totally, in the midst of my teaching and other commitments. But often, often, the notebooks were a great resource for my spirit.

To read, maybe?

To write, maybe?

To resume and continue living, certainly. "Ay," said Hamlet, "there's the rub." How can one pick up pieces when an alabaster vase has been shattered? How can one rebuild a house after hurricanes?

For one thing, maybe, by regular conferences with a pastor or a more mature widow? Perhaps to set up a schedule and see such a counselor as regularly, after an amputation through death, as you would see a physician during other convalescences? Maybe every few weeks at first, and then at lengthening intervals?

Maybe by some memorial gifts, carefully chosen and significant? At the funeral, perhaps friends were told that they might make certain memorial gifts. Maybe now a very special gift, which you will arrange with more of an opportunity to think about it, will be a therapy to you as well as a lasting memorial to him. Anyone who has not been through the grief process may think that "in memory of" is an empty phrase. And it may be, in some callous fund-raising organizations. But love and thought and prayer about a memorial can be really important to the donor's growth as a person, growth into emotional strength. Recently a missionary nurse told me, with incredulous awe, about a $2,000 contribution she had just received for hospital equipment to take back to Taiwan. It was a memorial gift, a mother's gift in memory of her child. Having given it will heal and heal, in the mother's mind as well as in the hospital corridors! One person might think of a memorial tree, for campus landscaping; of books for a church library; of a scholarship fund. Whatever it is, the feasibility of it should of course be checked first with the proposed recipient; some gifts do not fit easily nor appropriately into existing channels of financing and planning.

Sometimes a memorial deed may be more right than a check written or letters on a plaque. A special kindness done to an international student might be "in memory of," though you are the only one who knows it. To place a lovely wreath of yew twigs on his grave for his birthday might be a good memorial; to invite for dinner a young family who seldom get to eat out might be a better memorial.

Let's think a little further, now that I've just mentioned a dinner, about your invitings.

As I think about all the widows and widowers I have ever known, beginning with my tiny white-haired grandmother and continuing to a minutes-ago telephone conversation, it seems to me that St. Paul's phrase about being "given to hospitality" is a remarkably clear dividing line between those who have been the happiest, the most contented, and those who were the self-pitiers, the selfish, the narrowed. If other people come and go from your door, you're not as likely to recede into pathological grief.

I think of gracious Alice Hoiles, in whose home I spent two of my college summers. Her Sunday breakfasts were a pleasant simplicity, but how people enjoyed them! She and I would set some things out in readiness on Saturday night. On Sunday morning, we would carry trays and the Silex coffeemakers out to the little paved terrace in her back yard, and wrens or cardinals or mocking birds provided the background music. People didn't go away thinking of her as widow, needing commiserations; they thought of grace and wisdom and courtesy and courage.

I think of a home where I have often been welcomed with a cup of hot wassail, from a jar kept ready-mix-full of blended instant tea and spice and Tang. My handicapped hostess is not able to handle meals, but she is able to give love and welcoming attention.

I think of Christmas dinner, this past Christmas, when several of us brought our casseroles and pans and jars for a festive meal in front of Mrs. Wilson LaDue's fireplace. Sequential hospitalizations have made her put aside her cookbooks, but her home zestfully, eagerly welcomes many comers.

In contrast, Mrs. A. In twenty years and more that I knew her, did she ever make a cup of tea or hot chocolate, even, for anyone except herself? A well-hidden secret, if she did! Nor, to tell the truth, did we ever feel that she wished she might.

Mrs. B. A superb cook, people said, while Mr. B. was her inspiration; afterward, planning menus for one seemed to take all of her attention.

Mrs. C. "Come and see me sometime," she urged, and I said that I would. I truly meant to, but I never did, and I never got to know the warmth of her heart, the sparkle of her mind. If she had telephoned and asked if I would be free for tea next Sunday at four, I probably would have made myself free. And the lines of sadness might have been a little less deeply etched in her face.

Mrs. D., though. The fame of her hot rolls among college girls who knew her brings a lilt to their voices when they reminisce about dormitories and college courses.

As you can, as is right and good in the present chapter of your life, do you share yourself and your home and your wisdoms through your hospitality?

Along with the invitings, and out beyond them, are you continuing to make new overtures in friendship? People you knew during the married era (and long before) are good to keep knowing. What about the new encounters? People at church, people you have been bowling with, people in civic groups? Someone you chat with during a Sierra Club tour and invite over the next Thursday for coffee?

And already I am suggesting another query. What about the new experiences, the new opportunities? Circumstances vary in every possible permutation, of course, but to be single again can make things possible which just could not have been done during homemaker years. There's Julia. If you had talked about a trip to Mexico a few years ago, or to the Canadian Rockies, she would have smiled placidly and told you she was not interested. Her housework kept her very busy. A while after William's death, though, she started looking at travel folders. Then she did more than look. And now she has been on junkets all around the globe, into countries she did not know were on the map.

There is Miss Lillian Carter, who went to India with the Peace Corps.

There's Celia, who started back to college within months after her husband's sudden going. "Just to take some courses," she assured me when we talked for a long time over her first registration. "Something to fill up some of the empty space." Not a degree program. And, horrors, no, not a teacher's certificate! But she soon found that the ozone of literature courses was her right kind of climate, and she did get the degree and the certificate. She was the only one I've ever had

choose to write a term paper on obscure poet Thomas Lovell Bed-
does, and it was a brilliant paper.

There is my mother. When Daddy died, she had been his faithful
nurse for the nine years that he lived, semi-invalid, after his open-
heart surgery. Before that, she had been looking after turkeys and
lambs and colts and crops and children on a western Kansas farm. In
widowhood, some of her previous longings to be in active Christian
service surfaced, and she made contact with a rescue mission in
Chicago. Yes, they felt that she could be helpful. And — over the
rather dismayed protests of her protective children — she went off to
Chicago for several different stints of several months at a time.
When, reluctantly, she decided that she should stop before she
became a burden to the staff, she had gathered a whole set of new
prayer topics; a store of experiences to remember; a valued group of
new friends whom she had worked with at the Olive Branch Mission.

Not every widow should be a volunteer worker in a mission. There
is no one new interest for everyone. But thank God for the new
interests, and for the new persons who find them!

In that small doxology, I am now including Mrs. Wilson LaDue.
In the last few years, since Uncle Wilson has been gone, Aunt Mary
has turned to gardening. (The titles are honorary; in affection, they
became aunt and uncle to half of Bond County and to decades of
students.) Aunt Mary can't use hoe and spade and fertilizer herself,
but she pores over seed catalogs, makes deals with muscular helpers,
and then triumphantly displays the harvest of what she has super-
vised. Her gardens have brought zucchini and tomatoes, parsley and
green beans and peppers, to visitor after visitor. There is a Ceres-like
glow about her as she puts her splendid vegetables into brown bags
for us; one thinks of a Mother Nature figure, filling cornucopias.

That new gardening interest, she would quickly assure you, is a
part of Mrs. LaDue's commitment to victorious Christian living.
I have heard her speak of "happy widowhood" as a rightful way of
life. She has not come lightly to that term. The agony of her bereavement was immense, and to be alive is still to miss Uncle Wilson with
all of her emotional intensities. But her life reaches out constantly to
other lives, pouring strengths into them, and her dependence upon
God is utter.

New interests, then, as a part of the inner growing that can happen
to widows.

And new learnings, too. New books, new magazines, new study
projects.

Last fall when Parents' Weekend happened on our campus, one
grandmother of a freshman came along. She saw me at a campus
dinner and talked to me, with delight and splendid elation, about

the reading she had just been doing because of her granddaughter's work in my course. In a compilation of the great literature of the Western world, we had read part of the book of *Job*. On hearing about the project, the grandmother had been stimulated to get out a study Bible and some other study materials, and she was more than pleased to report on her new knowledge. What a tonic!

In contrast, I think of a time when I, just back from my first time on the continent, was taken by a mutual friend to a neighbor's home. The neighbor had no shred of interest in Venice or the Rhine River or Paris or Capri; my small overtures of comment dropped straight to the floor one by one, like pricked balloons. I was amused but not amused when she asked with some excitement about yet other neighbors, and whether they were back from their visit to their Michigan relatives. Michigan did not invite new learnings, and she could cope with Michigan, but to think one thought about Venice or Capri would have required some small opening of her closed mind, and all its apertures were rusted shut. Or so it seemed to me, with cathedrals and Alpine glaciers and castles and mosaics still a very euphoric jumble inside my mind.

To read.

To write.

To entertain.

To find the new interest, to know the new knowing.

What else?

Well, in a way that only a widow can, to become a special instrument of comfort to other persons.

In a recent telephone chat, Aunt Mary (our same Aunt Mary LaDue of whom I keep speaking) told me about a poem she has clipped to her refrigerator door, which she wanted to share with me. In mentioning it, she mentioned a habit she has fallen into, of mailing some of her favorite bits of poetry to the newest widows among her acquaintances in our town. To reach and to reach the hand of sturdy help — who could know how much it means?

The Reverend Lyle C. Hillegas — formerly the president of Westmont College; formerly and still my good friend — impressed upon me one of the principles of his belief: that God brings into our lives people to whom he would have us minister; they are not always people we would choose, says Lyle. I think he is right. And I think that widows or widowers, who have been through the furnace fires of bereavement, may be the precision-tuned metals for some ministries which no one else can perform.

For the Christian, the death of a spouse will surely become a time of new covenants with God, of new explorings in ultimate meanings, of new submissions to his sovereign will. When the greatest grief comes that can come, he is there. His relationship to the mourner may be baffling for a while. (C. S. Lewis found it so, for a while; his gropings, his yelling out against God, which he so candidly reported in *A Grief Observed,* have been very hard for some of his Christian readers to understand.) Whether one comes to the realization quickly or very, very slowly, we can be sure that the one who goes away goes into the loving hands of God, and the one who stays is also in his very hand.

"Why?" the mourner may be screaming, inside himself or aloud. "Why did God take *my* dearest one?" To such a mourner, I would pass along a comment from a conversation on the second floor landing of the Hogue Hall stairs one day. I was mentioning to colleague Dan Jensen a friend's outcry of just that sort, and Dan looked very thoughtful. "I don't think God ever *takes* anyone," he said quickly. "I think God *receives* him." There's a difference. We are within his love, when accident comes and the laws of physics are at work; when disease comes and the laws of biology continue to exert their forces; when sin puts weapons into murdering hands. He made us for himself, and he receives us to himself.

As for those who stay, a few minutes with a concordance will remind us that widows have a special place in God's care and love and concern. As he loves, we should love; widows are, to us also, his dear and special people.

*   *   *   *

It is evening. This morning began with blue phlox and a black butterfly on a placemat. Before thought drifts off into dreaming, I think I shall light for a while my tall triple-angel candle. While that symbol glows, I'll read again from my battered copy of the booklet, "For Those Who Mourn," and I shall commend to God's love some of the people I know who mourn. I shall remember that those of us who are still in now are privileged to worship him, we are told, in the company of "angels and archangels, and all the company of heaven." And I shall be glad, very glad, and at peace.

Notes to Chapter 27

1. C. S. Lewis, *A Grief Observed* (New York: The Seabury Press, 1961), p. 49.
2. Lewis, *A Grief Observed,* pp. 57-59.
3. Lewis, *A Grief Observed,* p. 57.
4. Sheldon Vanauken, *A Severe Mercy* (New York: Harper and Row, 1977), pp. 231-232.

Single Again: Divorced **28**

Dear Margaret,

Oh, my *very* dear Margaret! How I wish you were right here in my living room! How I would glow, if the next ringing of the doorbell were at the touch of your fingertip. You have been in my mind over and over and over since we talked on Thursday evening. Long before dawn this morning you were in my mind. Long distance telephone wires are great, but they do have their limitations. I just wish I could fling a greeting arm around you, and grip your hand now and then while we talk, and hand you the Kleenex box when you need it, and pour you some Lemon Lift tea, or a cupful of my special peppermint coffee. My dear. My dear.

Well, let's talk anyway, in this fashion. And call me again sometime soon?

I wrote a short story once which I titled "The Ugliest Word." In it, I had one character asserting that *divorce* is the ugliest word in the English language, and truly I believe that it is. We get angry about divorce statistics when they are news items in the newspapers, but when someone we love is a statistic, the word stabs and tears. I feel now as though someone had been beating me with fists, and what I feel isn't a thousandth part of what you have been going through for these months, I know. Oh, Margaret.

Look, let's. . . .

I interrupt myself. There's a good verb, "look." Let me toss it in several directions with you, Margaret?

First, to look backward.

It hurts most awfully, I know, and there will soon be times to guard against the backward look. (Remember Lot's wife? The parallel isn't complete, at all, but for all of us the backward look can sometimes immobilize.) But right now you probably do need to do some very careful looking backward, preferably, I'd think, with a counselor whom you will see frequently for a while. From what you said of your pastor, maybe he is the one. Maybe a mature woman you know at church? Maybe a professional counselor?

If you can be starkly honest with yourself and get out into daylight exactly what became infected in your marriage, it will surely help the healing processes. With or without a counselor to help you, can you use some scribble notebooks and get into writing some enumerations of what it was in you, and what it was in Jerry, and what it was in other people, and what it was in events, that culminated in those pieces of paper the courts have now processed saying that you are not Mrs. Jerry any more?

Some of the things you will jot down will reach back into your dating time, and maybe on back into your teens and into your childhood. You always adored your father. Did you, maybe, try too hard to push Jerry into being a father-figure for you? Did it bother you when he didn't handle a household crisis in just the way your dad would have handled it? You said that Jerry started going out with other women quite a while ago, and I remember what you said about the grimy episode at the motel last August. But what were the causes behind the causes? Forgive me; let me be cruel to be kind. Did his early rovings coincide with your stint in city politics? Was he insecure about your affection for him?

In college, he was so very handsome and so much desired that jealousy nibbled at you. Did it keep on living in your kitchen cupboards?

Ask yourself the questions under the questions, and the questions behind the questions. (Maybe you are already well on the way through and beyond this looking into the past; if so — well, hallelujah and thank the Lord.)

Let's talk a little about why it is so very important that you do this exhuming. One of the deepest reasons would be suggested by a very significant chapter, "Forgiveness: The Aughts and Anys," in Catherine Marshall's book *Something More*.[1] (Let me suggest that you read her chapter half a dozen times, and soon.) The basis she works from is Mark 11:25: "And when ye stand praying, forgive, if ye have ought against any. . . ." She suggests very specific listing of the resentments, the grievances we have against anyone, anyone, and then the placing of those grievances in God's own hands as a needful step in our growth and wholeness as human beings, as Christians. Well, you have whole trunks full of "aughts" against Jerry, against his flirty women friends, against his family. If you can specify them to yourself and then specify them to God, and keep on putting all of them into his all-capacious, all-loving hands, you will find releases for your emotional self that don't now seem possible. I'm sure of it.

And you will need to think about your own bloopers, your nasty attitudes, your disposition sins, too, dear Margaret. You need God's forgiveness, and you need to be able to forgive yourself. That time . . . and that time . . . and that time. . . .

The more candor you can have now, the more it can help in the healing processes inside yourself, and in the help you will be able to extend to other hurting people in times ahead, and in all of your own new relationships that you will be building.

As you think and pray and make lists of "aughts" and commit, there is a principle of retroactive forgiveness which can be at work. Ruth Carter Stapleton has talked about "the healing of the memory."[2] Whether just in her manner or not, you can indeed invite the Lord Jesus Christ to be present with you as you think back to painful times, harsh scenes, dreadful episodes. You can ask his forgiveness for your part, and ask his love to encircle Jerry's part.

We started a while ago with the verb of looking. To look backward obviously leads quickly to a look within, and a look at other people. At Jerry. A forgiving look.

Are you clenching your fingers and gritting your teeth, dear Margaret? For Christ's will to happen in you, my dear, for his love to be at work in you, be open to letting his love flow through you in forgiving ways. You can't work it up of your own willing. It has to be his miracle. But it can come. You can be like a faucet which turns it off and turns it off, or you can open yourself to Grace and let God's love flow through you.

If you don't, bitterness and harshness and scorn can fill your days and you will become a lesser person than you are now, lesser than he means you to be. I think some of the ugliest, harshest tones I have ever encountered in human speech have been from divorced women; their anger was "justified," but it smudged and deformed them as it came through them. Dear Margaret, I don't want *you* to become snarling and vicious and emotionally deformed. Not you, not you.

You're protesting that I don't understand, at all; I've never lived with a Jerry and suffered from a Jerry and been humiliated by a Jerry. And that is true. But I do know something, Margaret, of the miracle of God's forgiving love. May I say a few small words? In July of 1975, a brilliant young former student of mine was murdered; I had been counseling with him, praying with and for him, sharing poetry with him, sharing his aspirations with him, and his death shook every corpuscle in my veins. In the course of events, I was a prosecution witness at the trial of each of the three young men who had, together, killed Danny Cade. When I saw those three faces successively in three court rooms, his very murderers, I truly did know the current of God's forgiving love. Truly, and in way that surprised me. I did know myself to be a faucet it flows through. I could pray (and I do, continuingly) that good might come to them, that God would forgive and touch and use them. Grief was still a daily, hourly agony, but it was an agony somehow cleansed by his presence.

"Father, forgive them, for they know not what they do" can be prayed daily, dear Margaret, as it was once prayed from a cross.

Sometime, you might like to read the "Pompilia" section in Robert Browning's great work, *The Ring and the Book*. Have you heard of it? It's no easy poem; you will need to dig for meaning, but it's worth the pickaxes. To summarize in tiniest brevity: Browning tells of young Pompilia, fatally stabbed by hired criminals at her husband's direction, after she had suffered many evil and cruel things from him. As she speaks from her deathbed, her pure innocence of spirit and her capacity for forgiving incredible wrong are from Christ himself. And what happened in Pompilia can find parallel in other lives that forgive great wrong.

To look back, then. To look within. To look outward, at other people. And to look upward, to our Lord, who is the center of all the looking, both for your desperate now and as the years will move onward.

Important looking upward, believe me, will often come as you look at your Bible.

Once when a student came to my home for a depth-level conferring, we read together some verses from Romans which had been much in my thought just before he arrived. He was deeply moved, and a sob caught in his voice as he said, "That is the first time the Bible has ever spoken directly to me."

The Bible is always ready to speak — the Lord is always ready to speak through his written Word — as we let him. Maybe you will like to work through Isaiah, or the Psalms, or the New Testament, with a special color of marking as key passages speak to your now. Before I went to Israel for a Christmas, I used a green pen for special attention and marked up my copy of the Revised Standard Version of the Bible with notes about all the spots I would be visiting. A green pen, for your now? A brown pen? More parallel would be the way I marked the Psalms once when certain desperate intercessions were going up from my home (yes: desperate, desperate) and I prayed my way through the entire Psalter during one long weekend. I look at Isaiah 43 right now, Margaret, and think about it for you. I look at various New Testament verses, and ask God to use them with you.

Talk with him, Margaret, daily and momently. He knows your raw pain, your angers, your fears. He knows the hurts that you may not even be able to pull out into daylight.

Maybe it will sometimes be a strength to you to write some letters to the Lord — to jot down the prayers of the moment. Sometimes the written prayer helps us to know our needs, our faith and our unfaith, more then we have known. In prayer he guides us.

And that leads toward the next look: *look forward.* When years have gone by, when this agony of now is long, long past, you will still need the *look forward.* We shall all need it, until we look right across the final river and into God's throne room.

I have been thinking and thinking, Margaret, about the forward look for you. (As I said, I was thinking about you long before dawn this morning!) I've been thinking about other women I have known, and men too, who have been working their way back from divorce. Let me mention a whole cluster of ideas. Some may be more useful than others. Pitch out, for now, the ones that are like crutches that aren't the right size at all.

Would Philippians 3:13-14 be a good motto for your now? Forgetting. Reaching. The past is not to become a void nor a blank; we're not intended to become amnesia victims. But there can be a forward focus which is right and good and wholesome.

And another motto? Try 2 Corinthians 1:3-4: "Blessed be God, even the Father of our Lord Jesus Christ, the Father of mercies, and the God of all comfort; who comforteth us in all our tribulation, that we may be able to comfort them which are in any trouble, by the comfort wherewith we ourselves are comforted of God." There is a ministry ahead for you, as he comforts you and you pass the comfort right on to other persons. "Any trouble." That's pretty inclusive. Through your help from him, you can become a helping person, in ways we can't possibly now predict.

While you are on your way to that, can you find your way into a small group of Christians who meet regularly for sharing and caring? Through your church or through other contacts, will that be possible? A little Bible study group? To be with a few persons you can really trust, with whom you can talk at deep levels, will be a great strength to you, and you to them.

Along with that, establishing and maintaining contact lines with a number of different people is important. Not that you will talk about Jerry to all of them, or to any of them; not that you will discuss the stages of your recuperation explicitly. But as you talk with Marie about recipes and Susan about patterns and Beth about new books to read and the Smiths about politics, you will be maintaining your emotional "support systems," — and they need maintaining. (I'm not thinking now about the other kinds of conversations you will need too, with lawyer and insurance man and tax consultant and all the rest. Can you find relatives or church friends to advise you about advisers, in the practical parts of life that you now face alone?)

Close sharing with a few is important, and broadening warm rap-

port with a good many. A word, though. Sometimes a divorcée or
widow finds a contact so helpful that she leans too hard, and smashes
or smothers a friendship. It can happen to any human being, of
course. In eighth grade and in high school, you probably watched the
"best friend" associations that went sour. But there's a greater need
for leaning when you are "single again," and the hunger for companionship as well as for someone to listen to you is so very great.
I'm thinking right now of — well, you wouldn't know her, but I'll call
her Cathy. Since her divorce, she spends most of her time alone or
with a few of her relatives. If any friend greets her on the street or
drops in at her apartment, Cathy's so insecure she usually gushes and
clings, until the friend feels awkward.

Can you think of your new singleness, Margaret, as a time for new
opportunities?

You will be shaping a new lifestyle, a piece at a time. Think of the
new opportunities that will be reaching out toward you.

Think, for example, of your opportunity to cherish and enhance
your secondary loves, now that the primary love is taken from you.
Your grandmother would value deeply, deeply, more notes and little
gifts and other remembrances. When did you last send her flowers
or a brooch or a sweater, just for love's sake? Your Uncle Bill. Not
many trickles of affection touch his life now. Your brothers. You
have a vast capacity for love inside you, and it needs to pour out and
to pour out. Remember what the doctors told your Mom when she
had her cardiac problem? — that exercise keeps little arteries stretch-
ing, and helps the one that's blocked? Your heart will function better
if a great many little arteries are exercised and keep opening, and
being stretched!

Have you thought about the ministry that you can have through
having people in at your apartment? (Maybe the guests you invite
will be arteries of third-level smallness.) Some you will invite,
frankly, because you feel you need them; the stimulus of congenial
persons is a worthy quest. Some you will invite because they have
needs: college students who would value your cooking; older widows
from your church, who would love being honor guests; young couples who would appreciate a change of scene from their own walls.

Maybe, maybe you will come eventually to have a special ministry, Margaret, among young wives. Early married years are stressful
for everyone. With your tact and grace, you may be able to strengthen
some other girls when fabric frays and strains. You know where
some of the danger spots are. You may become a very special
encourager, confidante, emergency baby-sitter, resourse person.

In that way and in other ways, are you starting to find new roles
of service in your church? As a matter of fact, you might want to

think about attending a different church now. For you, will it be therapeutic to stay among people you and Jerry have known together, or would it be more therapeutic to build a new set of contacts in your new singleness? You will want to think about it, and not to rush a decision — on that, or on scores of other decidings. One friend of mine — call her Kay — says it was one of the greatest things she did after she became single again, to establish a new church home; it helps Kay in living out Philippians 3:13, in forgetting the things which are behind.

Whether it's the old church or a new one, what about new ways to participate? It might help the whole set of adjustments if you, who have never sung in a church choir, would show up among the altos. (You sang in oratorios in college; remember?) Or the library committee, or a new class to teach. Newness, for now. New ways to let God's love course through you to meet human need.

What about new hobbies or new activities, now that you are single again? You will continue your job, I assume, but what about some evening classes at the university? Some correspondence courses in short story writing? Have you ever joined the local branch of the A.A.U.W.? New opportunities, in your new chapter of living.

Now, a couple of things to think about as you look in *all* these ways of looking: backward, inward, outward, upward, forward.

There will be the necessary tears and the inescapable sighs, but can you cultivate a good crop of chuckles and laughter, too? I was glad to hear some giggles in your voice on Thursday evening as you told about the awkward dividings of the wedding gifts. Laughter is one way of praising God, and of bringing joy to others. Do you take any newspapers or magazines with good cartoons? How about clipping them more often, and using them in your mail?

Along with humor, to live daily and daily with gratitude. Yes, dear lass, I'm saying gratitude. Praise. Thanksgiving. (Go ahead; get some Kleenex, and come back to the paragraph.) Praise God because he is, because you know him. Thank him for tiny blessings: a cardinal's song, a wisp of blue sky, the petals of daisies. Thank him for good experiences, when they come; for anticipations; for friends; for music; for — for all sorts of things. Especially for the growing that you will be doing, through some of the hardest and the bitterest of times.

Humor. Gratitude. And pride in yourself. Good, joyful, wholesome pride.

A woman who has been through the terrible amputation of divorce, when the legal process has wielded surgeon's tools on the "one flesh" relationship that God himself fashioned, may well find that her self-concept has been badly, badly damaged. If that is true for you, let your humor be a medication. Let gratitude be constantly at work, and don't hesitate to build little lists of "Thank God for me." Maybe you should start putting little slips of paper in a bowl on top of the refrigerator, with written gratitudes: thank God for my office skills; thank God for the eyes I see in the mirror; thank God for the calmness he gave me this afternoon; thank God for hair that behaves.

The divorcée with children has both blessings and huge problems you won't be facing. Maybe one of your ministries will be to help some other divorcées with their single parenting: to joy in their joys, to tug at their burdens. They will need not to let their children become too totally their whole world; maybe you can help.

Courage to you, my dear.

And know, always, that you do not walk any road alone. No Christian walks alone.

Notes to Chapter 28

1. Catherine Marshall, *Something More* (New York: McGraw-Hill Book Company, 1974), pp. 35-57.
2. Ruth Carter Stapleton, *The Gift of Inner Healing* (Waco, Texas: Word Books, 1976).

For Married People Only **29**

Charles Lamb, the delightful and whimsical British essayist of the nineteenth century, once wrote with merry malice a "Bachelor's Complaint of the Behavior of Married People." I'm not quite ready to borrow his title, but I would like to converse candidly with the two-thirds of American adults, on behalf of the one-third.

Other singles might give you other viewpoints. Feel free to ask them!

To begin with, let it be noted that you need us and we need you. Let's start with the first half of that assertion — and assume, at the outset, that each of my comments is open to qualification and exception.

You need us.

The "nuclear family," as sociologists like to call it, can whirl inward and inward, in centripetal circlings with constant attention to its own discipline problems, budget problems, little tensions, and big aspirations. It can become so self-centered, so preoccupied with "we, us, my, our" that it is impoverished. To interact with a detached single outsider can bring a valued new openness, fresh breezes of understanding. Much of the family's social life will be with other couples, or with other families who have children in similar age brackets, and that is all to the good. But the nuclear family still needs the divergent, the different: the temporary aunt, the transient uncle, the borrowed grandparent, if you will.

The home-keeping wife especially needs at least occasional contact with a feminine mind which has other preoccupations from her own. Take Lucy. She was a brilliant grad student in history, let's say, when Jed found her. She loves Jed dearly, but she also loves the world of ideas. To have businesswoman Nan drop in unexpectedly between afternoon-off errands and chat about her committees, her appointments, what she has been reading, what she has been thinking can be a better tonic than any herbal brew or vitamin for Lucy. And Nan will be more likely to drop in if from time to time Lucy has taken other initiatives toward maintaining their friendship.

Husbands can profit, too, from bachelor friends who share mind-interest or hobby interest but not parent-child-wife-husband syndromes of thought. Suddenly, thinking about this fact, my mind skips back across decades to our western Kansas farm home, and the great satisfaction my father found in talking theology on Sunday afternoons with—um, what was his name? The genial, well-informed, earnest "hired man" over at the Woodbury ranch. Lee. That's it. Lee Lohmeyer, I think. Daddy liked to talk with anyone; he enjoyed the times with the men who brought their wives and their denim-covered children, too, but there seemed to be something very special to him about unattached Lee and his free, clear mind.

And your children need the singles. They need to learn outgoing warmth toward all sorts of human beings, not just their own play-mates. Can any child have too many uncles and aunts? Can parents have too many people who will support their children's crucial decisions with prayer? Maybe the single whom you invite over for a snack after church next Sunday will be the confidante, the stabilizer, to whom your little blonde toddler of today will turn, a dozen years from now.

Gerta and Ted had welcomed me into their home a good many times, I remember, when their Ruth and their Raymie were little kids. Those home times made it natural enough, later on, for Ruth to collapse sobbing in my arms when her college years hit one of their worst crises and my office was a haven she could come to. I suppose I've never been gladder that I have arms than when Ruth's brave-tense-dismayed-desperate face appeared at my office door and I asked quickly, "Oh, Ruthie, what *is* it?" And when little Raymie became big Raymie, and went through an identity crisis of agonizing proportions while he was off at his university, he let Gerta know it was a stability to him that "Dr. Mac" greeted him with warmth when he came back to our town. (How could I else? My heart was break-ing too, with him and for him; with Gerta and Ted, and for them.)

Okay. You need the singles. Oh, another thought, before we move on. You need the singles, too, when they may be the uncongenial ones, the ones you don't get strength from in obvious ways. You need them because Christ is in them, and you need him. You need them as receivers of Grace that flows through you.

Now, you'd expect me to say, and I shall say: the singles need you, too. Any person who is an "I" in most of his social contacts needs sometimes to be a "we." Whether it's a teen-age secretary who is away from home for the first time, or a nurse who is 28, or a business man who is 36, or a widow who is 84: the single needs, sometimes, to be included in a family circle. He needs to feel little fingers curling inside his fingers, sometimes, instead of lab equipment or golf clubs. She needs to hear family chatter and family teasings. They all need to feel the pulsing rhythms of family growth and family change: seasons, holidays, birthdays, special times.

Socializing with the singles seems to be a skill that some families develop more easily and practice more naturally than others. Ed's an extreme case; he freezes if a single woman is seated across from him and Junetta at a banquet, and he finds it hard to talk with the single women who serve on church boards with him. I don't know whether he's insecure inside his own masculinity, or whether he doesn't trust Junetta to trust him. In contrast, Roy and Barbie seem as natural with singles as with their own ears and lungs. It was so even before they were engaged; I remember an evening when I was seated in the front row of the balcony in LaDue Auditorium, await- ing a college concert or lecture, and glanced up to see Roy and Barbie cheerily asking if they might join me. Now their home wel- comes me with great eagerness, and they are most delightfully extro- verted in letting me know that they count an evening more fun when I join them for it. I have had happy times with the two of them; with them and another couple; with them and two other couples.

Dean and Ann are adept, too, at socializing with singles. I remem- ber an evening when a faculty throng was moving en masse from our college dining room to H. J. Long Gymnasium, half a block away, for an evening lecture or concert; I don't recall precisely the event, but I do recall the deft courtesy with which Dean asked if I wouldn't join him and Ann for the program; getting from place to place can be much smoother, sometimes, for a three than for a one. And trudging along among many people — many nice people — isn't like being so graciously asked to join two of the people. I remember a visit to their home when they were living, once, where I could pause to see them on my way abroad; I remember the eagerness with which Ann took me to help her buy a coat, the good woman-woman talk with Ann, along with all of the good person-person and Christian- Christian talk that Ann and Dean and I were having threesomely.

If, thus far in your lives, you haven't found it very easy or natu- ral as a couple to socialize with singles, how about giving it some practice? Tennis isn't easy at first, either, nor Scrabble, nor piano, nor anything else.

Of course the threesome needs to be under the discipline of Christian conscience and of common sense. Follies can happen, and have happened. But the Holy Spirit can be guardian and guide and, yes, chaperon, for the three-way friendship which can be an enrichment to everyone.

I have spoken of Dean's graciousness. Let me mention that there can be — how to say it? — a hospitality that repels. Let's say that George (single) is clearing his desk on the day before Thanksgiving when Andy (much married) says, "Hey, what are you doing tomorrow?" "Oh, nothing much," says George. Actually he is basking in the thought of some splendid hours with his ham radio set, his darkroom equipment, and four new books. That night the telephone rings. "Hey, George," says Andy, "if you don't have somewhere else to go for Turkey Day, Louise says we'll have gobs; wanna come on over? Oh, sure, man, I mean it. Look, you *can't* just sit up there in your penthouse and eat wieners on Thanksgiving Day. . . ." And finally George goes, a little angry with himself, and a little angry with Andy, and maybe a little angry with God because thus far God has left him single. Andy's manifest pity rankles more than the cranberries satisfy.

Contrast this: a colleague, Dennis Brown, stopped me on the campus some eight or ten days before a holiday. He and Karen were planning toward a houseful of people, he said; could I possibly join them for dinner? They would love to have me. And I felt valued, deeply valued; I knew that they would be eager to share my thoughts, my life; it would be *koinonia*. And contrast this: Willa told me (radiantly) how friends two states away telephoned one time to say that, with Christmas coming, they had held a family council about Christmas company and the children wanted Willa more than anyone else. First choice. They called several weeks ahead, for emphasis. Her commitments made it impossible for her to go, but being wanted so graciously brightened that whole year-end time, and the rest of her life.

Suppose Kathryn is a widow, and her children can't come home for Easter, and Easter has always been special for them. Suppose Marian says, in a word or in tone, "Oh, are you going to be *alone* next Sunday? Oh, you poor *thing*! Why don't you come over and eat with us? Jerry won't mind. . . ." Kathryn will probably feel like throwing the little ham she has purchased right at Marian's chattering face, or like running to her bedroom and bawling. If, instead, Marian says sincerely, "Kathryn, *would* you be free to join us Sunday? It will make Easter so much more special for Jerry and me if you could," Kathryn will sing the anthems with an additional lilt in her voice. Or if a young family announces spontaneously, "We need a borrowed grandmother; could we *possibly* borrow you today?" she may sing especially well.

When an invitation seems to demean and to pity and to make one an object of charity — alas. But it needn't.

Maybe you have noticed that I have been speaking about the single who is invited singly: George, Willa, Kathryn, me. It's on purpose that I speak so. Maybe you will invite another widow, Alice, when you invite Kathryn, and it's certainly okay if you want to do so; maybe you will invite Bill when you invite George. Fine. And if you're confident enough of the chemical balance, you may want to invite Alice with George or Bill with Kathryn. Fine. Excellent. But please know that a single person is a wholeness, an entity, who comes and goes individually. Pairing us off around your tables isn't really necessary, is it? Not always.

While we are still thinking about the invitations, I do hope you have warm and generous feelings for that person you have had over 16 times, and you have never once been invited back. "Not once, Harold," you tell your husband mournfully. "Well, I mean. . . . I know there are five of us, but after all. . . ." And you do get tired of cooking, and Genevieve ought to realize it. (Or Arthur ought. Or Kathryn.) I don't know all the nuances of the situation with you and Harold and Genevieve, but I can conjecture a little. Genevieve feels more insecure than you would ever guess about cooking for five; you cooked for one, and then two, then four, and then five. Now you're constantly in practice. Genevieve is a social worker, let's say, and is usually at her desk finishing the reports she brought home in her brief case until the hunger pangs drive her to the kitchen. Then she opens a can of soup or makes a peanut butter sandwich. Or maybe she has a TV dinner — and enjoys it thoroughly, having decided just at the right moment that a Mexican TV dinner would taste great, and that she can do another report while it bakes. She really likes to cook, but cooking full-scale meals for one person doesn't make much sense. And now she feels rusty about full-scale meals. And you have intimidated her (you really have!) at the practiced ease with which you have always tossed rolls and meat and three vegetables and two desserts in front of your family and the guests. And there are the limitations of her apartment, which she wonders about and worries about when she thinks of entertaining.

Well, that's the way it is. Keep on loving her, even if you start giving her a cup of tea after Sunday evening church rather than roast beef after the Sunday morning service. Maybe soon she will have a different apartment and a different job and more courage. Maybe soon she will discover some ingenious simplicities in hospitality which you will all enjoy. Meantime, if she brings her overflowing affection for your growing family, and brings her need of you; if she is meeting social needs that you and Harold have; if she is an inspiration to your children; if she's one to whom our Lord Christ is reaching out through you — well, maybe she is one of the ones, for you, through whom "thou shalt be blessed," as Luke 14:12-14 promised. Genevieve is not "the poor, the maimed, the lame, the blind" in physical appearance, but sometimes she is all of that within her psyche, and in her present circumstance it seems to her that indeed she "cannot recompense thee."

Sam couldn't either; I saw Sam not long ago, and I worry about him. He is a musician who truly lives for his composing. He almost goes into trances of preoccupation. His friends say they never see him at local restaurants. I wonder if he even remembers to eat. Certainly he wouldn't think to reciprocate, or know how, if you'd invite him over. But the blazing creativity of his artistic mind could make a difference in your children's perceptions of music for the rest of their mortal lives.

Kenneth couldn't recompense you, either, or wouldn't. He is a slim white-haired widower, past seventy. People in his town say he does his own housework, mostly, but I doubt whether he has invited anyone to a meal since the times when he provided living room conversation while his wife made the gravies.

Beyond the invitings, let's think about something else.

Your children and the singles.

I've already said that there is mutual need and opportunity for mutual enrichment. I believe it, deeply. But might I murmur one soft word of caution? Please realize, when your single friends are with you, that your children just are not the center of all worlds for them. During a brief visit, the baby's tooth or the baby's newest word should have some attention, certainly, but you will all grow more if the conversation is not totally pabulum and diapers and "gitchee-gitchee-goo." Or, 15 years later, if the conversation is not *all* about Johnny's grade cards and Johnny's camping trip and Johnny's dental retainers and Johnny's piano lessons. Our grandparents went too far in their dictum that children should be seen and not heard, but some hospitable households seem to go to the other extreme and feel that their single adult guests should be seen and not heard. A healthy balance, please?

That plea to some homes, for some of the time. Now, if I may, a different plea — for more homes, more of the time.

Would you permit and encourage your children to develop their own friendships with us? Rapport between a child (toddler or teen) and an older adult cannot be programmed, of course, but it can be expected and encouraged, or it can be unintentionally short-circuited and expected not to happen. Few scenes in mortal experience are more beautiful when they happen.

I think, for instance, of Danny Cade's quiet but intense joy as he (age 23) showed me a poem he had written about Esther Wright, age 2½; he told with some awe how she had perched on his lap, how her prattlings had totally enchanted after he had been a dinner guest at the Wright home. It was probably one of the brightest events of his entire life.

The parental encouraging toward rapport may be very incidental. It can recognize that the child is a person to be valued, that the single adult is a person to be valued, that they have something to share with each other. A quiet paragraph of spoken comment ("Bobby, this is Mother's friend Muriel; she has been off on a trip to Brazil; maybe she would like to tell you about some of the things she saw in Brazil. . . .") can lead to continuing links of warmth and identity and self-valuing that both Bobby and Muriel will cherish for a long while. My mind skips back to the puckish fun on Steve Leierer's face, age seven or so, when he quizzed me about whether I had seen leprechauns in Ireland, and then memory flips to a few months ago when his mother, long distance from the West Coast, was saying, "Someone here has something to tell you," and Steve was reporting the acceptance of a graduate school paper by the *Athletic Journal*.

I think of crayon-drawn art work I have received; of little gifts pushed into my pockets; of Sherrie's bright excitment when she got to sit with me in the dining hall of the writer's conference her father was directing, for which I was a speaker.

I think of two particularly treasured notes of congratulation that came to me in November of '77, after I was "This-Is-Your-Life-d" — on our campus — two notes from teen-agers, each of whom wrote with sparkly originality and spontaneity.

Thank you, married people, whose children are becoming, in their own persons, the friends of your single friends. May your tribe increase!

Obviously you will need to use common sense and obey the nudgings of the Holy Spirit, in this as in all else that you do. My friends Don and Carla, for example, attend a medium-sized church which probably has, at a quick estimate, some 40 to 60 single persons among its frequent attenders. Don and Carla also have three youngsters whom everyone tends to describe as "such *wonderful* children." They will quickly become less "wonderful" if they are encouraged to adopt 50 or 60 new aunts and uncles in the immediate future. At the moment, however, I wonder if Don and Carla have had even one or two or three singles at their dining table in the last six months. I wonder if Don and Carla sometimes introduce their youngsters to adult friends before or after church, in ways that would build toward sustained and continuing friendships.

Now another something.

I talked a while ago about Roy and Junetta, and how they are not (yet, anyway) at all skilled in socializing with singles. Maybe, although I haven't ever heard him say anything to evidence it, Roy is one of those persons who is too quick to impugn the attitudes of other people. Please *do* maintain, utterly the sanctity of your marital relationships; please *do* be alert to anything in yourselves or in others that could become a smudge or a taint upon the sacredness of the home. But may I plead with as much intensity that you please, please *don't* be too quick to misjudge us?

Like an episode at a college banquet. The juniors had invited all of us to their junior-senior banquet, and I went along cheerily to their festivity. At the banquet hall, I was directed by the junior hosts to a particular table, where I was genuinely pleased to find Kenneth and Marilee already seated. They were alert people, exemplary Christians, and I always enjoyed their conversation in social groups. I uttered some little pleasantry (I thought) about my good fortune in sharing the table with them; I still wonder what I said — or what Kenneth heard. Well, I started glancing around to enjoy the decorations, to wonder what students would come to the same table, when suddenly Kenneth spoke to me, with a tense rapidity which made me think afterward that he must have rehearsed his words about 15 times in his mind while I was doing my amiable glancings around the room. He wanted me to know, he said — in a cutting and eloquent little paragraph, he wanted me to know — that Marilee might have her faults, but jealousy was not one of them. I was astounded. I don't know what I replied, if anything. Probably just a blank and startled "Oh," as students started filling the chairs around us; anything more, then or later, would have seemed to give my unfortunate pleasantry even more attention than it deserved. (Or so I thought. Maybe I was wrong.) Well, Kenneth apparently forgave me, for I had a good many calm and easy encounters with them both before those juniors graduated. I'm glad Kenneth was chivalrous about Marilee, but I still could wish that he hadn't been quite so ready to think evil of me. Please don't impugn us too quickly?

My insouciance on that banqueting occasion might point toward another comment, another request.

It is my perception that we singles have a continuing need for family-type feedback about how we are doing. In this human life, just about everyone needs encouragement just about all of the time. (That's a McAllaster proverb that I have been murmuring to assorted listeners for several years now.) But two-thirds of the American everyones have spouses to praise, to chide, to question, to exhort, to encourage. According to all the evidence, from Chaucer's humor backward and forward, in the annals of literature, some spouses are much better than others at giving useful feedback. Granted. But that still leaves the singles living with their wonderings: How *did* I do in that report to the school board? *Did* my part in the panel discussion go okay? *Was* I as useful as I wanted to be in the skits for the Christmas party? *Did* I wear the right outfit for the mayor's lawn party? *Was* I too intense in arguing for the new Christian Education curriculum?

And the brotherly or sisterly word of praising or chiding, of encouraging or admonishing, can be valuable. Sometimes it will be painful for the moment; sometimes it will be judged a faulty evaluation, after it has been duly considered. But valuable, nonetheless. It is a startling thing, sometimes, to catch a glimpse of one's own face in a hall mirror, or in the reflections of a plateglass window. It can be just as startling, sometimes, to get a cue about an impression one has made. It can also be very helpful to know that things went right, when they did.

I was really amused (with an alum-flavored or persimmon-flavored kind of amusement) one time to receive a letter from a good friend of mine who lived many, many miles away from where I was working. He was hearing, he confided, that "everyone" in my locality thought I ought to do thus-and-so about a particular matter.

Well, that was one way for my local associates to give me the feedback: to write to a mutual buddy, or deliver a state-of-the-union message about me over hamburgers when "everyone" saw him somewhere. That was one way. There must be more effective ways! And, in truth, I have been fortunate in having colleagues who were like family to me, brothers and sisters in Christ who have indeed performed the service that I am pleading for.

Thanks for listening, all of you people. Thanks for your friendship.

May each single to whom you reach out hands of comradeship be a genuine blessing to you, and you to them.

Amen.

Amen.

Interlude with a Restless Wife **30**

Esther is vexed with me, writes a mutual friend. For several days, I have been thinking about Esther's vexation and feeling some prickles of conscience. Recently Esther read some things I had written about single serenities, and my paragraphs have apparently stung some of her habitual feelings about her marriage into acute nettle-blisters of discontent.

Alas.

While I think about Esther, I remember a very intense letter I received one time after a national magazine had carried an article of mine. The sender had numerous children, impossibly heavy housework, great longings for contact with the kinds of music and literature my article had talked about, great wistfulness for some of the choices that her marriage had blotted out from her potentiality.

I think about a book of fiction I read last night, Rumer Godden's *Take Three Tenses,* and the character Griselda, wife of a wealthy London businessman, whose wistful inner thoughts kept being stifled by her wife-mother roles. Well, Griselda Dane was fictional, and her author-inventor caused her to be a stifled wife; I can push thoughts about her away. But I can't so easily push away the thoughts about Esther. And from Esther I must think further about tensions in homes all across America. I think sadly about advisers like Gail Sheehy, with her brittle, cynical overreadiness, in her much-discussed volume *Passages*, to see divorce as the solution.

Esther's morale.

Esther, Esther. I wish you were in my town today. I wish you could sit here in the big green chair in my living room and talk some things out — I in the brown chair, which has heard so many personal conferrings all through its several years.

For you, Esther, for any other Esthers, might I say a few thoughtful words? I am not a marriage counselor, but I have watched a few thousand marriages at fairly close range, and I have had to think some thoughts.

First, a practical proverb. I grew up on Scotch-Irish proverbs and Pennsylvania Dutch proverbs and other proverbs, out there among the buffalo grasses and wheat fields of a western Kansas farm. An earlier chapter talked about one of them: "Comparisons are odious." It was invoked often, briskly and firmly, when one of us six McAllaster youngsters thought a sibling's pancake to be larger or a stint of chores to be smaller. It was invoked if we thought a neighbor's pastures and cattle to be better than ours. It was invoked if one of us reproached another for doing less well than a classmate in "speaking pieces" at school, or in a spelling match. We used that proverb so often that our McAllaster flair for the hilarious got away with us, and someone (age 8 or 10 or 12) translated it "Comparisons are odorous" and then "Comparisons stink!"

Well, dear Esther, sometimes comparisons do stink. The person who constantly compares any experience he hears about with his own experience, any gift with his own gift, any opportunity with his own opportunity, is opening a door wide to covetousness and envy, two of what our fathers called "the seven deadly sins." When we can observe objectively what is happening in another life, without adding the subjective measurements of comparison, we are much healthier. A simple illustration. Two neighbors drop in for coffee during the morning. Vada says, "Oh, what lovely new curtains! You have such a cheery kitchen, Esther!" (Result: peace and joy.) Thelma says, "You have new curtains. You have so much more light and space to work in than *I* have, Esther!" Result: envy, discontent.) Further, when we can praise God for what he is giving to another life, or doing in it, without tacking on the comparison, we're better off. ("Mary has received a scholarship; thank the Lord!" Result: general gladness. "Ethel's painting won a prize; thank the Lord!" More gladness. "Mary has received a scholarship; Ethel wins prizes; *I* have to work for every dollar, and *I* never win anything." Result: pain and inner friction.)

Okay, let's be candid. If you compare your lot with the circumstances of any Susy Single, you can cause pain. "Susy is touring Israel during her vacation, and if I didn't have Tom and the kids *I* could do something exciting." "Susy has her interesting job now, at a downtown bookstore, and here I am, washing diapers and coveralls." And so on.

Instead of the hurtful comparings, can you learn to praise God for Susy's glad times, and to enjoy them vicariously with her? When she goes to Israel or to a book fair, can you plan with her, ask her about her schedule, find out about her best experiences? Can you live with extra dimensions through her living?

In that vein, can you help your own morale frequently, Esther, by keeping in touch with several of your single friends? Their comings and goings can give you windows on larger worlds. Ask Marcia over for coffee on her day off, take Susy to the park for a picnic, telephone Ruth and Kate and Jill from time to time. Interview them. File away ideas from one conversation to ask about or argue about in another.

Is part of your present restlessness, Esther, related to your whole readiness for a better chapter in your marriage?

I don't know just what you have been reading, and whom you have been conferring with. Are you aware enough that many good marriages go through their times of deep, deep tension and stress? Some wives, you know, are still too deeply conditioned by all the Grace Livingston Hill books they read as adolescents, or by Hollywood's improbabilities, and they may come to marriage without clear notions of all the mundane that lies beyond the white satin and the wedding march. Some wives live with pretty deep guilt feelings, thinking that theirs is about the only marriage in town with such stress, along with the ecstasy.

I'm thinking now of the intensity with which Annette, the gracious wife of a distinguished minister, once said to me, "I *thank God* for saving our marriage!" She was so fervent in her earnestness that I was really quite startled. (You, Annette?) Her mountain-huge stresses were behind her when we talked, and few of her friends know, I'd imagine, either what she has already worked through or how she still works creatively at her "wifing." I'm thinking of Martha, 40 years married, who still quivers to recall how often she wanted to give up, during the earliest years. I'm thinking of Charlotte, whose marriage many observers assume to have been a very model for two decades; Charlotte's pastor knows, and I know, that she and David are now working through crucial new growth patterns, with immense emotional cost to both of them.

So don't berate yourself too much over your wifely tensions and frictions and angers, dear Esther. Recognize that many good people and many good marriages know their desperations. But can you start, and continue, some constructive action?

Have you been to a good bookstore lately, and to your library? Have you gleaned specific ideas, and talked them over with Tom? Some books with which you disagree strongly may contain paragraphs which will help you toward new quotients of contentedness. Have you secured a copy for Tom of Dan Benson's *Total Man?* And for yourself a copy of Elisabeth Elliot's *Let Me Be a Woman?*

I myself am not about to offer full-scale advices on your marriage, you may be sure. But one curiosity wells up.

Are you getting more and more adept at *praising* Tom? Over and over. Creatively, diversely. At home and in public. Expressed loyalty and expressed admiration have a wonderful capacity for enhancing good qualities, for causing good new qualities to sprout and bud and blossom. Or, to change the metaphor, praise has a wonderful way of knitting up raveled fabric and of reweaving torn places.

Your face tightens. Is he, then, so hard to praise?

That's a part of the pain, then, in the wish to be single that still tangles through your married love. He is not as admirable as you wish he were, nor as wise. He disappoints you. You have to recognize that you yourself are often the clearer thinker, the better executive. Sometimes you know real despair at being married to . . . to . . . well, to a clod, a lout, a boor, an oaf. A very dolt.

Go on. There's more terror and more hope in the next noun. You're married to a sinner. But there's hope, in Christ, for sinners. We are tainted and we blunder, but we are still only a little lower than the angels. God's grace and human love — your love — can redeem and keep on redeeming.

A reminiscent smile. In his poem "Locksley Hall," Tennyson had a very disillusionsed young man say of his cousin Amy,

"As the husband is, the wife is; thou are mated with a clown,
    And the grossness of his nature will have weight to drag thee
        down."

One time I paraphrased that couplet merrily for a close friend, when she had just decided to marry a man whose worth some people questioned; I assured her,

"As the wife is, so the husband; he is mated with a saint,
    And the sweetness of her nature will soon make him what he
        ain't."

And Joyce's marriage has been wonderfully durable and good. She has known how to praise, how to encourage, how to believe in his strengths, how to adore Tim during their dissensions, how to trust him with decisions, how to give ideas without destroying his, when to hold out for her own viewpoints and when to yield. No, I don't know everything about their household counsels, of course. But I am sure that from what I have seen, Joyce's wisdom has been a gyroscope on many occasions that I don't know about.

What Joyce has been for Tim makes me think about Robert Louis Stevenson's tribute to his wife, Fanny. Maybe it says something, Esther, about what you are and will become for your Tom:

Trusty, dusky, vivid, true,
With eyes of gold and bramble-dew,
Steel-true and blade-straight,
The great artificer
Made my mate.

Honor, anger, valor, fire;
A love that life could never tire,
Death quench or evil stir,
The mighty master
Gave to her.

Teacher, tender, comrade, wife,
A fellow-farer true through life,
Heart-whole and soul-free
The august father
Gave to me.

(Long pause. Slow fingerings of the silver candle holder I take
from the maple table beside my chair.)
Esther, my dear.
Are you keeping constantly, constantly in mind that your marriage is man-God-woman and woman-God-man, not just woman-
man? Is your marriage a daily new experiment in practical prayers?
Prayers about your most subtle attitudes toward Tom, as well about
bills and job decisions? Prayers about what the two of you are doing
together to touch other people for Christ? Prayers about the thousand reachings and aspirings within you, some of which cannot come
to fruition in one lifetime, and would not in twenty lifetimes?

Is the principle of finding new ways to obey the Holy Spirit your
constant principle? I don't know what he will be teaching you about
new wifeliness, but it could be an adventure to discover.

I almost hear a soft creak-creak as you stir in the platform
rocker. "Yes," you scoff. "It's easy for you singles to talk about
obedience. You have only yourselves to please. You have things so
easy."

I pick up a New Testament and thumb to John 21:22. "What is
that to thee? Follow thou me." Isn't God's word to Peter the important word to you also, Esther? What is he asking of you? How are
you, now, to follow him?

What are your right roles for you, as our Lord Christ directs,
and as your Tom desires the roles to be?

Yes. As Tom desires.

Does your face darken? No, I do not know just how dictatorial
Tom likes to be. I do know that your supreme happiness will lie in

the building of his supreme happiness. You are his wife. If you denigrate him, or try to build your own fulfillments at the cost of his, you will deny your own best fruitions. When you come to new interests and new skills, there will be more of you to love Tom with; thank God for that. But do you remember always that your wife self is your most queenly self, the highest identity of your Esther-hood?

You shake your head and grimace. "Idealist!"

Well, yes, I think I am. I think, too, that those ideals were taught to me by God's own Word, and by the idealisms that he has implanted in the Judaeo-Christian tradition for these centuries. Husband is to wife as Christ is to his church, St. Paul said.

So I made you restless, did I, in talking about what God has done through some singles, and about rich blessings he has given to some singles? But we are we, dear Esther, and you are you, and each believer is to follow with utter care the instructions that come to him individually.

When I was a youngster on the farm, sometimes it was my task to fill out order blanks for shoes or shirts or linens to be purchased from Sears Roebuck and Montgomery Ward. On the rural route, and more than 20 miles from the post office, those two great mail-order firms were very important to us. When I was 8 or 10 or 12, it gave me a curious little pang to letter "Rural Route 2, Box 64" in the designated blank, and I felt somehow cheated because other people got to use the alternate line. Other lucky people had street addresses; we didn't. Later on, I came to realize that some people with streets and house numbers would like to be able to write from an R. F. D. location. They couldn't use both blanks, either. To each his own. For you, dear Esther, your life — as God has chosen, and as you have chosen; for me, my life — as he has chosen, and as I have chosen.

If you were indeed in my living room, I would probably be asking quietly, "Shall we talk with him about all this before you go?" Shall we, indeed?

Lord God. . . .

From A to Z, and 31
Back Again

This morning I turned in my last grades for the second semester. Yesterday was our Commencement, with a congressman speaking to the seniors about the caring persons they are to become, with caps and gowns being photographed all over Scott Field after we left the gymnasium. Now, from our Greenville College campus as once from Queen Victoria's Diamond Jubilee,

> "The tumult and the shouting dies,
> The captains and the kings depart."

Not exactly kings for us, as in Kipling's "Recessional," but the eminent alumni and the jubilant seniors have departed.

And I am so eager to resume conversations with you that I have a tray beside me here in my study; from time to time my fingers leave the typewriter keys to pick up another carrot stick, or to lift the mug of hot bouillon. No discussion-filled lunch at the college snack bar today.

It's Mother's Day plus eight, and for these eight days I've been wanting to ask how Mother's Day went for you this year. When you're a single woman, the way you spend a Mother's Day can be an interesting index to your whole lifestyle. It may be a time for new perspectives and new resolutions, too. The fiction writer within me is clamoring for a chance to speak. After all I've been reading and hearing and discussing and thinking about singles, shall I let the fiction writer speak today? The fiction writer will speak from what some periodicals would carefully label as "Fiction Based on Fact," believe me.

Which one were you, this year?

*   *   *   *

Alice glared at her clock on Saturday night and carefully did not set the alarm. "Mother's Day," she told her roommate fiercely, "is the day I hate most in the whole year. If you make one sound before noon tomorrow, I'll do something drastic."

"No church?" asked Beth.

"Definitely no church. If I'm lucky I'll sleep all day. They make all this silly fuss about Motherhood, and I hate it more every year."

"You wouldn't hate it if you were a mother. . . ."

Alice glared and banged her first against the light switch. "That's the point, stupid. We're singles, remember? I'm not a mother, and not about to be one, am I?"

*   *   *   *

"Yes, two white gardenias," said Christy to the florist. "And you'll deliver early on Saturday evening?" One more time, she told herself as she hung up the telephone. I've honored Mother's memory for these 20 years, but the habit wears thin. At my age, I should be getting flowers from my own kids. My church is always ridiculing the singles, and what they do on Mother's Day is the worst of all. One more time, and if they're as crude and cruel as usual I may never go to church again.

*   *   *   *

Della left her house early. She was picking up a young Vietnamese family she has been seeing in the laundromat. "They have three darling boys," she had told her pastor earlier, "and they don't know about our American Mother's Day. I hope we can make it really special for them. Maybe they will keep on coming to church with me."

*   *   *   *

Ethel celebrated Mother's Day on Saturday. She took her neighbor's girls, age seven and ten, to a shopping center and helped them find gifts for their mother.

*   *   *   *

Frances sang the morning hymns more absent-mindedly than usual. Two rows ahead of her was Gretel, whom she knew well in high school. Gretel looked so worried and flurried that Frances couldn't keep her mind on the liturgy. Gretel's husband isn't well, and her children looked grubby, and Gretel needed a shampoo. "And I spent three hours reading stupid magazines last night," thought Frances. "Dear God, forgive me! Gretel's mothering is so hard for her. I could do more things with her than I do. Next year . . . or next week . . . or tomorrow. . . ."

* * * *

Hannah made a point, as she usually does, of getting to the narthex early. She is not on any official greeting committee, but she likes people, and she likes greeting them as they arrive for Sunday services. Today her face was almost incandescent as she saw young people, home for the weekend, whom she knew in cherub choir; as she exclaimed over her friends' corsages; as she admired crayoned greeting cards being brought from Sunday school in chubby fists.

* * * *

Isabel wrote a note to her pastor this afternoon. She prayed very carefully first, and may yet tear it up rather than mailing it.

Isabel is shy and sensitive and earnest.

Isabel is 32 and not currently dating. She broke off with Tom, because she could not accept an agnostic husband. She broke off with Fred when he wanted her to try marijuana with him.

Usually Isabel is calmly confident that God is guiding her personal life.

But this morning her pastor talked so exuberantly about how every woman, every woman, should know the joys of motherhood that Isabel found herself wiping away tears all afternoon.

* * * *

Joyce heard the same sermon that Isabel heard.

Joyce is reckless sometimes and adventurous sometimes and a little rebellious most of the time.

Joyce did not write a note to her pastor this afternoon. She telephoned Hank, whom she met on a cruise along the Maine coast last summer, and said okay, she will go to the mountains with him next weekend, after all. Why not?

"I'm still young enough," Joyce wrote in her journal. "Up to now I've played it cool, but since Pastor himself has said that being a mother is the highest good there is for a woman, then by golly, I'm going after the highest good. I know Hank would marry me if I'd get pregnant, so here's hoping. Maternity ward, here I come. Nine months and six days from now, the Lord willing. Yeah, the Lord willing. Nice irony, huh?"

* * * *

Kathryn wrote a stack of notes this afternoon. She kept thinking about the women she knows for whom this would be the hardest

Mother's Day ever. Lois, whose husband was killed in an auto accident in March. Martha, who still lies awake through the nights and
cries her way through the days, since her young daughter's death.
Nan, whose mother was buried at Christmas time. Opal, whose long-
planned-for first child was stillborn in February.

*   *   *   *

Peggy decided several years ago that she would regularly adopt a
mother for each Mother's Day. This year she adopted a retired missionary whose income is somewhere between meager and tiny.
Peggy sent her a potted geranium, took her to church, took her out
to dinner. Peggy thinks maybe her church should have Mother's
Day two or three times a year.

*   *   *   *

Queen Jezz, they've been calling her in the singles bar where she
most often goes on Saturday nights. Her parents named her Jessamine, but her motto could be one that other young adults have
waved on their banners, both before and after Robert Louis Stevenson went through his years of storm and stress and used it: "Disre-
gard everything our parents taught us." And her christened name
is one thing Queen Jezz disregards.

She knew it was Mother's Day weekend, because she has been
wrting advertising copy about posh lingerie and jewelry. Her elegant
face was scornful while she wrote the ads, and after she left the
office at 4:30 on Friday she carefully ignored any Mother's Day
thoughts.

Queen Jezz hasn't been to church for three years and six months
— not since she found an apartment in a complex which advertises
itself as the latest syllable in liberation.

But this morning when Queen Jezz awakened in yet another bed,
with yet another man whose name she isn't sure she remembers, a
radio somewhere nearby was clearly audible. Some announcer with
a very resonant voice was announcing "Childhood Memories."
Queen Jezz shivered a little, and swore a little under her breath, and
listened against her will. Then two other sounds blurred in with the
radio. Somewhere in the far distance a church bell was ringing, and
somewhere in a nearby motel room a baby cried. And suddenly
Jessamine knew, as certainly as though she were Joan of Arc affirming the voices of her saints, that she wants motherhood; that it still
might come; that she must make herself ready and worthy, in case
it does.

She dressed quickly and asked at a service station about churches
nearby.

*   *   *   *

Ruth telephoned a former high school teacher of hers, whom she talks with three or four times a year. Neither of them said "Mother's Day" to the other, but both were gladder.

*   *   *   *

Susie is angry, really angry.

She will probably talk with the church board members, one by one.

This morning their church gave out corsages and other citations for "Oldest Mother," "Youngest Mother," and a whole row of other titles.

"Mother's Day has its merits," said Susie to her friend Tricia this afternoon, "but don't they think of the implications? Don't they think at all? There was Ula Mae, 16 years old and married for two months before the baby came. Is that what we honor? There was Vivian: eight kids, and eighteen grandkids, and not many of 'em ever come to church with her, and all of them on welfare, and Vivian gets a big plant to take home to say that she is a model of excellence. Is that what our church delighteth to honor? I ask you, Tricia. Dogs and cats and rabbits and gorillas can produce offspring; Christian people ought to have some other ideas of merit! And, sure, they will say it's sour grapes if you and I say anything about it, since they think *we* ought to be pining after motherhood, but I'm going to say something this time. I really am."

*   *   *   *

Wilma is the sponsor of a youth group. She stopped by the prayer chapel of her church this afternoon, and used her attendance file as a prayer list while she thought and prayed about her group, one by one by one. They talk with her sometimes about drugs at school, about hassles from their pagan parents, about dates and lack of dates, about their vocational dreams. Although she is very sensitive about seeming to compete for their affection, Wilma is more of a mother to some of them than their own mothers know how to be.

Afterward, she telephoned Xena, and they talked about their mutual concerns.

*   *   *   *

Xena had a busy day, today.

In her devotions this morning, she prayed very earnestly, very pointedly, about the use of this segment of eternity. The answer seemed to her to be very clear: she was to do some mothering, and she was to strengthen some other women for their mothering.

In the early afternoon, Xena spent a half hour with a highschool boy whom she has been tutoring in Latin, and another half hour with three semi-orphaned girls whom she sometimes takes to concerts or to art shows. Today they wanted her to see their newest book reports and home economics projects.

Later on, Xena spent a while with her address book, her stationery and her telephone. The Smiths, whose sons are so fiercely rebellious right now. Mrs. Jones, whose daughter has leukemia. Mrs. Brown: her daughter was in court last month for marijuana possession. Mrs. Doe, the widow whose income does not grow at all while her four boys get taller and taller. Long distance, then, to Ms. Roe; 13 years ago, Ms. Roe decided to keep her illegitimate son rather than giving him up for adoption, and now every day is a welter of conflicting emotions for her: anger, gladness, pride, hate, shame, grief, satisfaction, dismay. She's usually too proud to ask outright for any advices from Xena, but she values postcards and Christmas notes and telephone calls, and Xena knows she does.

*   *   *   *

Yvonne had a hangover.

She spent Saturday night in a singles bar again, and the bruising of her ego was worse than usual while men surveyed her appraisingly, and she drank more than usual. She spent all day in bed, feeling tawdry and dull when she wasn't nauseated. Sipping black coffee in the twilight, she thought a semi-prayer: "Well, thank God I wired flowers to Mom, anyway. What she doesn't know won't hurt her. But it hurts me. Oh God, oh God, oh God. It hurts. Why are the churches so black and blank on Saturday nights, when nice people need to meet some nice people? If I'm still a nice people. Oh God, oh God, oh God."

*   *   *   *

Zelda shrugged her way through a Mother's Day, again. She is getting more practiced, year by year, in insulating herself from all emotion. She went to church as usual. As usual, she joined two or three other spinsters in her usual pew. As usual, she said neutral "Good Morning" greetings that carried no glints of emotion to anyone. As usual, she listened to the announcements with neutral indifference. As usual, she found the Mother's Day sermon unimportant and irrelevant and boring.

Most sermons are unimportant and irrelevant and boring to Zelda. She comes to church because it is a habit, and habits are not easily changed at Zelda's age. Somewhere, far under the leather layers of indifference, Zelda has a lingering hatred for Mother's

Day — a hatred dyed from the same vats as Alice's hatred. But Zelda would never admit, not to her Siamese cats and not to herself, that maybe it is the one day in the whole year which she, too, hates the most.

For single women whose attention and affection turn inward rather than outward, it can be such a day.

Now it is two days past Commencement at Greenville College, or Mother's Day plus nine for this year.

The doorbell took me away from you yesterday. A college girl needed some candid conversation. We talked quite a while about the man she is dating — and I pause now to breathe a prayer that heaven will give her wisdom. (She needs it.) We talked, too, about how she feels toward her mom, about responsibility and independence and adulthood.

Now a tall orange candle flickers and glows in my study. It stands near a vase of flowers which I have been very reluctant to discard. They have brightened my life remarkably for these past ten days. You see, on Saturday night before Mother's Day, I was pedaling away on my exercise bike and chuckling over a witty P. G. Wodehouse story on Channel 9 when the doorbell rang. Two merry sophomores, as blithe as sixth graders at an end-of-school picnic, thrust into my hands a tall glass jar swathed in florist's green paper. Pink daisies, white daisies, yellow daisies. "For Mother's Day," the boys said. They watched the rest of the Wodehouse play with me, exploding with laughter over the quips and inventing others of their own. Then they hurried back to their dormitory, to study for finals.

Mother's Day: I think it's great. Even if that bit of blithe brightness had not come into my life this year, I would have said it can be a day of special opportunity for creative singles, from A to Z and back again. It can, if we will make it so. We need to remember that our Lord himself, the one great Single of all time and all eternity, came not to be ministered unto but to minister, and to give his life. We need to be giving our lives.

It is true, however, that Mother's Day is also a day on which some churches across America push crude and cruel discomforts upon their singles while they try to do honor to mothers. Churches need to think again about how they are being heard by the singles, from A to Z and back again. They need to reexamine their easy presuppositions that motherhood is all splendid, and splendid for all, from A to Z and back again. Some singles need to speak up and ask for the reexaminings.

How was Mother's Day for you, this year?

About *Karass* and *Granfalloon* 32

A few months ago I mentioned to my colleague Dale Martin that I was feeling certain pangs about my ignorance concerning the writings of a much-discussed contemporary author, Kurt Vonnegut, Jr. Minutes later, Dale — who reads piles of science fiction — was at my office door with a helpful little grin on his face and a tall stack of paperbound books from his crammed shelves.

Well, yesterday I had some hours available to reduce my ignorance, to travel a little in the zany, satirical, witty, brilliant, often irreverent company of that particular author. Not books I could or would write, I told myself, but certainly books I can learn from. "A far-out imagination," says one of the book blurbs. Yes, certainly that. "A mind-jolting experience." Right. I'd agree.

This morning as my jolted mind was climbing back into consciousness from the deep depths of night, one Vonnegut term kept tangling with the chirping of cardinals and the dawn breezes. *Karass.* My *karass.* Your *karass.* The *karass* of the nameless narrator in a science fiction novel.

Vonnegut carefully did not explain how he invented the word. Perhaps, as my Greek-teaching colleague Jim Reinhard quickly conjectured when I mentioned it to him, it was a very direct borrowing from *charis,* the New Testament word for *grace.* In his handling, as the narrator of *Cat's Cradle* explains, *karass* is a concept in his own non-Christian religion; as a Bokononist, he believes humanity to be "organized into teams, teams that do God's will without ever discovering what they are doing."[1]

Karass.

Whether he borrowed it from a Greek New Testament or not, it's a term worth borrowing from Kurt Vonnegut — worth detaching from an invented and contradictory Bokononism; worth considering in Christian dimensions in real life.

Who are the persons in your *karass*, in my *karass*? Who are the persons providentially linked with you, or with me, to do God's will?

People in the local churches we attend? Some individuals there, certainly, and more of them as we obey our Lord more fully. But some of the attenders are mere associates, not a soul-linked team. Not yet. Not yet persons really bound together to do God's will.

Almost as soon as my head, filled with its half-thoughts about the implications of *karass*, was off the pillow this morning, and actually before I had reached for a washcloth or a toothbrush or a vitamin pill, I found myself reaching again for my heavily underlined copy of Thomas Kelly's *A Testament of Devotion,* and his remarkable essay on "The Blessed Community." "Within the wider Fellowship emerges the special circles of a few on whom, for each of us, a particular emphasis of nearness has fallen," wrote Kelly.[2] His version of *karass*?

Thank God for the few, when one finds them. Thank God for every linking, in the doing of God's will. Thank God for the discipline, the contacts, the opportunities, that lead into new linkings.

And, I'd say, thank God especially for the *karass* of right now, for the present opportunities. There can be gratefulness, certainly, for every close linking of other times, other places. (A former pastor? Were you in a very special team-relationship with him? A 10-years-ago neighbor? An Inter-Varsity associate in summer school, once at a university?) But it is now that is now; from this point in this life, the doing of God's will can flow out or can be dammed up, atrophied, stymied, repulsed.

More about the now-ness, after a bit. First, to think more about the who-ness.

Who is in my *karass*?

The people I pray for, surely. The people whom the Holy Spirit brings to mind with a poignance, an intensity which is not to be ignored. Two days ago, thoughts of a troubled eighth-grade girl of my acquaintance were impelling my mind to cry, to wail, "Oh God . . . oh God . . . oh God." Awakened momentarily once very early this morning, I found myself returning toward slumber with a litany echoing unaccountably in my head: "Bless Eugenia Price today — bless Eugenia Price — today — Bless Eugenia Price — today. . . ." I haven't seen Eugenia Price for quite a few years, haven't read one of her books recently, but she is a part of my *karass* today. Linked together, to do his will.

The people I see, meet with, talk with, because of my work? Yes, surely, some of them. In varying degrees, as we learn how to open heart to heart and mind to mind. It isn't always a matter of tenure together; sometimes the very newest associate may be closely, truly, amazingly, a sharer and a teammate. Such sharing is always partly a miracle, and not just proximity, not just a habitual association. Such sharing isn't automatic. The deep level of fellowship comes with response to response: my response to God, and my response to another's response to God.

People I write to. People who write to me. They're part of the linking. Or they may be. Perhaps, as with the people I see day by day, there is association but not an effectual linking. Vonnegut's narrator in *Cat's Cradle* has a word for the superficial association also: a *granfalloon*, "a seeming team that was meaningless in terms of the ways God gets things done."[3] Some of my letters are *granfalloon* letters. (Aren't yours?) Sometimes family reunions or college reunions are *granfalloon* events. (Aren't they?) Sometimes Sunday school class socials are terribly *granfalloon*. A lot of the after-church greetings on any Sunday morning are *granfalloon* greetings. (Aren't they?)

Still, any *granfalloon* contact might be transformed into *karass*, and any letter might become a part of the deep welding of spirit with spirit with spirit.

And a beauty of it is that in very truth, as in the made-up science fiction sect of the Bokononists, one can be a part of a team without ever knowing it. Some things, as Christians, we see and comprehend about how our lives are fitting into schemes of things. Some things we do not see, do not comprehend. Not now. So, yes, people I hear from may be part of my *karass*.

And people, also, who touch the lives that my life touches. They, too, may be part of it. They may be beyond my choosing, often beyond my knowing, yet not apart from my love, not apart from the tendrils used by the Holy Spirit to bind life to life, in the teams that are to do God's will.

I thought of something like that yesterday when, out for an errand, I noticed a single concrete block perched on a retaining wall at a college residence hall. At first, that concrete block sent a tremor all through me, and my impulse was to ask someone to hide it; I wanted to be a brawnier person, so that I myself could hide it. (Somewhere! Anywhere! Hide it! Take it away!) I had seen a block just like that one in courtrooms during murder trials. A block just like that one was used to weight down the body of my friend Danny Cade when murderers flung two corpses into the Kaskaskia River.

But as I looked again, as I thought about it, the inner shudders subsided and the concrete block seemed to become a sort of altar stone. Because of Danny's death, various other people who were close to him, or to the event, impinged upon my life in new ways. My *karass* changed and shifted and grew and intensified, as I had opportunities to "weep with those who weep," to counsel, to comfort, to intercede. And later, because I had been initiated into such a grief at that season, other persons have identified me as one who could walk into their dark, dark trails with them, and they, too, have come into my *karass* for a time.

Who is in my *karass*? Maybe some persons who do not use the religious verbalisms that I use. Maybe some persons who are the "other sheep" of our Lord, whom he has allowed to pasture beside me for a while, whom he is using with me in ways I do not know.

No doubt some persons would be counted in your *karass*, or mine, whom we deliberately and consciously encourage and try to challenge; some to whom we speak our appreciations; some we plan with in conscious Kingdom strategy — or what we hope to be Kingdom strategy. Maybe sometimes our Lord sees the planned efforts to be self-conscious, cocky, empty posturings on our part. Maybe the posturings will lead, though, to the unexpected *karass* of real linkings, into other and real teams that can actually do God's will at another time.

At another time. At another time. The linkings change, shift, merge. As I've thought about it, since those first cardinal-call-filtered thoughts of dawn today, I recurringly see this *karass* to be a present tense experience. And that concept can help us, in letting us let go of connections that were for another time, another place. For example, in straightening a file recently, I came upon a manila folder marked with a name that used to be very important to me. (Another time, another place.) One impulse shoved me, hard, toward cynicism and anger: all that we shared, all that we talked about, all that we prayed about, all the trying-to-be-helpful notes I wrote, as these carbons affirm; and now a silence, a separateness, a disconnected distance, from a distance. Well, *karass* thoughts say, that's all right. Quite all right. We were linked for then, to do the Lord's will. For now, let me be open to God: to the now-linkings, that are for now; to doing his will, for now.

A new gratitude permeates my day. Thanks, Dale Martin, for the use of your paperbacks. Thanks to a science fiction writer for certain coined words. And thanks — great thanks — to God for the opportunities he has given to me, to you, to all of his children: to be part of the linkings together of mortals, who do his immortal will.

Notes to Chapter 32

1. Kurt Vonnegut, Jr., *Cat's Cradle* (New York: Dell Publishing Co., Inc., 1970), p. 11.
2. Thomas R. Kelly, *A Testament of Devotion* (New York: Harper and Brothers, 1941), p. 85-86.
3. Vonnegut, *Cat's Cradle*, p. 67.

A Doxology Day *33*
For Singles

Every day of the Christian's life is a doxology day. "All blessings" happen continually. But what would you think of inventing a new national holiday, a doxology day for singles?

What would you think of each single person's Doxology Day as a specific and individual celebration? No, not something else to add to the printed calendars which observe Arbor Day, National Secretaries' Week, and Frances E. Willard's birthday. How about each single's using his semi-annual birthday as his Doxology Day? That is, if you were born on April 10, then on October 10 you and your friends could do the special praisings and celebratings.

Friends, too?

Of course. Why not? Single friends. Married friends. Maybe especially the marrieds. You help them to celebrate their special days, with the showers, the weddings, the anniversaries. If you decide to have an open house or a dinner party, do think about including some married friends.

"A partying, then, is what you mean by a 'doxology day'?" wonders a dubious voice. Oh, not necessarily. The possibilities are unlimited. But the merry festivity of an open house might praise God through the chips and dips, mints and punch, that you will serve.

Maybe you will like to buy yourself some Doxology Day gifts — some special equippings to serve God and his other children more truly, more adequately. A magazine subscription, maybe, to help equip your mind? A new supply of candles, to use during your year-long hospitalities? Books or records that you can use over and over, and lend often?

Maybe you will want to spend a part of the day with a pen in your hand, making some visible lists of present praisings. Some zany ones? Some very individual ones?

If you are a formerly married person, you may want to linger for a while in quiet praises for past blessings: for tremulous first-date gladness, wedding flowers, vacations together. You may want to praise the Lord particularly for the new growings and steadyings he is bringing to your inner self now, since the shattering of your world. You may want to praise him for the new ministries he is opening out before you, in the present chapter of your life.

Maybe you will like to have a brief worship service, with some friend leading a litany of veritable doxology and of dedication. You might use a nearby chapel, or let your living room become a chapel. You might ask a ministerial acquaintance to participate. Stereo records could substitute for organs and choirs. If you like, the leader of the litany could modify extemporaneously the script that you have prepared. For any Christian single, a Doxology Day service might go something like this:

Organ prelude.
Hymn, "Praise to the Lord, the Almighty"
Psalm 103, or 148, or 150
Hymn, "O Come, Creator Spirit, Come"

Leader: We have come together today to join our friend (Name) in his/her day of special rejoicing, and thanksgiving, and festivity.
Let us pray.
Lord Jesus, who walked our human earth as a single person, we bring you praise today for your sustaining love and grace to each single person who names you as Lord.

All
participants: We bring you praise.

Leader: We bring you praise today for (Name), for his/her gifts of mind and spirit, of personality and creativity.

All: We bring you praise.

Leader: We praise you for what (Name) has learned of your grace and your guiding through all the years of his/her life. We praise you for the decisions he/she has made, that have brought him/her to this present hour in your kingdom. We praise you for what he/she has learned through all his/her times of personal difficulty and stress. We praise you for your grace, which is now at work in (Name's) life, in eternal ways.

All:	With love and gratitude, we praise you for the life of (Name) among us.
All:	The doxology: "Praise God from Whom all blessings flow."
Leader:	(Name), on this festal day, I call upon you to praise God for specific blessings which he has poured into your life during the past year.
Celebrant:	I do praise him. I praise him for _____, and for _____, and _____, and _____.
Leader:	I call upon you, (Name), to renew your commitment as a Christian disciple. Will you seek to discern the will of our Lord Jesus Christ more fully in the coming year? Will you endeavor to obey the guidings of the Holy Spirit more closely?
Celebrant:	I will endeavor so to do, God being my helper.
Leader:	(Name), in the providence and guidings of Almighty God, you are a single person. Your singleness gives you distinctive opportunities in Christian service. While you are free to be a single person, will you commit your life to his special service, as he may direct you?
Celebrant:	I will.
Leader:	Will you endeavor, as you can, to strengthen other single persons in their Christian walk? Will you endeavor to be a continuing benediction to all families, and to the larger units of the body of Christ?
Celebrant:	I will.
Leader:	Let us praise God for this renewed commitment which our friend (Name) has made. Let us praise God for what he will do through (Name) in the coming year.
All:	The doxology: "Praise God from Whom all blessings flow."
Benediction:	Numbers 6:24-26.

* * * *

Maybe a litany is not a celebration you will choose. Maybe a beach picnic with quiet sharings around a campfire will be your way of praising. Maybe you would like to reaffirm your confirmation vows, or to have a simple communion service.

Maybe guitars or banjos will speak your praisings, and songs that are not usually labeled "sacred."

Maybe you will choose to celebrate your day by attending a football game, or by playing in one.

What will affirm to yourself, and to God, and to your world, your gladness for what you are?

Oh, a small practicality. If this whole idea, or any part of it, catches your interest, what about the single whose birthday (like my own, on August 30) does not have a half-year counterpart? Well, August 28 and 29 and 30 and 31 could all be celebrated on February 28, couldn't they? Maybe sometimes groups of November-birthday singles will all celebrate their singleness together in May festivals. Why not?

"Look," says someone. "I don't like being single, and I don't like having attention called to my singleness at any time, and I'm not about to throw a hypocritical party to celebrate what I hate, nor to praise God for it! I am not!"

Okay, okay. You're free *not* to celebrate, too.

But keep thinking, friend. The Christian way of life is to praise God in all things. And singleness is a specific gift from God to some of his people. (You might want to look at 1 Corinthians 7:17 again.) How you accept and use his present gifts to you will make a great difference in your whole relationship to him; in your eternal self. Birthdays and half-birthdays are transitory, but what you do with them will last beyond stars and moons, beyond this little earth. Would a Doxology Day help to prepare you for doxologies among seraphim and cherubim?

Blessings to you, all of you, for all days and in all ways. I have just realized, with a start, that I have been doing this brain-storming about celebrations on a mini-Epiphany. It is June 6. Now it is the ending of a summery day, rather than the dawning of a wintery one. I reach for my clipboard and look again at all the names I jotted down, in scribbled green ink, on January 6. The list has been here on my clipboard, under the rustle and swish of other papers, during these intervening months. I circle a name, and a name, and a name. This one seems much closer to God than he was in January. This one is engaged now, and so is this one. Another is married, very joyfully. This one has had her illegitimate son. This one has a new job, and has just bought a house. This one, and this one. . . .

Bless them, O my Father!

Can you use some of my words from these circling months to help them in their daily circumstances?

On this small Epiphany, would you give to them a new revealing of yourself?

When they read what I have been writing, would you let the reading be another and continuing Epiphany?

For these, whom I know and care about. For the others, whom I do not know, but you know entirely. Bless them, Father!

Amen.
Amen.